Francis Frith's

Cornwall

A Century Ago

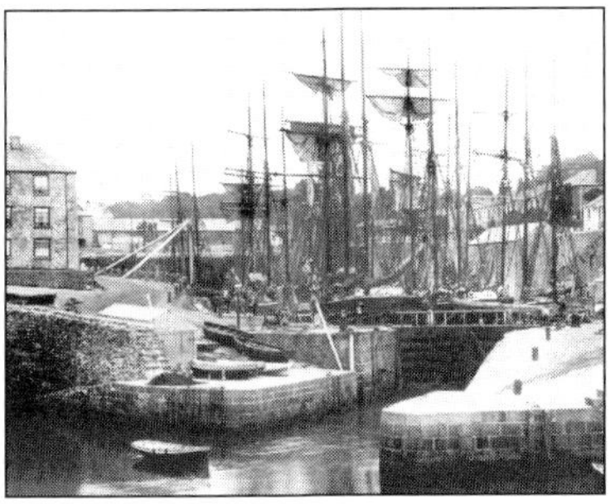

Photographic Memories

Francis Frith's
Cornwall
A Century Ago

Peter Stanier

THE FRANCIS FRITH COLLECTION

First published in the United Kingdom in 2001 by
Frith Book Company Ltd as Victorian & Edwardian Cornwall

ISBN 1-85937-252-X

Hardback Reprinted 2004 as Cornwall a Century Ago

British Library Cataloguing in Publication Data

Francis Frith's Cornwall a Century Ago
Peter Stanier

Frith Book Company Ltd
Frith's Barn, Teffont,
Salisbury, Wiltshire SP3 5QP
Tel: +44 (0) 1722 716 376
Email: info@frithbook.co.uk
www.frithbook.co.uk

Printed and bound in Great Britain

Front Cover: LOOE, *The Harbour 1906* 56404

The colour-tinting is for illustrative purposes only, and is not intended to be historically accurate

AS WITH ANY HISTORICAL DATABASE THE FRITH ARCHIVE IS CONSTANTLY BEING CORRECTED AND IMPROVED AND THE PUBLISHERS WOULD WELCOME INFORMATION ON OMISSIONS OR INACCURACIES

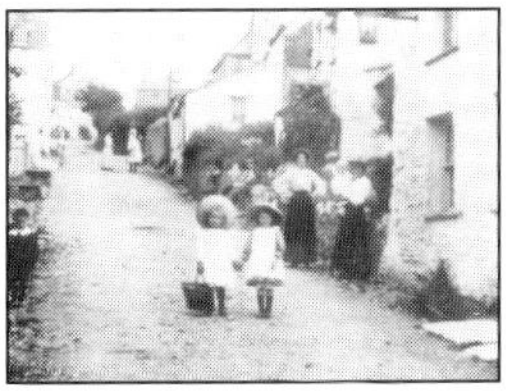

Contents

Francis Frith: *Victorian Pioneer*

FRANCIS FRITH, Victorian founder of the world-famous photographic archive, was a complex and multi-talented man. A devout Quaker and a highly successful Victorian businessman, he was both philosophic by nature and pioneering in outlook.

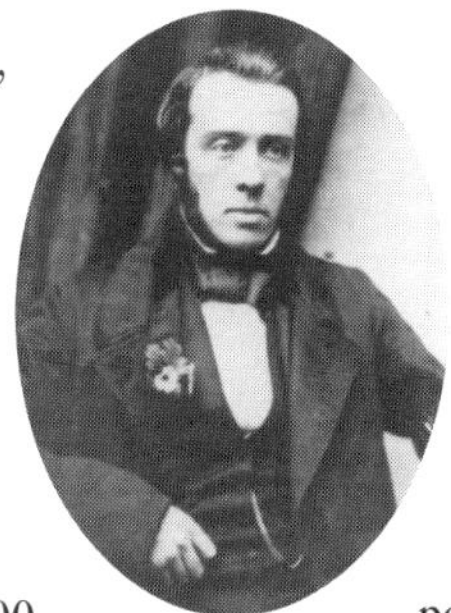

By 1855 Francis Frith had already established a wholesale grocery business in Liverpool, and sold it for the astonishing sum of £200,000, which is the equivalent today of over £15,000,000. Now a very rich man, he was able to indulge his passion for travel. As a child he had pored over travel books written by early explorers, and his fancy and imagination had been stirred by family holidays to the sublime mountain regions of Wales and Scotland. 'What lands of spirit-stirring and enriching scenes and places!' he had written. He was to return to these scenes of grandeur in later years to 'recapture the thousands of vivid and tender memories', but with a different purpose. Now in his thirties, and captivated by the new science of photography, Frith set out on a series of pioneering journeys to the Nile regions that occupied him from 1856 until 1860.

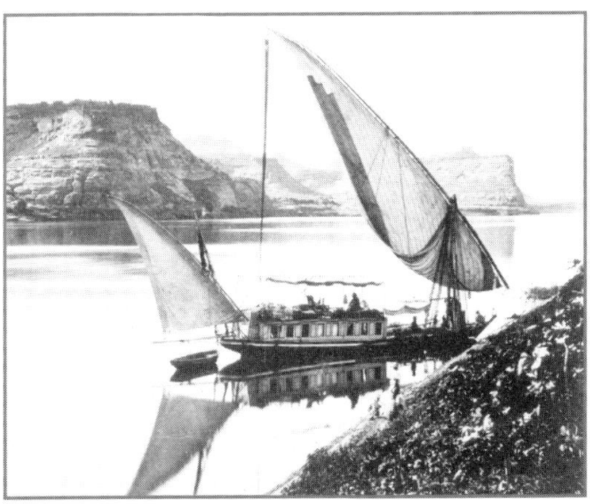

Intrigue and Adventure

He took with him on his travels a specially-designed wicker carriage that acted as both dark-room and sleeping chamber. These far-flung journeys were packed with intrigue and adventure. In his life story, written when he was sixty-three, Frith tells of being held captive by bandits, and of fighting 'an awful midnight battle to the very point of surrender with a deadly pack of hungry, wild dogs'. Sporting flowing Arab costume, Frith arrived at Akaba by camel seventy years before Lawrence, where he encountered 'desert princes and rival sheikhs, blazing with jewel-hilted swords'.

During these extraordinary adventures he was assiduously exploring the desert regions bordering the Nile and patiently recording the antiquities and peoples with his camera. He was the first photographer to venture beyond the sixth cataract. Africa was still the mysterious 'Dark Continent', and Stanley and Livingstone's historic meeting was a decade into the future. The conditions for picture taking confound belief. He laboured for hours in his wicker dark-room in the sweltering heat of the desert, while the volatile chemicals fizzed dangerously in their trays. Often he was forced to work in remote tombs and caves where conditions were cooler. Back in London he exhibited his photographs and was 'rapturously cheered' by members of the Royal Society. His reputation as a photographer was made overnight. An eminent modern historian has likened their impact on the population of the time to that on our own generation of the first photographs taken on the surface of the moon.

Venture of a Life-Time

Characteristically, Frith quickly spotted the opportunity to create a new business as a specialist publisher of photographs. He lived in an era of immense and sometimes violent change. For the poor in the early part of Victoria's reign work was a drudge and the hours long, and people had precious little free time to enjoy themselves. Most had no transport other than a cart or gig at their disposal, and had not travelled far beyond the boundaries of their own town or village. However, by the 1870s, the railways had threaded their way across the country, and Bank Holidays and half-day Saturdays had been made obligatory by Act of Parliament. All of a sudden the ordinary working man and his family were able to enjoy days out and see a little more of the world.

With characteristic business acumen, Francis Frith foresaw that these new tourists would enjoy having souvenirs to commemorate their days out. In 1860 he married Mary Ann Rosling and set out with the intention of photographing every city, town and village in Britain. For the next thirty years he travelled the country by train and by pony and trap, producing fine photographs of seaside resorts and beauty spots that were keenly bought by millions of Victorians. These prints were painstakingly pasted into family albums and pored over during the dark nights of winter, rekindling precious memories of summer excursions.

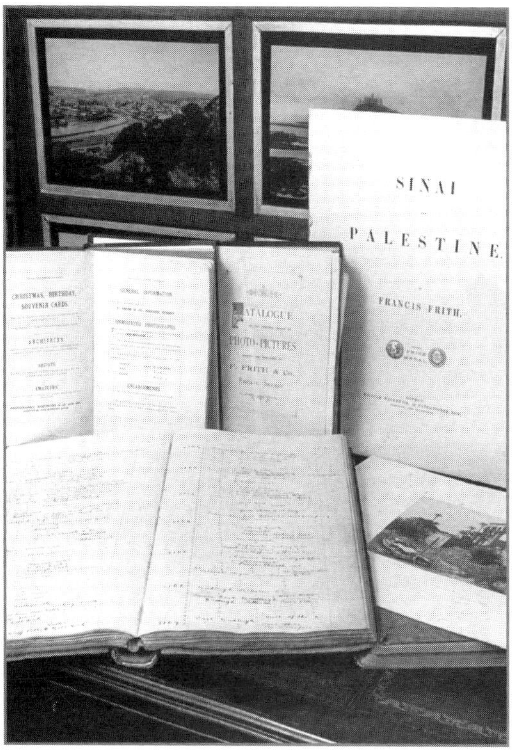

The Rise of Frith & Co

Frith's studio was soon supplying retail shops all over the country. To meet the demand he gathered about him a small team of photographers, and published the work of independent artist-photographers of the calibre of Roger Fenton and Francis Bedford. In order to gain some understanding of the scale of Frith's business one only has to look at the catalogue issued by Frith & Co in 1886: it runs to some 670 pages, listing not only many thousands of views of the British Isles but also many photographs of most European countries, and China, Japan, the USA and Canada – note the sample page shown on page 9 from the hand-written *Frith & Co* ledgers detailing pictures taken. By 1890 Frith had created the greatest specialist photographic publishing company in the

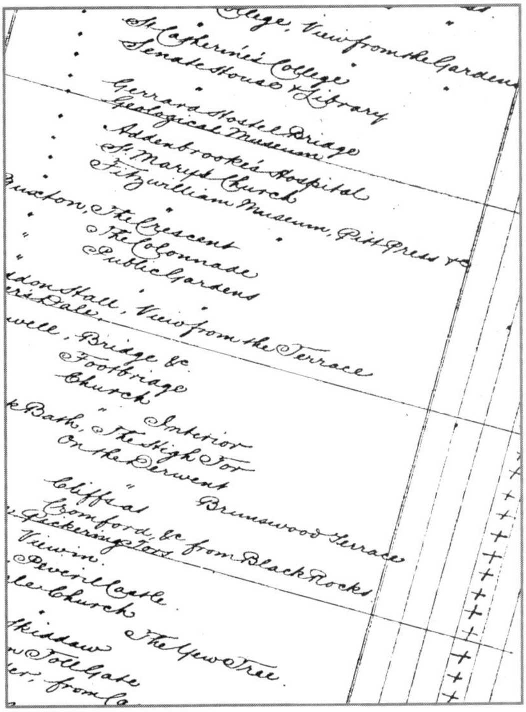
...llege, View from the Garden
St Catherine's College
Senate House & Library
Gerrard's Hostel Bridge
Geological Museum
Addenbrooke's Hospital
St Mary's Church
Fitzwilliam Museum, Pitt Press &c
...uxton, The Crescent
The Colonnade
Public Gardens
...ddon Hall, View from the Terrace
...well, Bridge &c.
Footbridge
Church
...k Bath, " Interior
The High Tor
On the Derwent
Cliffs at " Brunswood Terrace
Cromford, &c from Black Rocks
...Pickering Tor
View in
Peveril Castle
...le Church
The Yew Tree
...Toll Gate

world, with over 2,000 outlets more than the combined number that Boots and WH Smith have today! The picture on the right shows the *Frith & Co* display board at Ingleton in the Yorkshire Dales (left of window). Beautifully constructed with a mahogany frame and gilt inserts, it could display up to a dozen local scenes.

Postcard Bonanza

The ever-popular holiday postcard we know today took many years to develop. In 1870 the Post Office issued the first plain cards, with a pre-printed stamp on one face. In 1894 they allowed other publishers' cards to be sent through the mail with an attached adhesive halfpenny stamp. Demand grew rapidly, and in 1895 a new size of postcard was permitted called the court card, but there was little room for illustration. In 1899, a year after Frith's death, a new card measuring 5.5 x 3.5 inches became the standard format, but it was not until 1902 that the divided back came into being, with address and message on one face and a full-size illustration on the other. *Frith & Co* were in the vanguard of postcard development, and Frith's sons Eustace and Cyril continued their father's monumental task, expanding the number of views offered to the public and recording more and more places in Britain, as the coasts and countryside were opened up to mass travel.

Francis Frith died in 1898 at his villa in Cannes, his great project still growing. The archive he created continued in business for another seventy years. By 1970 it contained over a third of a million pictures of 7,000 cities, towns and villages. The massive photographic record Frith has left to us stands as a living monument to a special and very remarkable man.

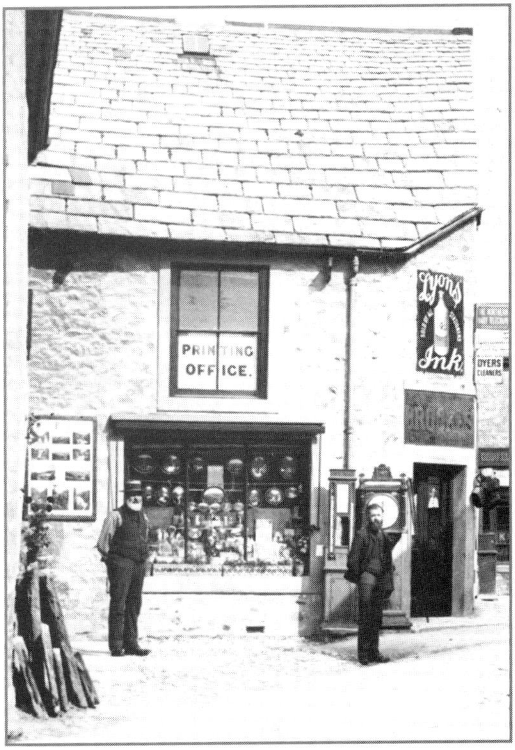

Frith's Archive: *A Unique Legacy*

Francis Frith's legacy to us today is of immense significance and value, for the magnificent archive of evocative photographs he created provides a unique record of change in 7,000 cities, towns and villages throughout Britain over a century and more. Frith and his fellow studio photographers revisited locations many times down the years to update their views, compiling for us an enthralling and colourful pageant of British life and character.

We tend to think of Frith's sepia views of Britain as nostalgic, for most of us use them to conjure up memories of places in our own lives with which we have family associations. It often makes us forget that to Francis Frith they were records of daily life as it was actually being lived in the cities, towns and villages of his day. The Victorian age was one of great and often bewildering change for ordinary people, and though the pictures evoke an impression of slower times, life was as busy and hectic as it is today.

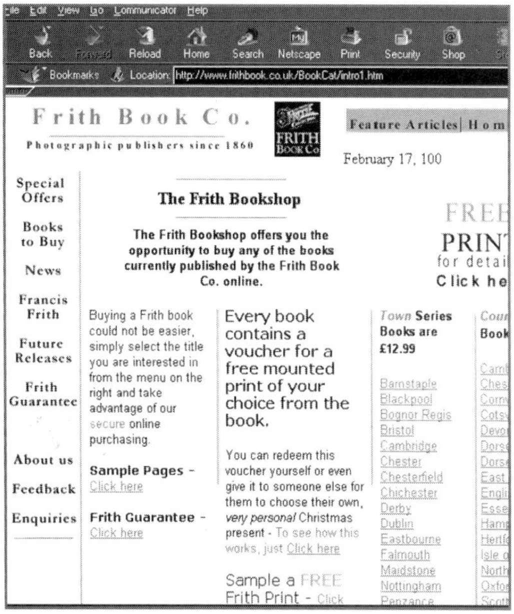

See Frith at www. frithbook.co.uk

We are fortunate that Frith was a photographer of the people, dedicated to recording the minutiae of everyday life. For it is this sheer wealth of visual data, the painstaking chronicle of changes in dress, transport, street layouts, buildings, housing, engineering and landscape that captivates us so much today. His remarkable images offer us a powerful link with the past and with the lives of our ancestors.

Today's Technology

Computers have now made it possible for Frith's many thousands of images to be accessed almost instantly. In the Frith archive today, each photograph is carefully 'digitised' then stored on a CD Rom. Frith archivists can locate a single photograph amongst thousands within seconds. Views can be catalogued and sorted under a variety of categories of place and content to the immediate benefit of researchers.

Inexpensive reference prints can be created for them at the touch of a mouse button, and a wide range of books and other printed materials assembled and published for a wider, more general readership - in the next twelve months over a hundred Frith local history titles will be published! The day-to-day workings of the archive are very different from how they were in Francis Frith's time: imagine the herculean task of sorting through eleven tons of glass negatives as Frith had to do to locate a particular sequence of pictures! Yet the archive still prides itself on maintaining the same high standards of excellence laid down by Francis Frith, including the painstaking cataloguing and indexing of every view.

It is curious to reflect on how the internet now allows researchers in America and elsewhere greater instant access to the archive than Frith himself ever enjoyed. Many thousands of individual views can be called up on screen within seconds on one of the Frith internet sites, enabling people living continents away to revisit the streets of their ancestral home town, or view places in Britain where they have enjoyed holidays. Many overseas researchers welcome the chance to view special theme selections, such as transport, sports, costume and ancient monuments.

We are certain that Francis Frith would have heartily approved of these modern developments in imaging techniques, for he himself was always working at the very limits of Victorian photographic technology.

The Value of the Archive Today

Because of the benefits brought by the computer, Frith's images are increasingly studied by social historians, by researchers into genealogy and ancestory, by architects, town planners, and by teachers and schoolchildren involved in local history projects.

In addition, the archive offers every one of us an opportunity to examine the places where we and our families have lived and worked down the years. Highly successful in Frith's own era, the archive is now, a century and more on, entering a new phase of popularity.

The Past in Tune with the Future

Historians consider the Francis Frith Collection to be of prime national importance. It is the only archive of its kind remaining in private ownership and has been valued at a million pounds. However, this figure is now rapidly increasing as digital technology enables more and more people around the world to enjoy its benefits.

Francis Frith's archive is now housed in an historic timber barn in the beautiful village of Teffont in Wiltshire. Its founder would not recognize the archive office as it is today. In place of the many thousands of dusty boxes containing glass plate negatives and an all-pervading odour of photographic chemicals, there are now ranks of computer screens. He would be amazed to watch his images travelling round the world at unimaginable speeds through network and internet lines.

The archive's future is both bright and exciting. Francis Frith, with his unshakeable belief in making photographs available to the greatest number of people, would undoubtedly approve of what is being done today with his lifetime's work. His photographs, depicting our shared past, are now bringing pleasure and enlightenment to millions around the world a century and more after his death.

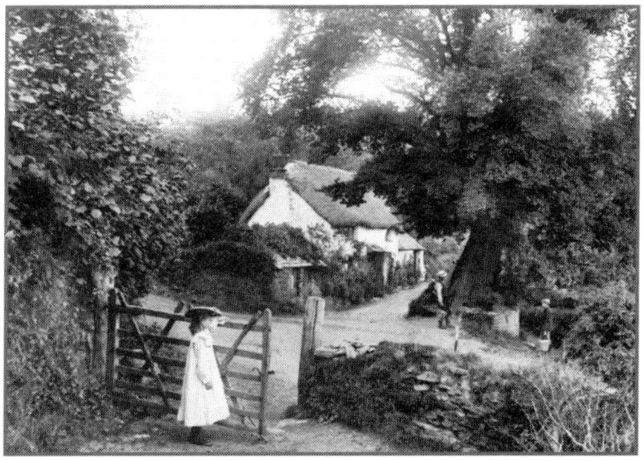

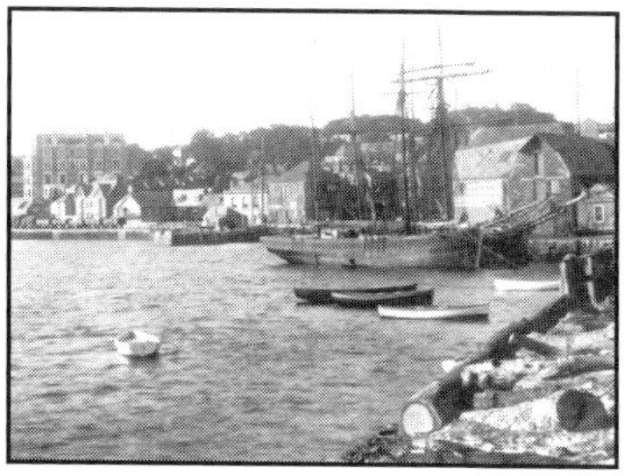

Introduction

MOST OF THE PHOTOGRAPHS in this collection were taken over a relatively short 20-year period between 1890 and 1910. The exceptions come from the 1880s, and two much earlier ones: Boscastle in c1871, and Polkerris c1876. We are seeing images of the late Victorian period passing into the Edwardian age, and some identical views taken a few years apart make good comparisons, such as at Callington, Penryn and Penzance. In most rural areas, changes came so slowly that there is probably very little difference, although two useful photographs do record the development of the cable station at Porthcurno.

The late 19th and early 20th century was a time of change in Cornwall. The great tin mining industry had all but collapsed; it is appropriate that there is only one picture of a mine, at Luckett, and that is closed. However, the towns of Camborne and Redruth or smaller places like Gunnislake owed their growth to the mining industry. Some ports also developed on the back of the mineral trade while it lasted. Fishing for pilchards and mackerel was important around the coast, although the old pilchard fishery was to collapse in the early 20th century. Agriculture was still the backbone of rural life, but it only really features in these photographs indirectly, on market day at Launceston or in the market halls here and at Bodmin and St Columb. Railways were already a familiar part of the county by the 1890s, although they had only just arrived at some places like Padstow or were yet to arrive (Bude). Their impact was mixed, but goods and passenger traffic on the main line continued to grow once Cornwall was joined to the rest of England's network. The railways helped stimulate tourism, and there are good examples of this new industry to be seen here.

One of the most striking features of all these photographs is the almost total absence of road traffic in the country and the towns, which occurs too often to result from the cameraman choosing all his views on a quiet day. There are a few horse-drawn conveyances to be seen - traps, carts, wagons and carriages - or, if they are missing, a common clue is the horse manure in the road! This period is at the very dawn of the motor age, and only two or three such vehicles are seen in any of the photographs. The motor revolution was about to change everything; within a few decades road surfaces were improved, and all sorts of motorised traffic could be seen. Gone are the days when one could pose safely in the road as a pedestrian or handling a pony and trap.

Some photographs are carefully composed, and at Launceston Castle or St Keyne's Well the cameraman has positioned children to enhance the charm of the scene. A view of the beach and headland at Polzeath stands out as exceptional because of a dramatic cloudy sky, not seen in other pictures. When it comes to street scenes, the photographer has taken time to get everyone out to pose; see the examples in Callington, Helston or Launceston, where the townsfolk are all standing along the length of the street. Of course, this was a time when there was no danger of being run over, but it is difficult to see how it could be achieved today: imagine holding up the high street's busy traffic while you set up a picture! It must have been exciting to know you would be in the picture, but patience was required by all; the occasional person is out of focus where they have moved during the camera's long exposure. There is usually someone appearing in even the smallest village pictures. There is a certain cheekiness in the group at Palmorla, where two boys are intent on being individuals by not facing the camera and have turned aside. The girls, on the other hand, are well behaved.

There are instances at Stoke Climsland and St Columb Major where you can almost see the cameraman asking at a house for the inhabitants to please come out and pose for his picture. The weather-beaten fisherman at Newlyn and the lady with her pannier donkey at Looe are two pictures that have been set up and deliberately posed.

Clothes and headwear give a real sense of period to all the pictures. Men are mostly hatted, and the shopkeepers' aprons are evident in many town scenes. Boys often wear caps, and the girls have bonnets. Fashionable long dresses and skirts are best seen in the pictures with ladies at Falmouth and on the Esplanade at Penzance.

The selected photographs have been grouped under broad themes, taking the Cornish landscape first. For the coast, there is no better place to start than the Land's End itself. We also see beaches and cliff scenery; the north is wilder in comparison with the calmer coast and quiet creeks of the south. It is comforting to see that some views are as familiar as ever, like Land's End and Logan Rock. The hands of time will have to work hard to alter these cliffs. St Michael's Mount in this section also seems to be everlasting.

The inland scenes open with the famous Cheesewring tor on Bodmin Moor, again little changed over the years. Few Victorian travellers failed to make the trip up to see this: among them was the author Wilkie Collins, who recorded his adventures here. Ancient

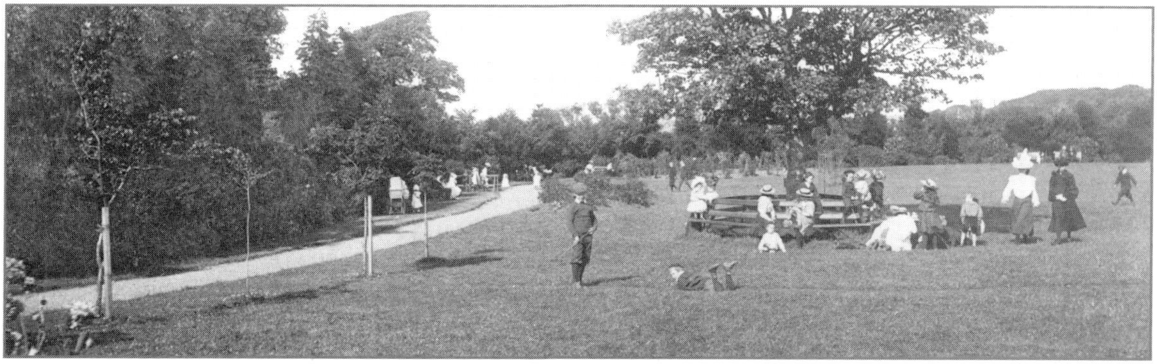

stone bridges are part of the Cornish landscape, and there are two nicely composed views of New Bridge near Callington and Lostwithiel's bridge, both unchanged today and carrying modern traffic. Landscape elements appear in many of the other photographs. For example, elm trees are now but a memory, but they are seen at St Clement village and in the asylum grounds at Bodmin.

Village life is depicted across the county from tiny hamlets to more substantial settlements like St Columb Major, which is almost a town. Churches and public houses appear, intentionally or in the background. Thatched roofs are a little unexpected for those who do not know the county well, but we see examples at St Keverne and Mullion on the Lizard and at Gulval near Penzance. Not all the villages can be said to be 'pretty', for there are many industrial ones like Gunnislake.

The selection of towns is also wide-ranging, from Bude in the north to Penzance in the west. Most of the street scenes will be recognisable today as, thank goodness, many Victorian buildings have been retained. There have been changes to the shop fronts and their uses, but the most significant difference is today's overwhelming traffic. Details to look for include billboards, posters, and gas street lamps, while the pavements and road surfaces are of varying quality. There are special buildings, such as hotels catering for commercial travellers and families, while at Bodmin the County Lunatic Asylum is an unusual subject for a postcard. A fine monument at Helston and a park at Camborne are reminders of other important features of the late Victorian town. The end of the 19th century saw the creation of several libraries and institutes by the benefactor John Passmore Edwards. Cornish-born, he became a London newspaper owner and returned some of his wealth to his county. His generosity is seen in the libraries at Camborne and Liskeard, and also the convalescent home at Perranporth. Other beneficiaries, not pictured here, were Bodmin, Falmouth, Helston, Newlyn, St Agnes and Truro.

Cornwall has a long coastline, and nowhere is far from the sea, so ports and shipping have always played a significant part in Cornwall's history. Coasting ships remained the vital carriers for many trades. They were hardly affected by railways, and only declined in the face of competition from motor lorries well into the 20th century. When the weather or tides allowed, small sailing craft called at open beaches, as at Port Isaac, or navigated to small quays on creeks such as Lerryn or Gweek. These boats provided a lifeline for remote

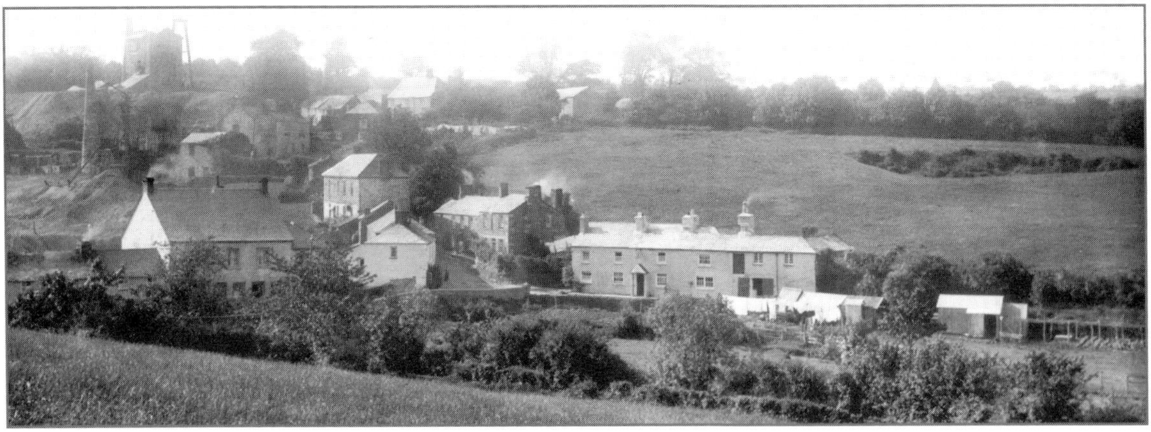

communities; the early photograph of Boscastle is a valuable record, as it shows sailing traders in the tiny harbour. In contrast, larger ports include Falmouth, with its large sheltered harbour and repair yard, or the china clay ports of Fowey and Charlestown, the latter a purpose-built dock. Newquay, usually seen as a tourist resort and fishing port, was developed for importing coal and exporting china clay and minerals. Portreath was entirely a mining port. We are also reminded that the quays at Looe were developed to serve the Caradon mining district, via a canal and railway; but by the time of the photographs the mines had mostly closed. Coal was still imported, but there was now room for the fisheries to take over.

The fishing industry was carried on from the tiniest coves like Porthgwarra, with its boats hauled up above the high tide mark, to the deepwater harbour at Newlyn, only just extended; here, record catches of pilchards, mackerel and other fish were landed in the early 1900s. We see drift net boats and the seine boats which worked off the beaches for pilchards at St Ives and Perranporth, while the Huer's House at Newquay is another aspect of the fisheries.

Travel by water was sometimes more convenient than by road. The theme of travel includes two contrasting ferries on the Fal estuary. The old King Harry horse boat is seen in its last days before the first steam chain ferry was introduced. It is one of the ancient ferry crossings of the south coast estuaries; this one provided a useful link to the Roseland peninsula. Higher upstream, a passenger boat steams down from Truro on a service that answered the requirements of tourists and was a passenger ferry in its own right. Railway travel was revolutionised by the opening of the Royal Albert Bridge at Saltash, taking the main Cornish line (Great Western Railway) right through to Penzance, its lofty viaducts crossing many valleys on the way. Branch lines are of special interest, like the old mineral railway from Par and St Blazey, which is seen serving passenger traffic in our superb picture. Then there is the opening of an Edwardian branch to Callington with the completion of Calstock viaduct: this one is built of concrete blocks, but is still a magnificent sight. Posters seen at Launceston market advertise Great Western Railway excursions, perhaps suggesting rivalry with the London and South Western Railway, a late comer to the town.

And so to tourism, which was already firmly established and set to grow in the late 19th century. Visitors had come to Cornwall long before, but improved railway access and the encouragement of the companies themselves brought more passengers to the far west. Once in Cornwall, excursions by road or on foot were a favoured activity; the Land's End and Logan Rock were on the itinerary of many Victorian and Edwardian tourists, both places having local guides on hand if required.

Visitors could promenade by the sea at Penzance, or enjoy the beaches of St Ives or Newquay.

The latter resort was already well developed by the 1890s, with large hotels and guest houses, and it is worth comparing it with Perranporth just down the coast. Of the late Victorian hotel developments, the Headland Hotel at Newquay is undoubtedly the finest monument to this period, extravagant in size and vision. It has succeeded because of its position in a major resort, while the remote Poldhu Hotel, despite its elegant interior, is no longer a hotel. The nature of tourism has changed in the intervening century, but it is now Cornwall's main industry.

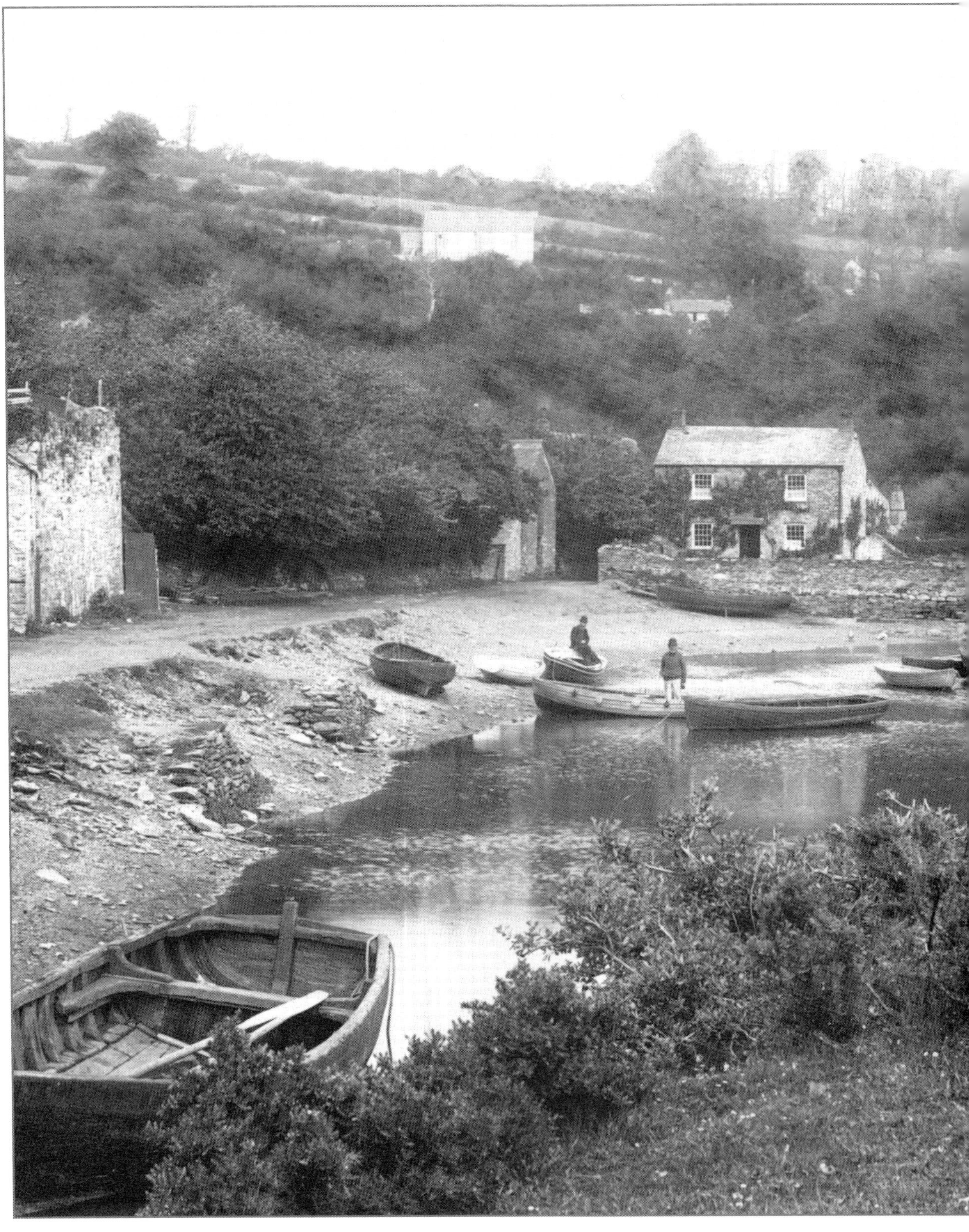

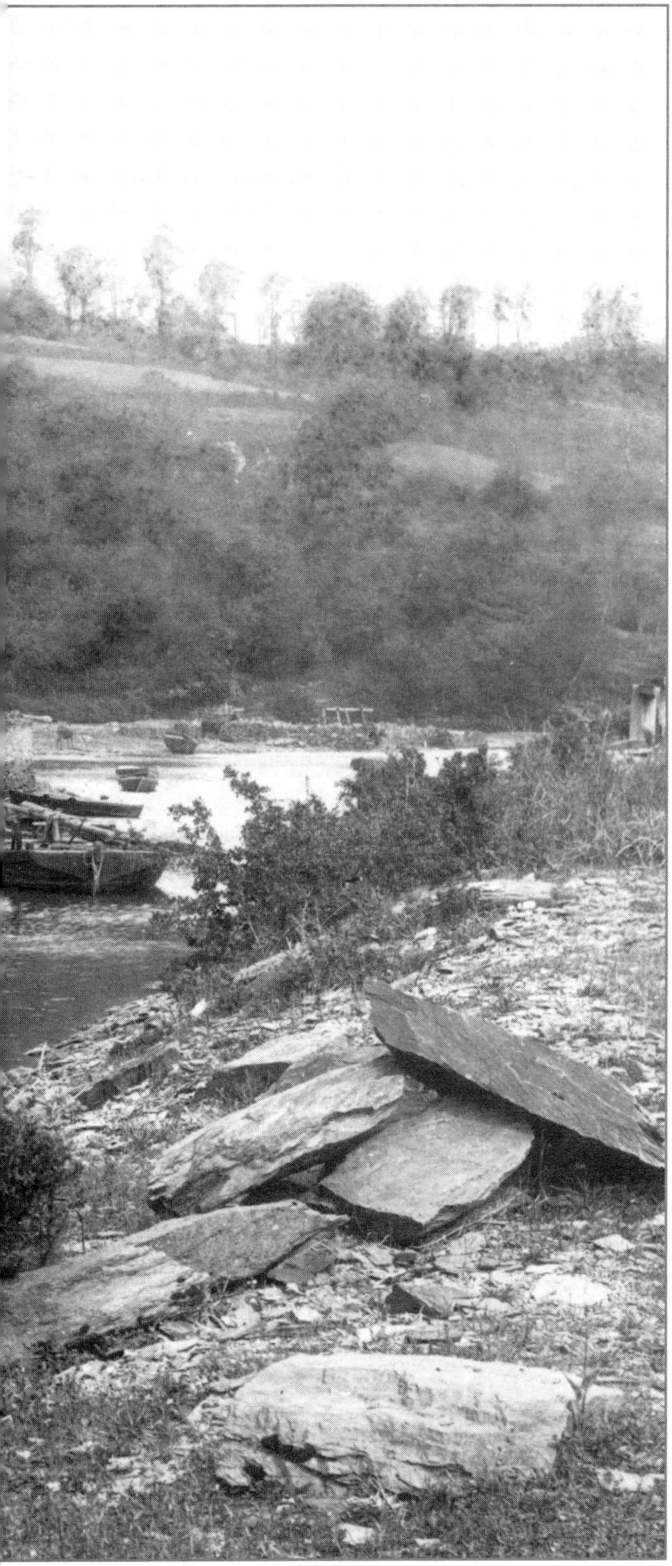

Around the Coast

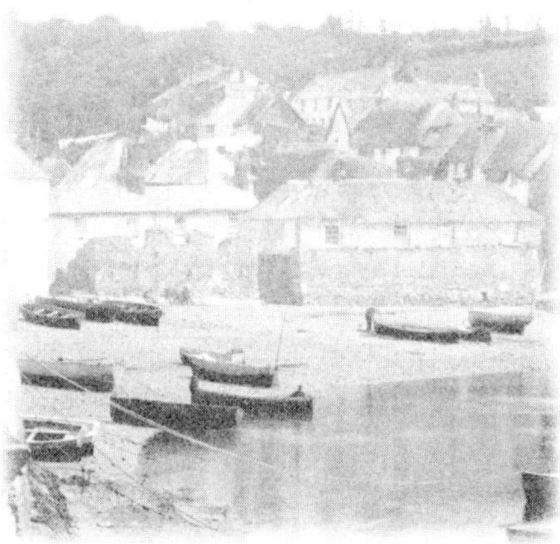

Golant, The Village 1891 29837
Also known as St Sampson's, Golant on the west bank of the Fowey was cut off from the main estuary, save for a bridge, by the embankment of the Lostwithiel to Fowey railway in 1869. This embankment, seen here on the right, enclosed a harbour around the old shoreline. The railway had become disused by the time of this photograph, and was not re-opened for another four years.

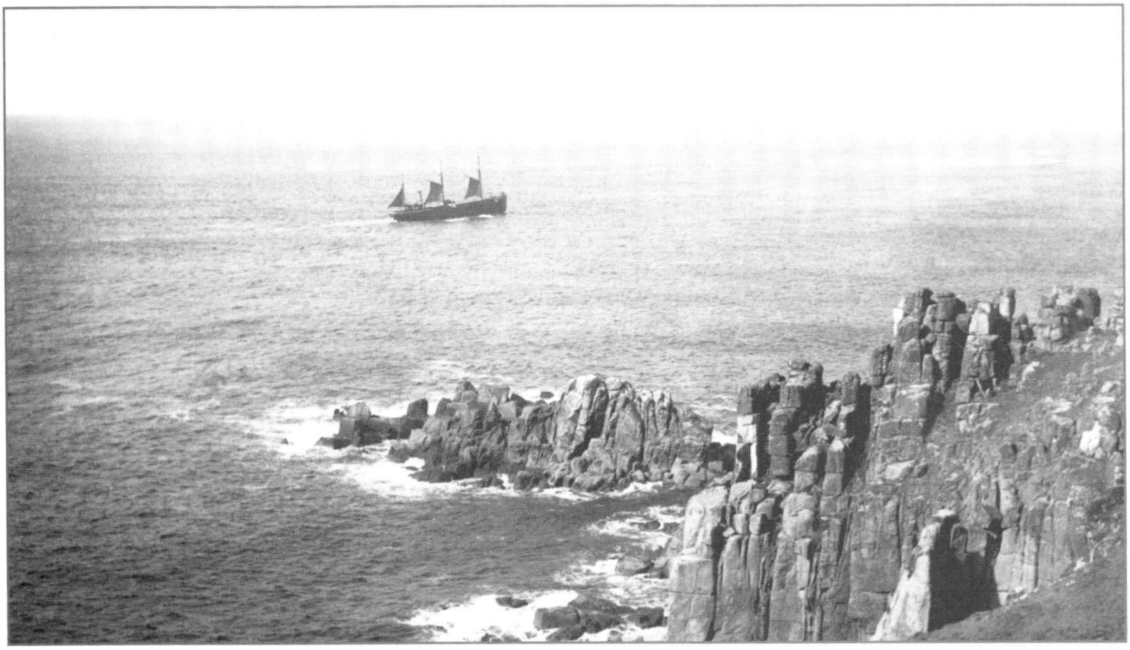

Land's End 1890 23004
Victorian travellers and writers, such as Dickens and Tennyson, all came to England's most westerly point and admired its rugged grandeur. The solid granite buttresses of the Land's End seem to have remained unchanged for ever, but it is the passing steam ship aided by three sails that puts this photograph into its period.

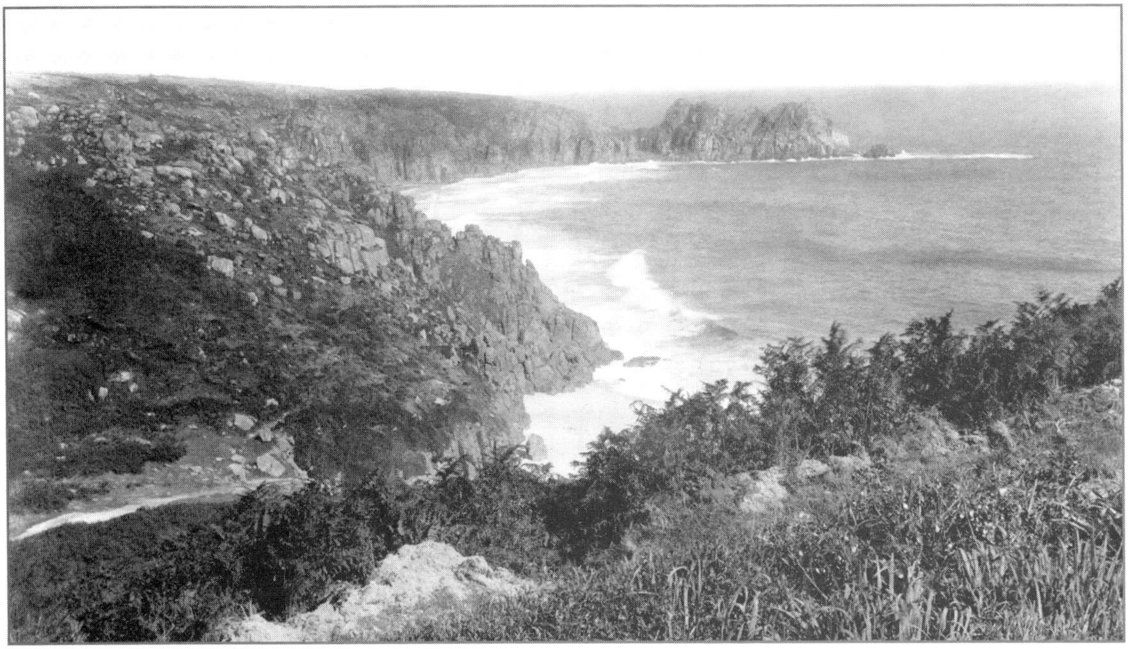

Porthcurno, The Bay and Logan Rock 1908 61262
Here we see the inspiring granite coastline near Land's End. Across the bay the rocky headland of Treryn Dinas is surmounted by the Logan Rock, a 60-ton block that can be rocked on its perch. In 1824, Lt Goldsmith and his crew managed to dislodge it, but the resulting outcry obliged him to hire tackle to lift it back.

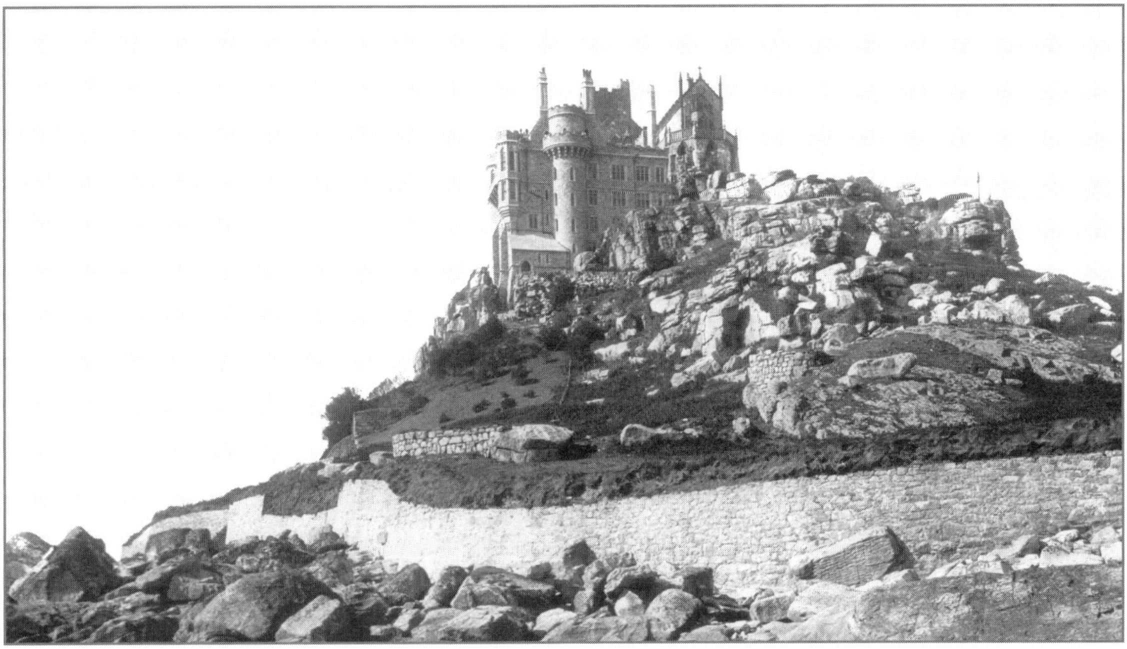

St Michael's Mount 1890 22993
An island at high tide, this famous granite rock is seen here from the eastern shore. We see the fairytale house and chapel built on the site of a Benedictine priory, with the south-east wing added by Piers St Aubyn in 1875-78. Landscaped gardens are among the rocks below.

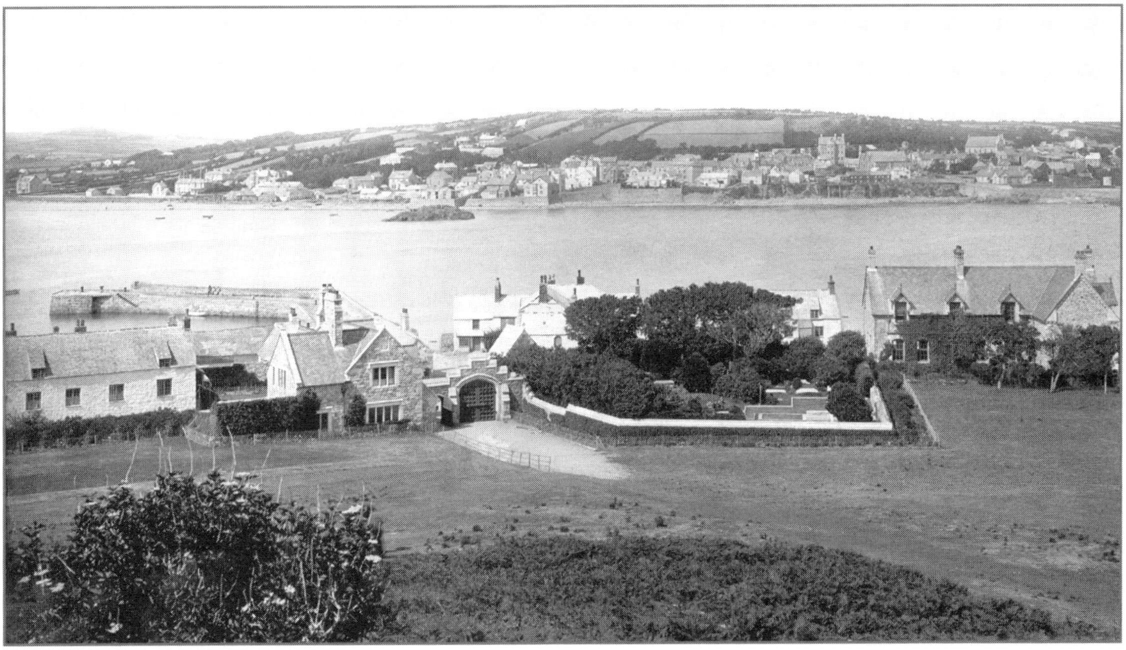

Marazion, From the Mount 1895 36182
The tide is in, covering the causeway and separating St Michael's Mount from the mainland. This unusual view shows the Mount's estate houses and a harbour wall, with Marazion stretched out along the coast and Trencrom Hill rising behind on the extreme left. This is a timeless view, for there are no people or traffic to indicate the date.

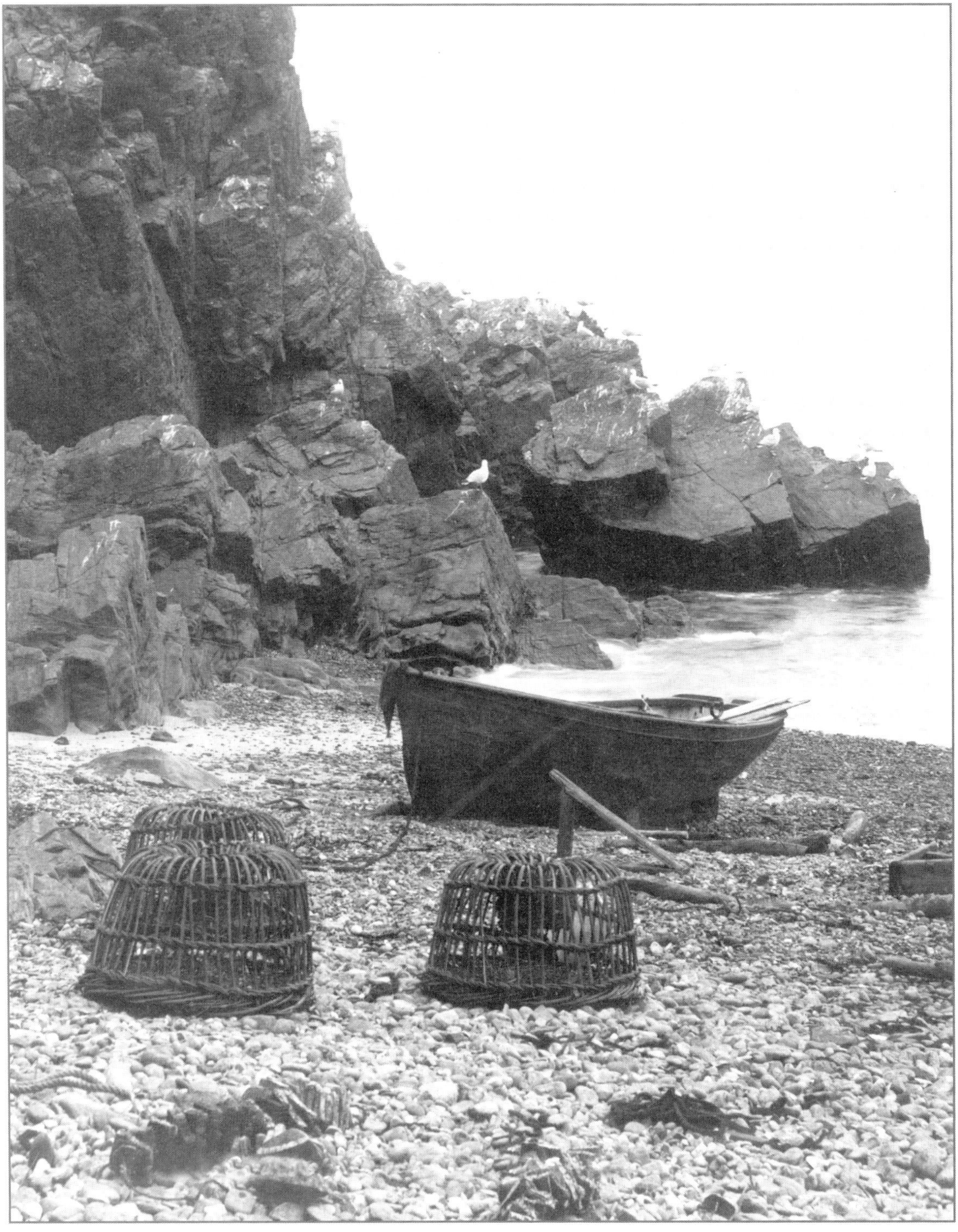

Cadgwith, Lobster Pots and Scavengers 1899 44189
Lobster or crab pots lie on the beach awaiting the next fishing trip, in a scene typical of many small fishing coves around the Cornish coast. Scavengers, the ever-present herring gulls, are perched on the rocks behind ready to grab any potential free meal.

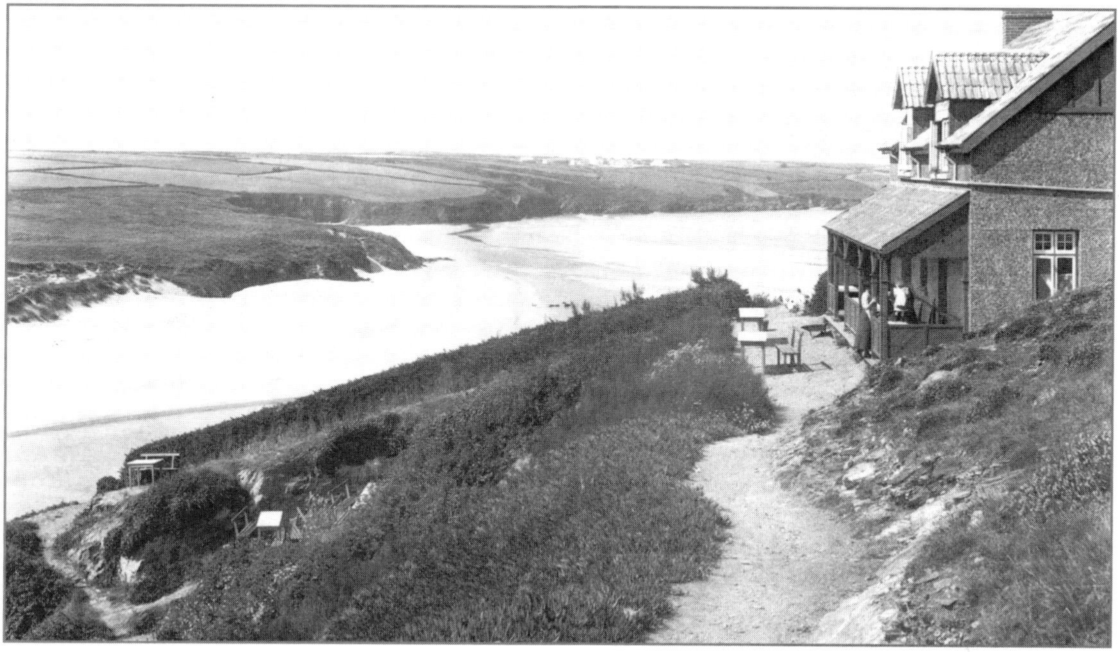

Newquay, Fern Pit and West Pentire 1904 52303
This uninterrupted view out over the lower Gannel estuary and the golden sands and dunes of Crantock confirms why Pentire became popular in the early days of housing development on the western outskirts of Newquay. West Pentire can be seen beyond the beach.

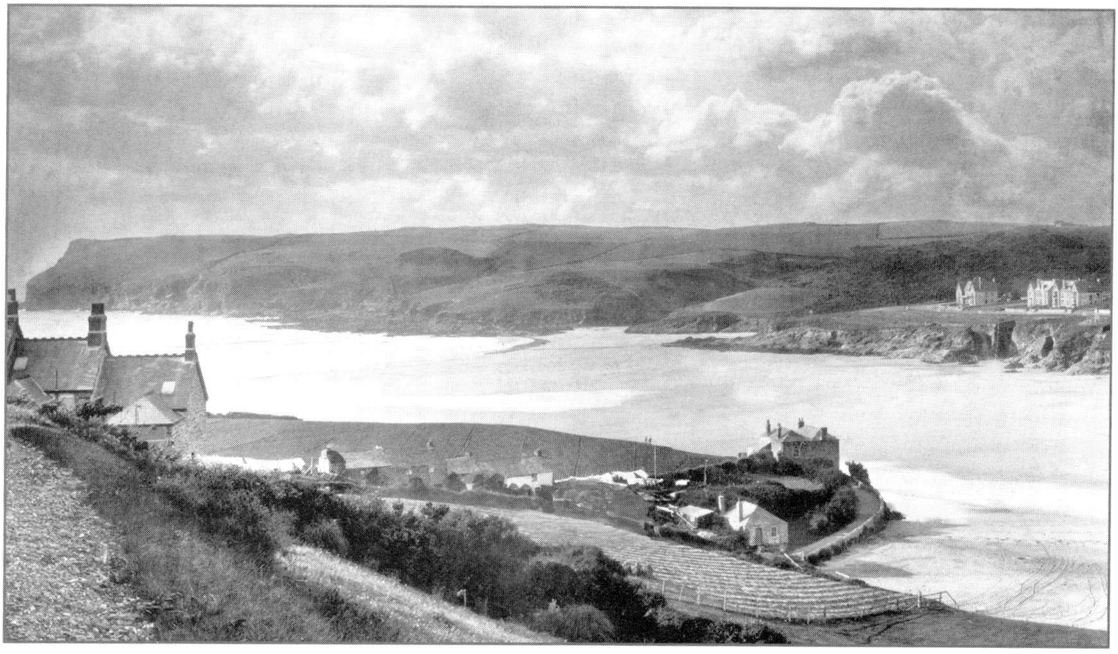

Polzeath, The Beach and Pentire Head 1903 49136
The beach is seen at low tide, with striking clouds and the sun glinting on the surf. Late 19th-century accommodation is seen at New Polzeath on the right, but the great Pentire Head remains as unspoilt as ever. Wheel tracks in the sand indicate that visitors were using the beach for parking, just as today.

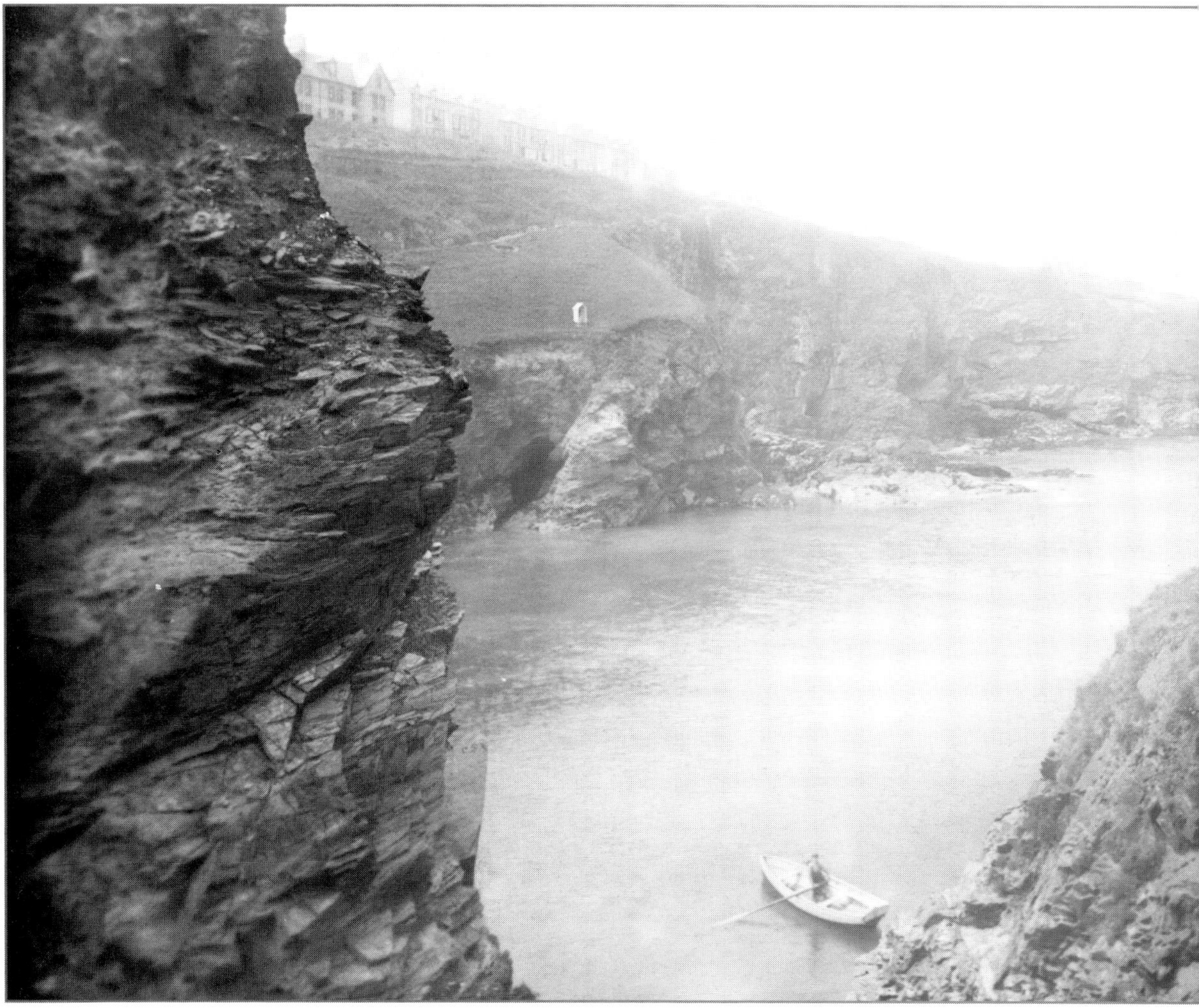

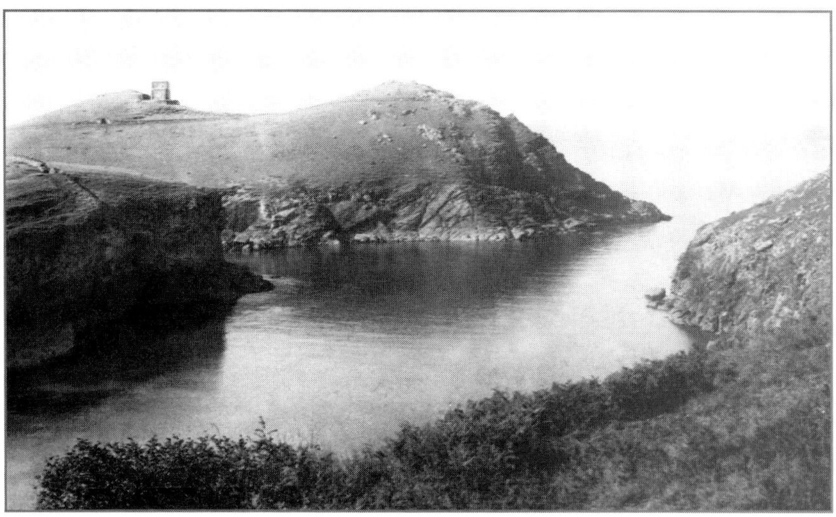

Doyden Castle, from Port Quin, 1895 37029
An amazingly calm sea hides the fact that this is on the rugged Atlantic coast. The so-called castle on Doyden Point is a folly, which was built in 1830 for parties.

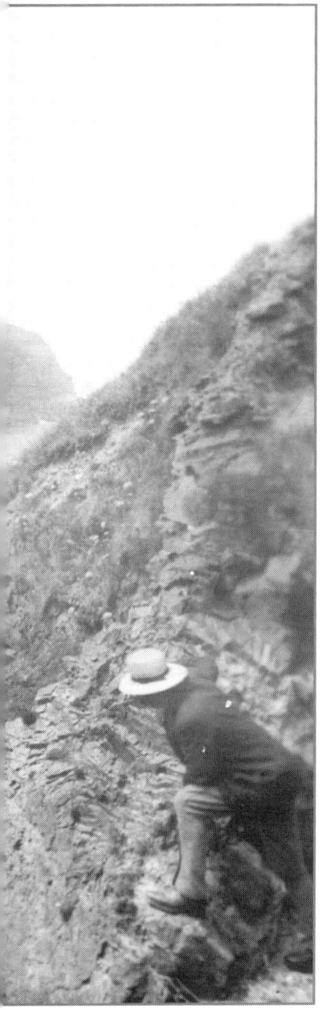

◄ **Port Gaverne The Cove 1906** 56188

We have a glimpse of the sea at the entrance to the north coast harbour inlet of Port Gaverne. Note the recent cliff top housing developments on the outskirts of neighbouring Port Isaac.

▼ **Trebarwith, The Strand 1895** 36991

This is a good view of one of the few places with access to a good beach for many miles of slate coast, although even then the sand is covered at high tide. Gull Rock is offshore. Numerous donkey paths descend the slopes on either side. The higher building on the left is now the Port William inn.

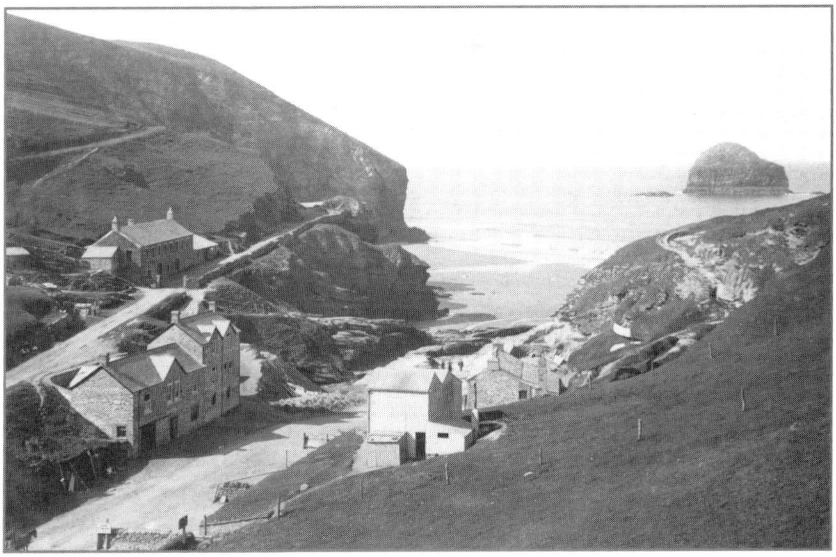

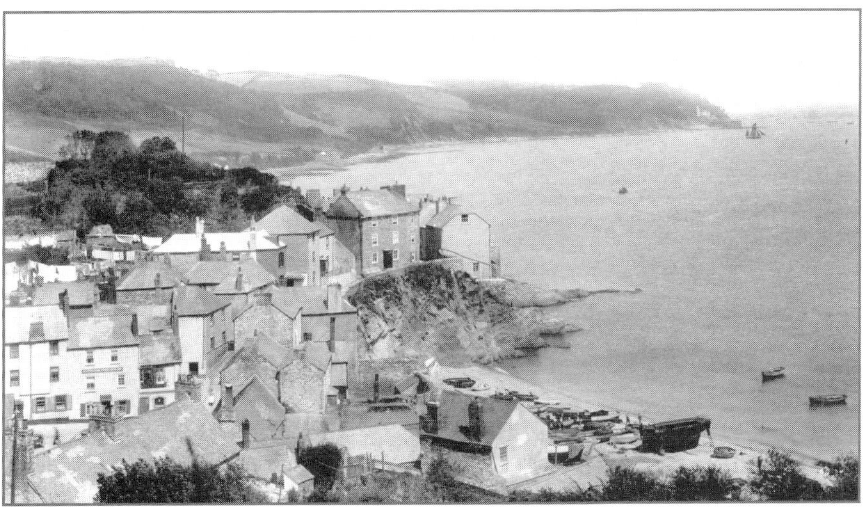

◄ **Cawsand and Kingsand, The Bay 1904** 52419

We are on the south-east coast at Cawsand Bay; the twin villages perched above the beach, where fishing boats are drawn up. The fields and woods of the Mount Edgcumbe estate reach down to the water. A sailing vessel is tacking out in the bay in front of Fort Picklecombe, one of the mid-Victorian defences to protect Devonport's naval dockyard.

▼ **Port Mellon, General View c1884** 16798

Just around the corner from Mevagissey, this charming view places the little cove and hamlet in their context admirably, with the outline of Black Head in the distance and a few fishing boats on the water out in St Austell Bay.

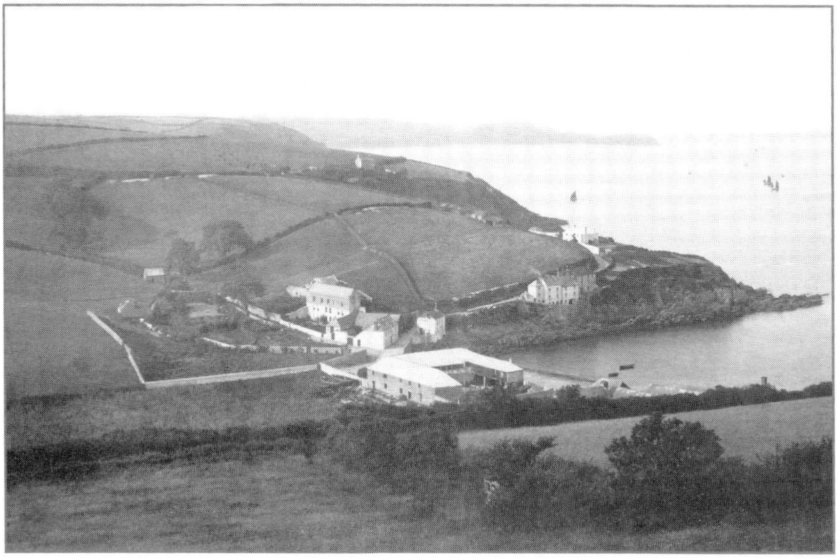

▼ **Lerryn, Looking across the River 1893** 32567

Set on one of the picturesque creeks branching off the Fowey estuary, Lerryn is seen at its best when the tide is high. At low tide there is nothing but mud in this creek. In the distance is the little 16th-century two-arched bridge.

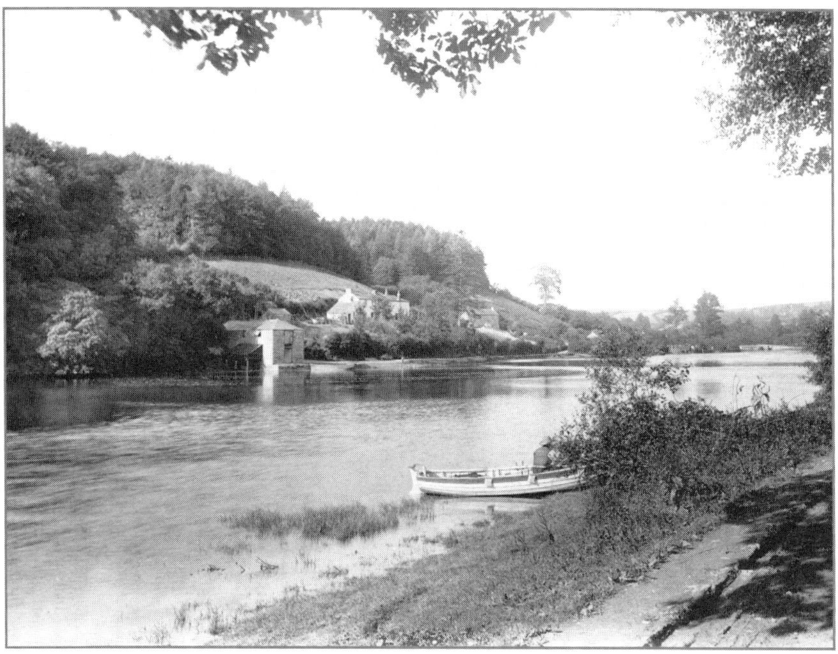

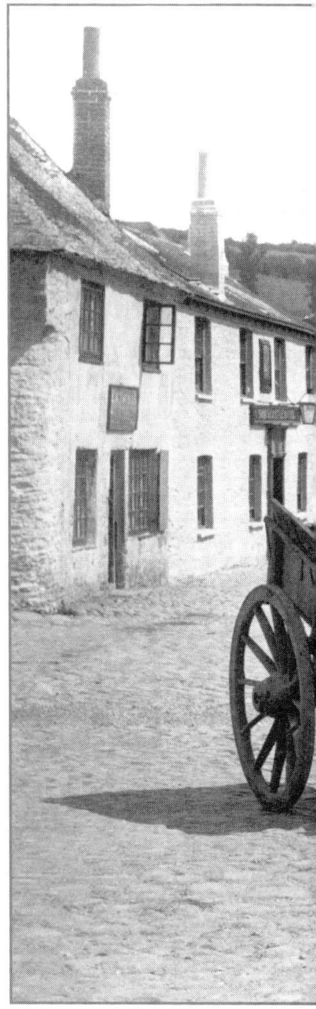

▲ **St Mawes, The Village 1890** 24232

St Mawes lies on a sheltered branch off Falmouth harbour. Here we see the as yet undeveloped village and waterfront from the pier. Behind the cart is the Ship and Castle Hotel: compare it with view No 52230.

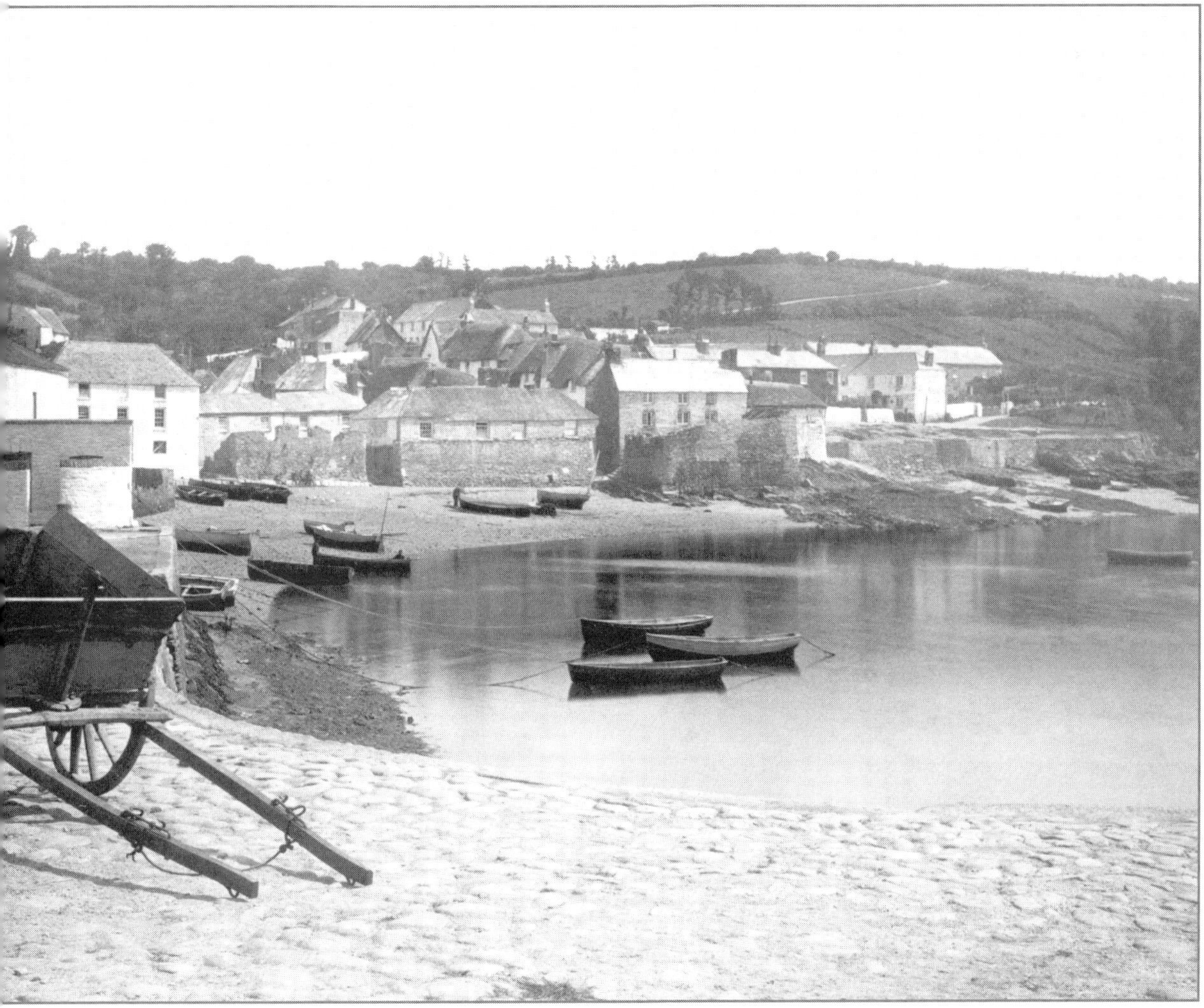

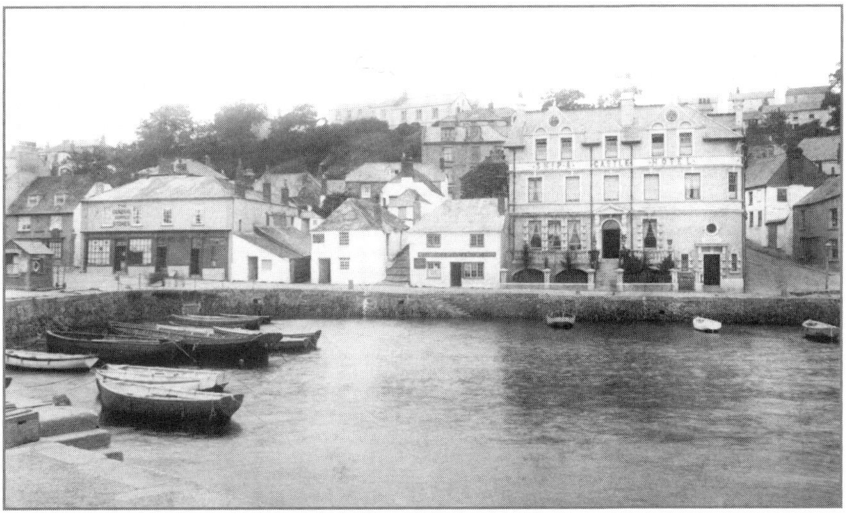

◀ **St Mawes, The Quayside 1904** 52230

The benefits of a growing tourist trade are seen with the rebuilt Ship and Castle Hotel on a prime harbour frontage. The small building to its left is the steamboat office and waiting room for passengers departing for Falmouth.

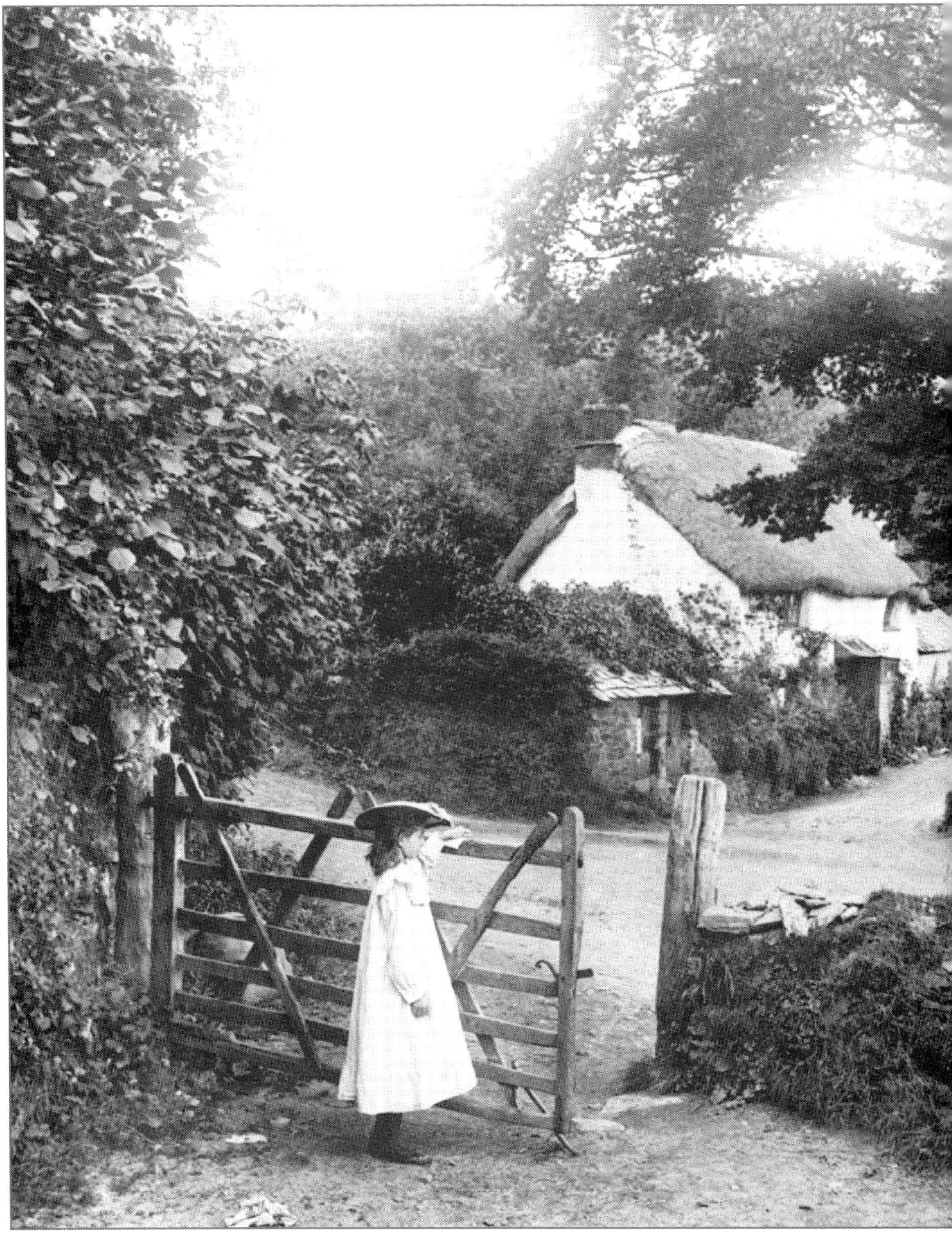

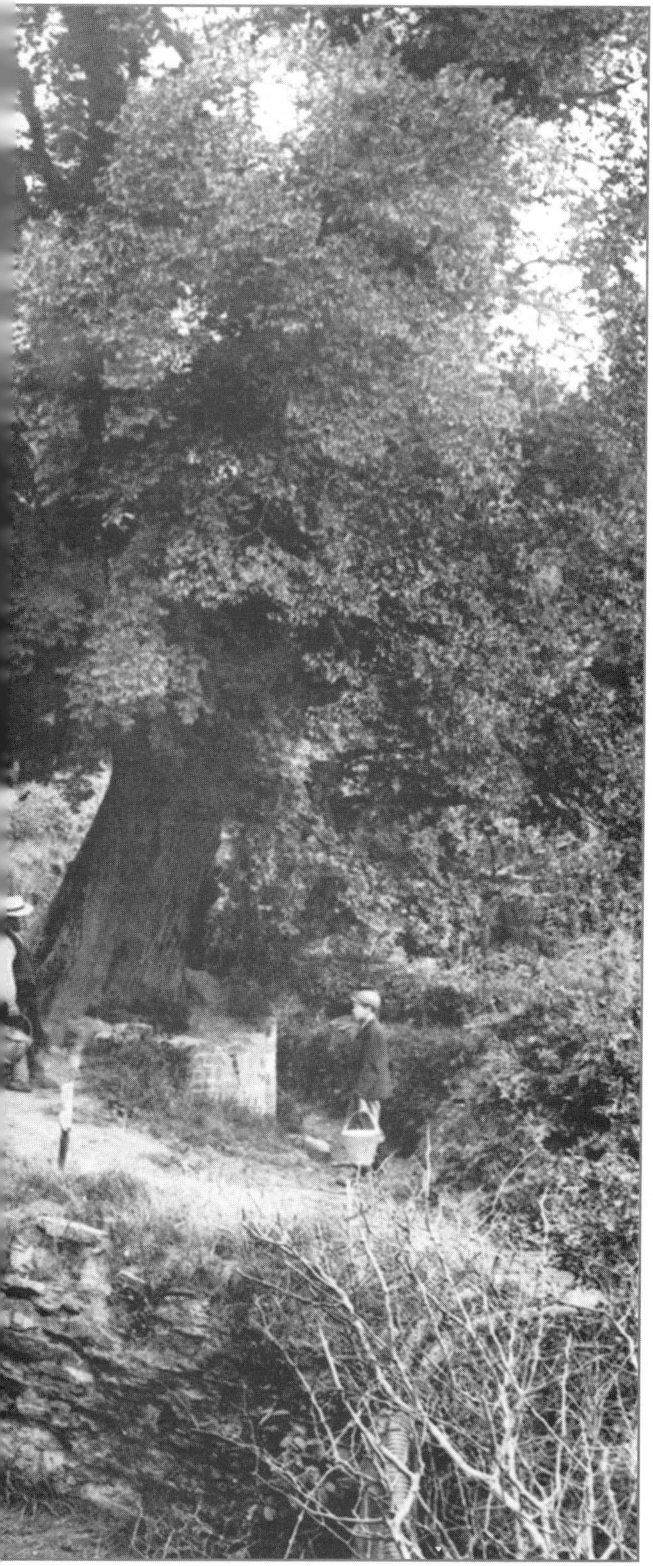

The Countryside

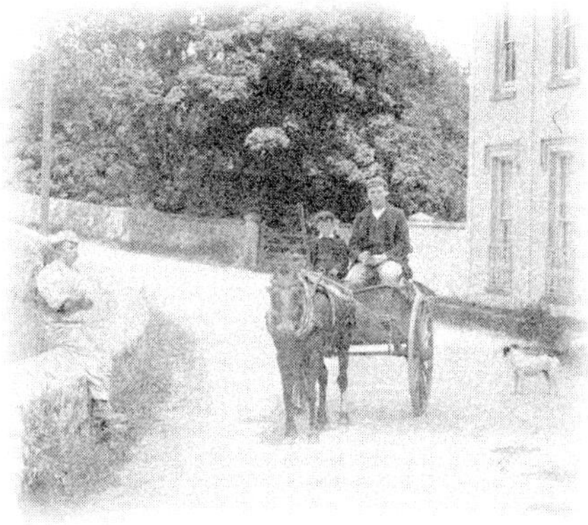

Liskeard, St Keyne's Well 1906 56313
This carefully-posed photograph shows the site of this historic well, which is situated a little way down a lane from St Keyne village in the East Looe valley. The man and boy wait with buckets at the well, which is just visible beneath the huge tree.

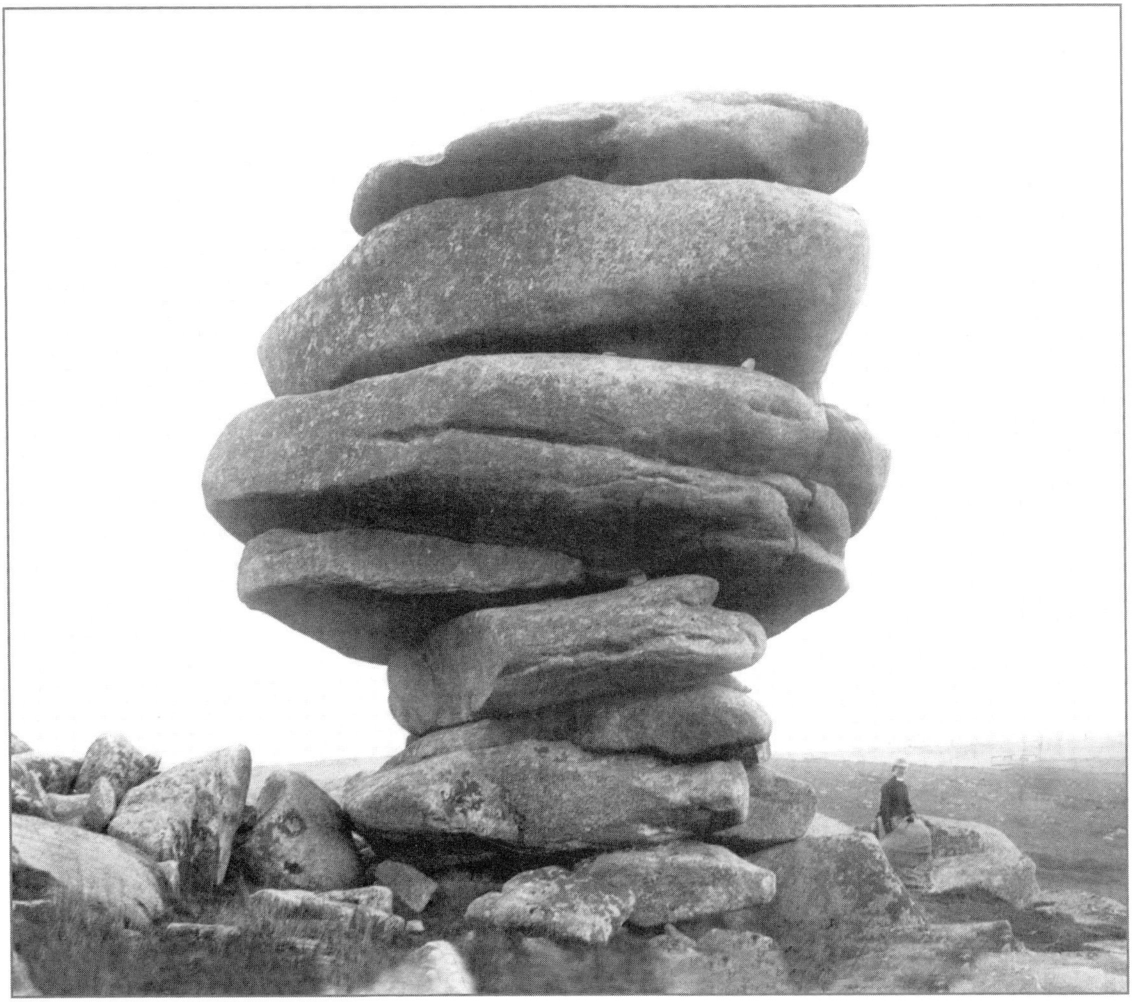

Liskeard, The Cheesewring 1890 24476

One of the strangest rock formations in the south-west, the Cheesewring near Minions on Bodmin Moor has been a place of pilgrimage for centuries. The overhanging slabs of this granite tor have been weathered naturally. This view, looking south, gives no clue of the vast Victorian granite quarry which comes almost to the Cheesewring on the far side.

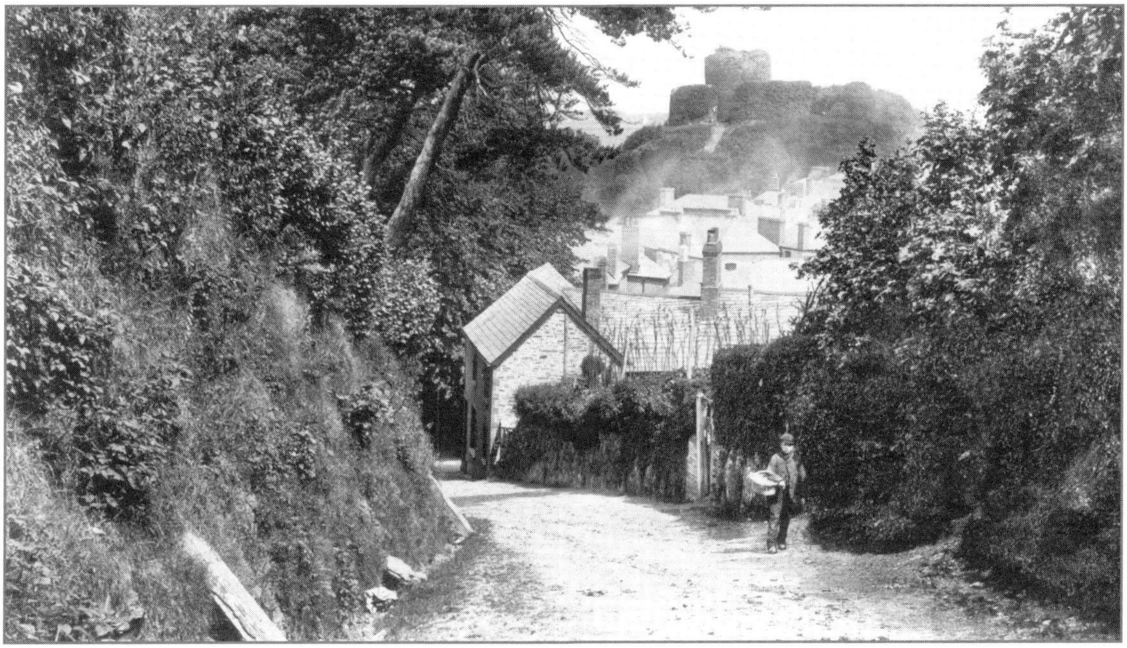

Launceston, The Castle 1893 32163
We have an attractive glimpse of the medieval castle keep on its mound, which dominates the roofs of the town and the surrounding countryside. The first castle was built at this border town within twenty years of the Norman conquest. A delivery boy with his basket completes the scene.

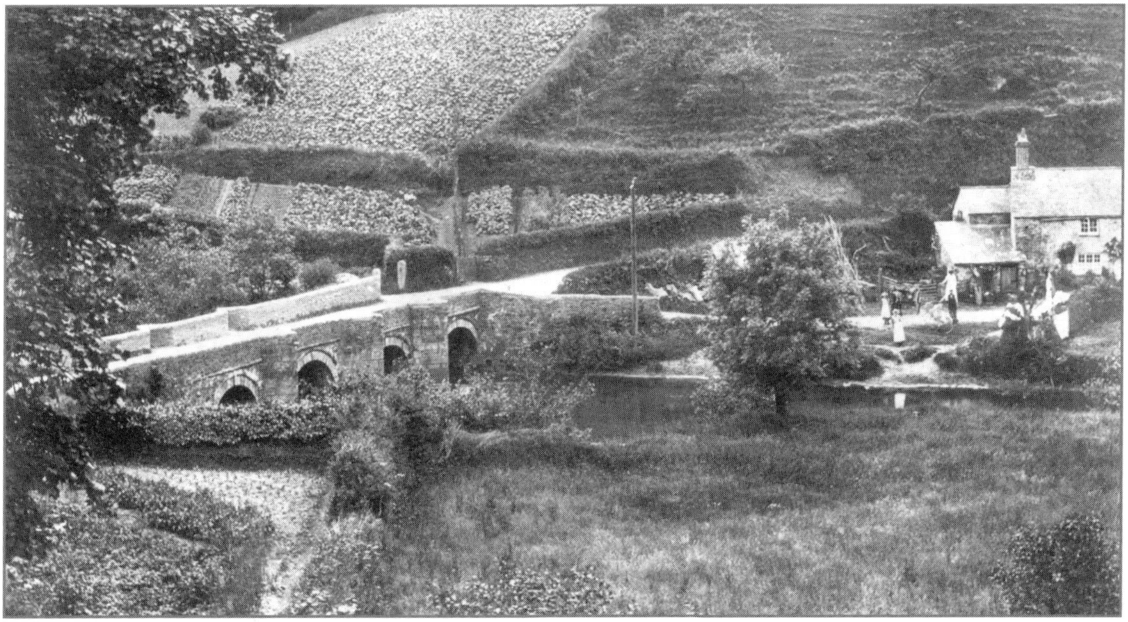

Callington, New Bridge 1904 51822
The Liskeard to Callington road crosses the River Lynher here on one of Cornwall's many historic bridges. First recorded in 1478, its granite arches were widened on the far, downstream, side in 1874. It is now busy with modern traffic, but this viewpoint emphasises the tranquil beauty of such crossing points. Note the garden plots on the hillside behind.

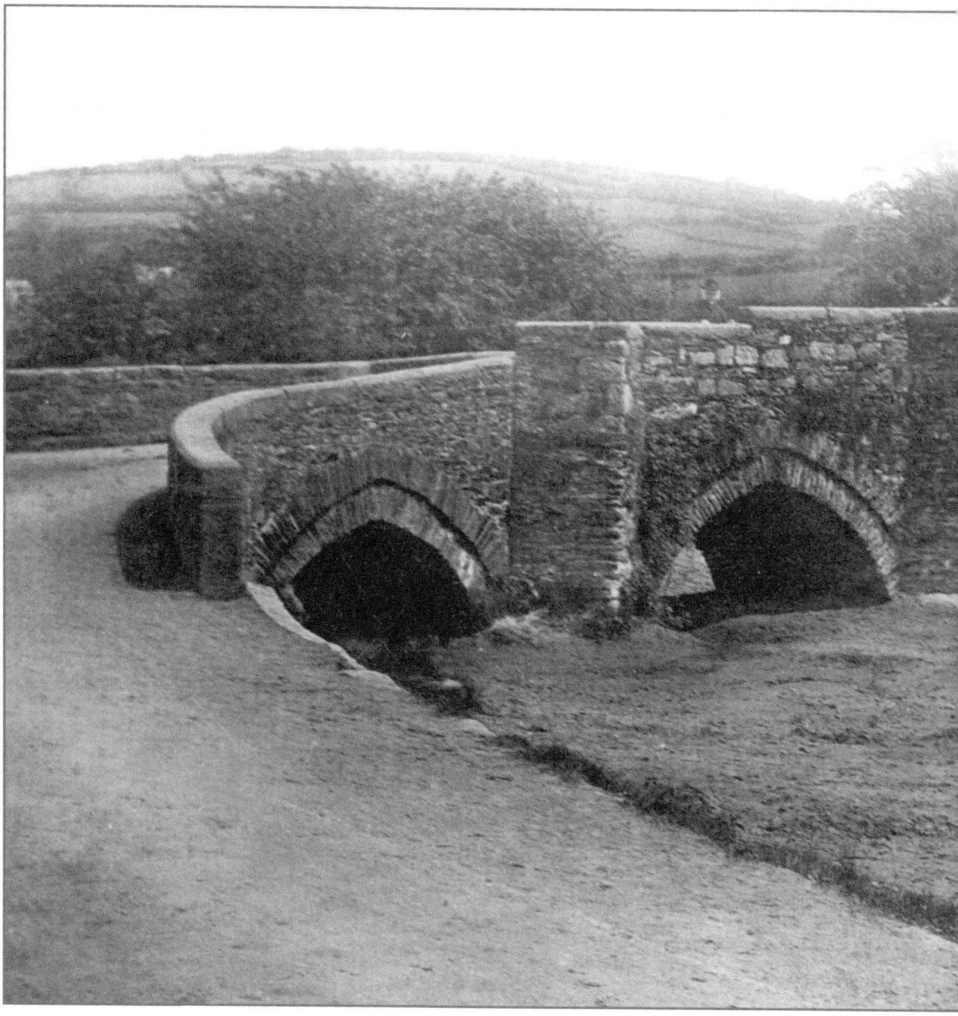

Lostwithiel The Bridge 1891 29844

This important mid 15th-century bridge at the lowest crossing point of the River Fowey links the two parts of Lostwithiel. This is also the highest tidal point up to which shipping once came; but as this view shows, the quays and channel became silted by material washed down the river. The cart may well be there to collect sand.

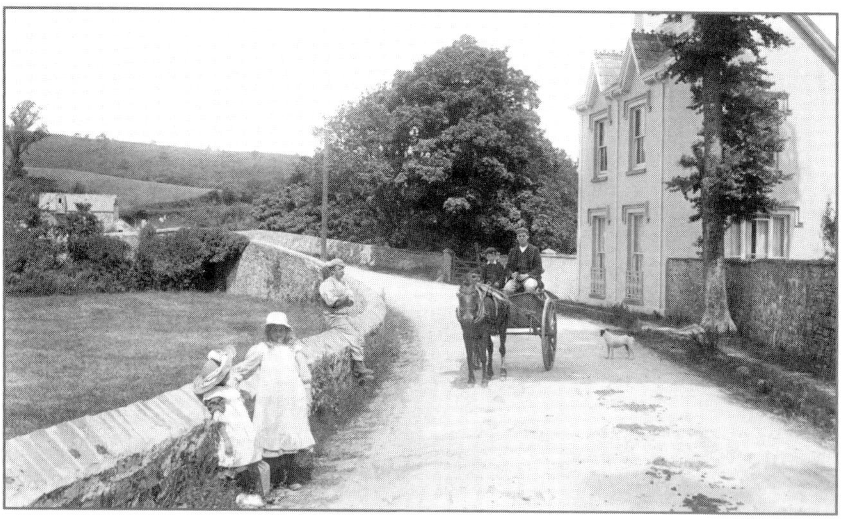

Bodmin, Dunmere Bridge and the Mill 1906 56290

Here we see a quiet summer scene in the valley bottom, where the Wadebridge road crosses the River Camel at the foot of a long descent from Bodmin. The mill is just visible beyond the bridge on the left. The bridge, hardly visible, was rebuilt after being destroyed in a flood in 1847.

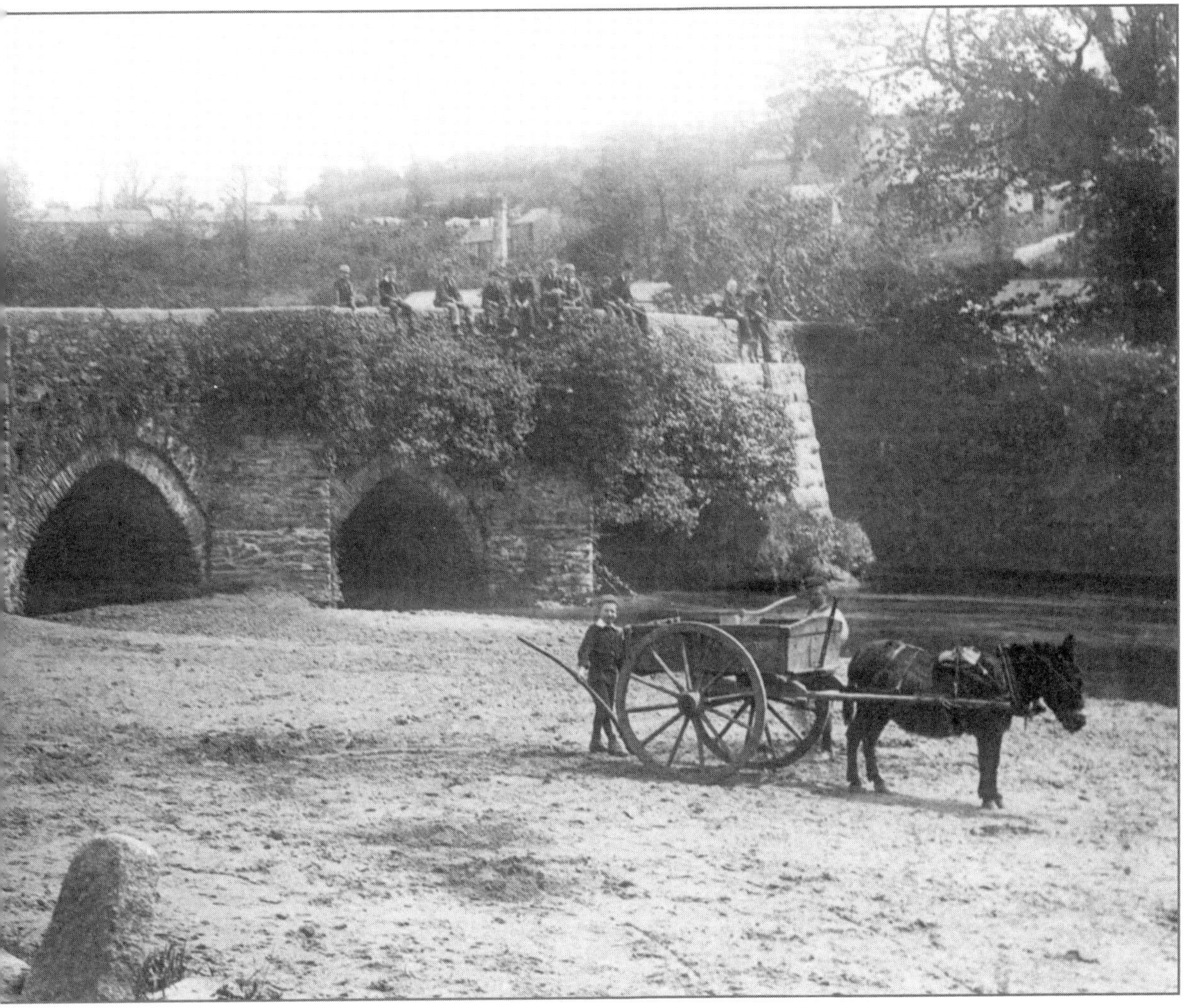

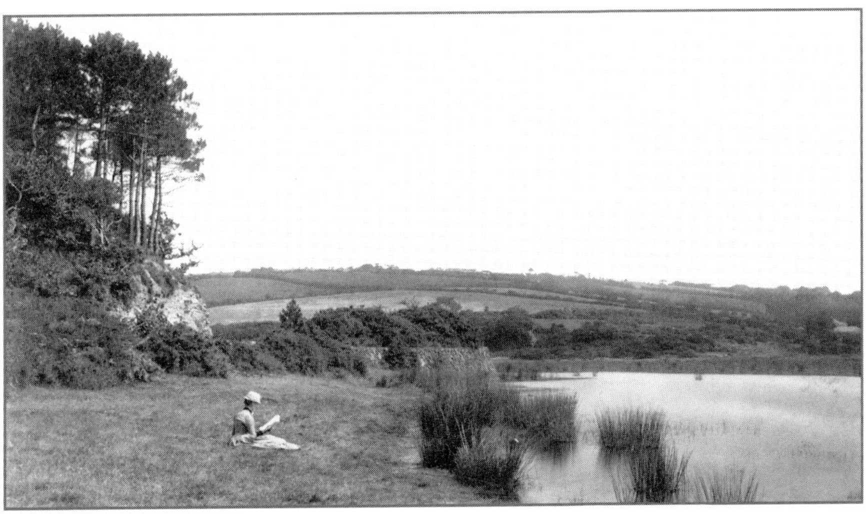

◄ **Helston, Loe Pool 1890** 24505

The Loe is the largest freshwater lake in Cornwall, and the shore can be a place of peace and contemplation. It is separated from the sea by the great Loe Bar, which blocked the Cober estuary to shipping in historic times. By an ancient custom the bar was cut to lower the water level whenever it threatened to flood Helston.

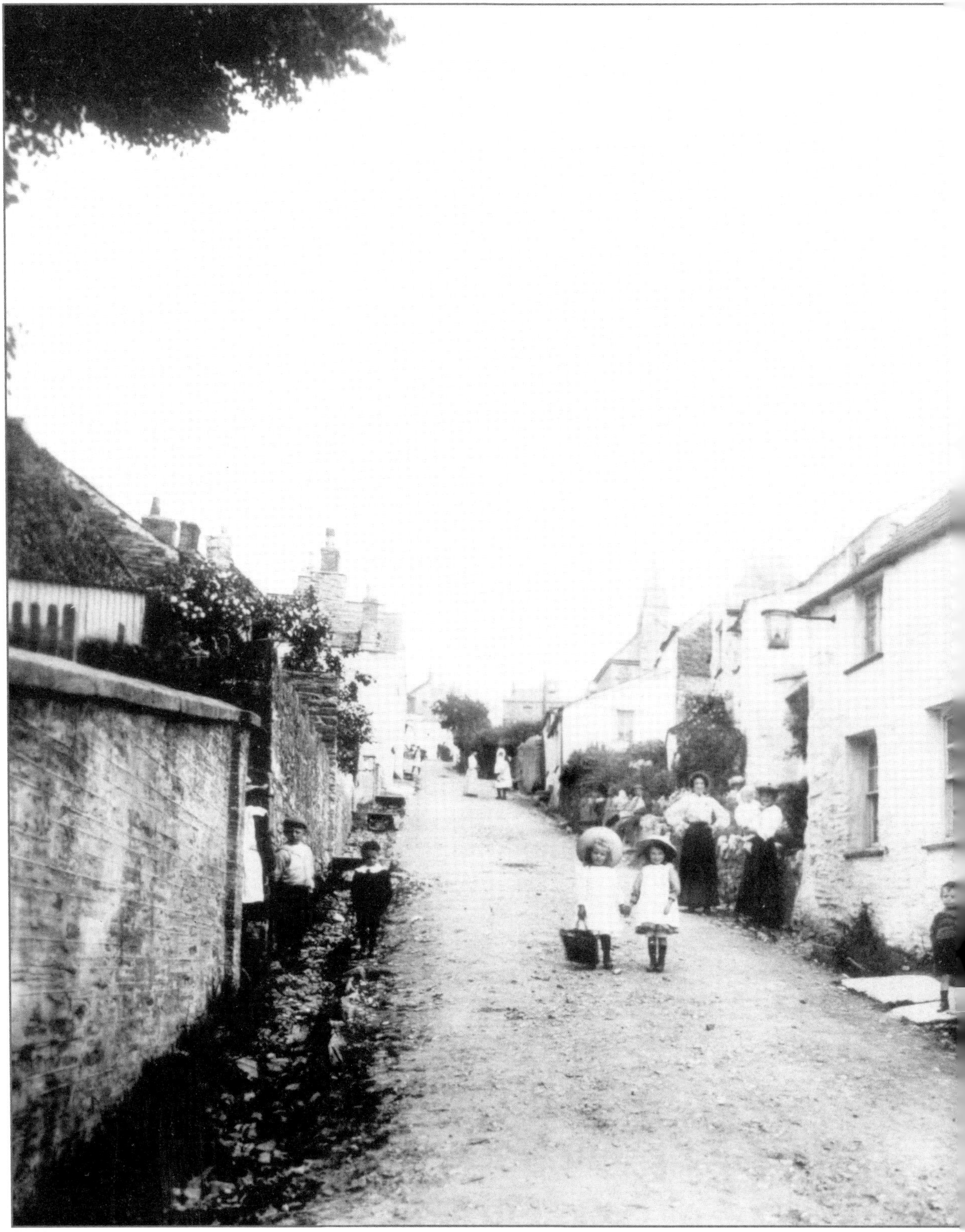

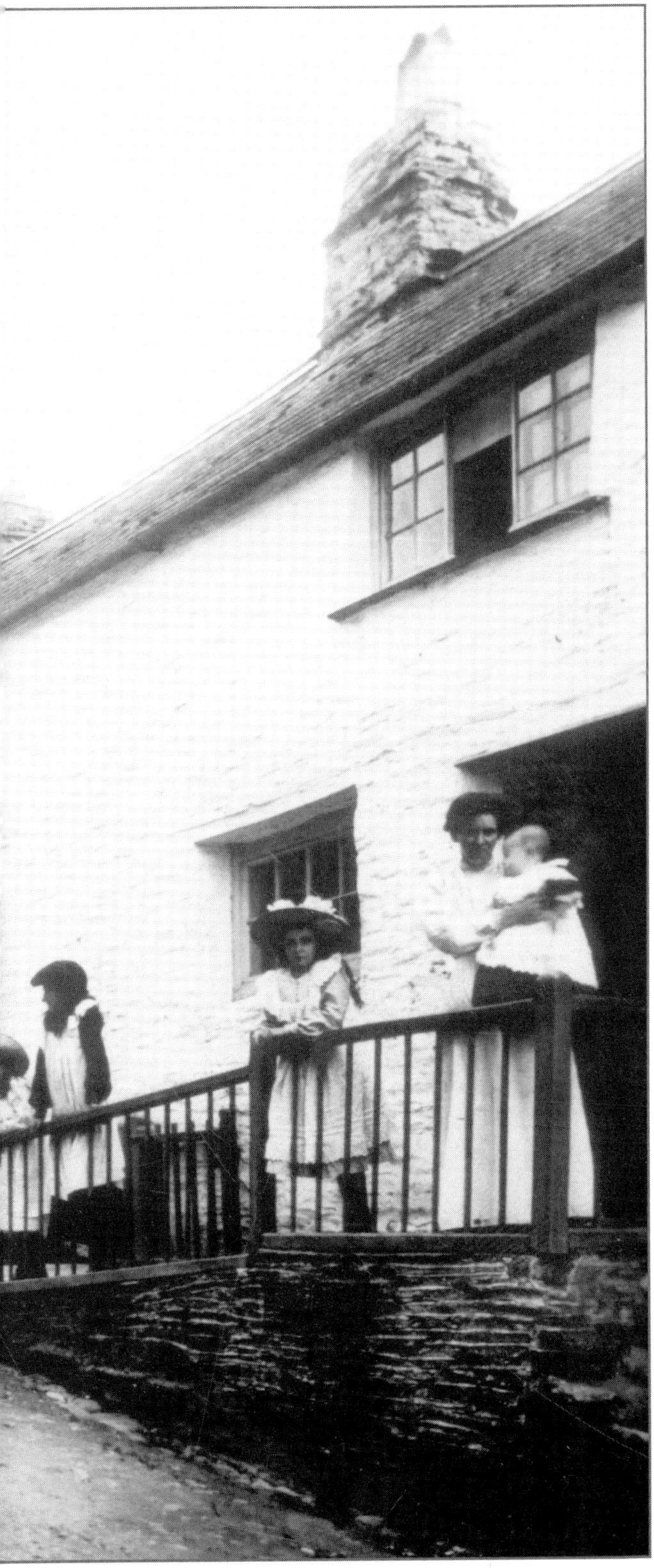

Village Life

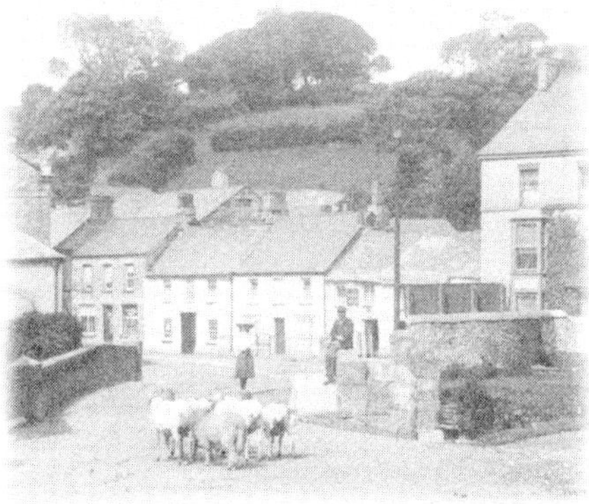

Boscastle, The Village 1906 56169
While the harbour area is well known to tourists, the true village of Boscastle climbs a steep hill to the south, where it was by-passed in 1886. Children and their mothers pose while the men are out at work, fishing or farming. Slate slabs form bridges over the roadside gutters.

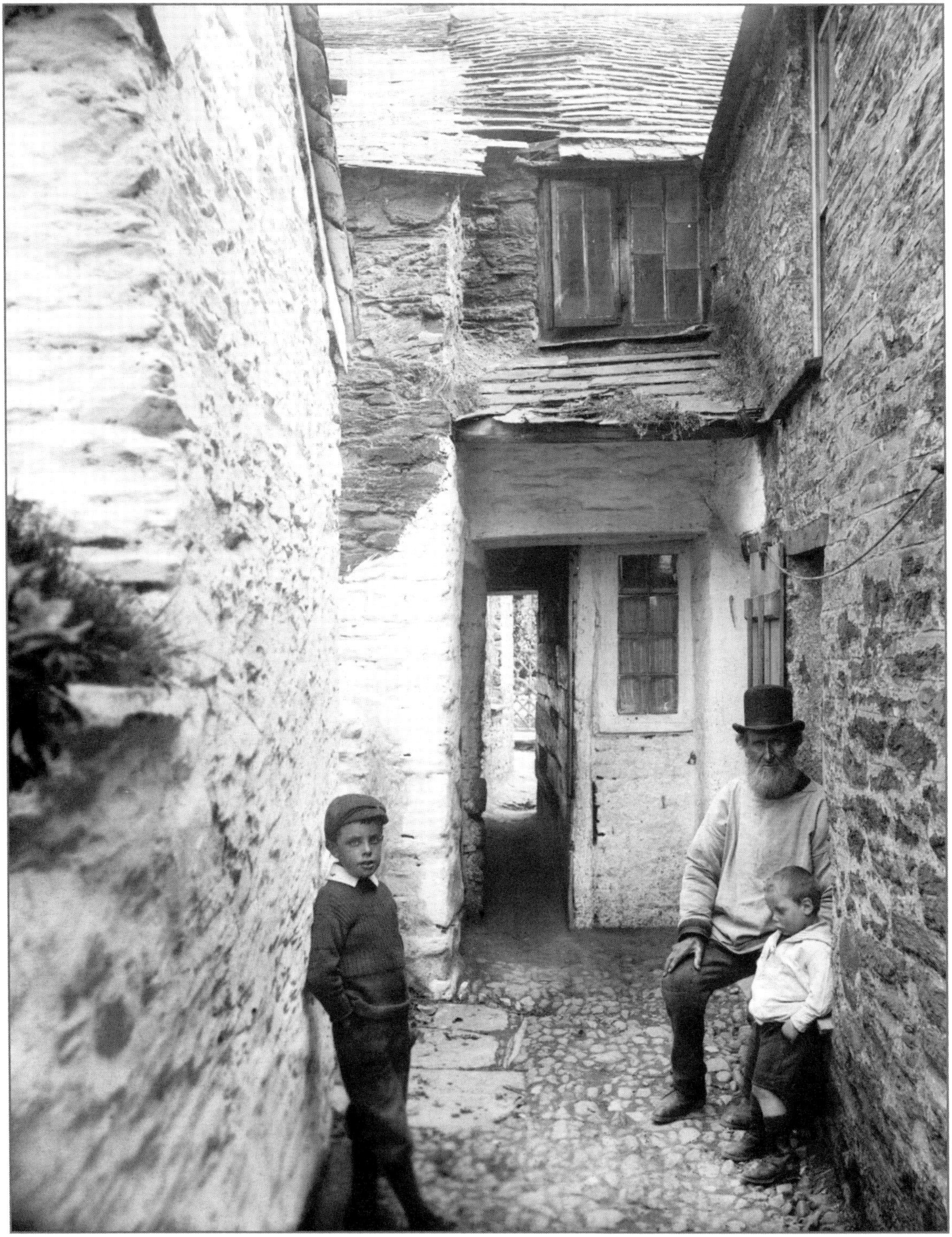

Port Isaac, Temple Bar 1906 56184
Closely-packed village houses built almost entirely of slate enclose a small cobbled courtyard. The youngest to oldest inhabitants are represented here.

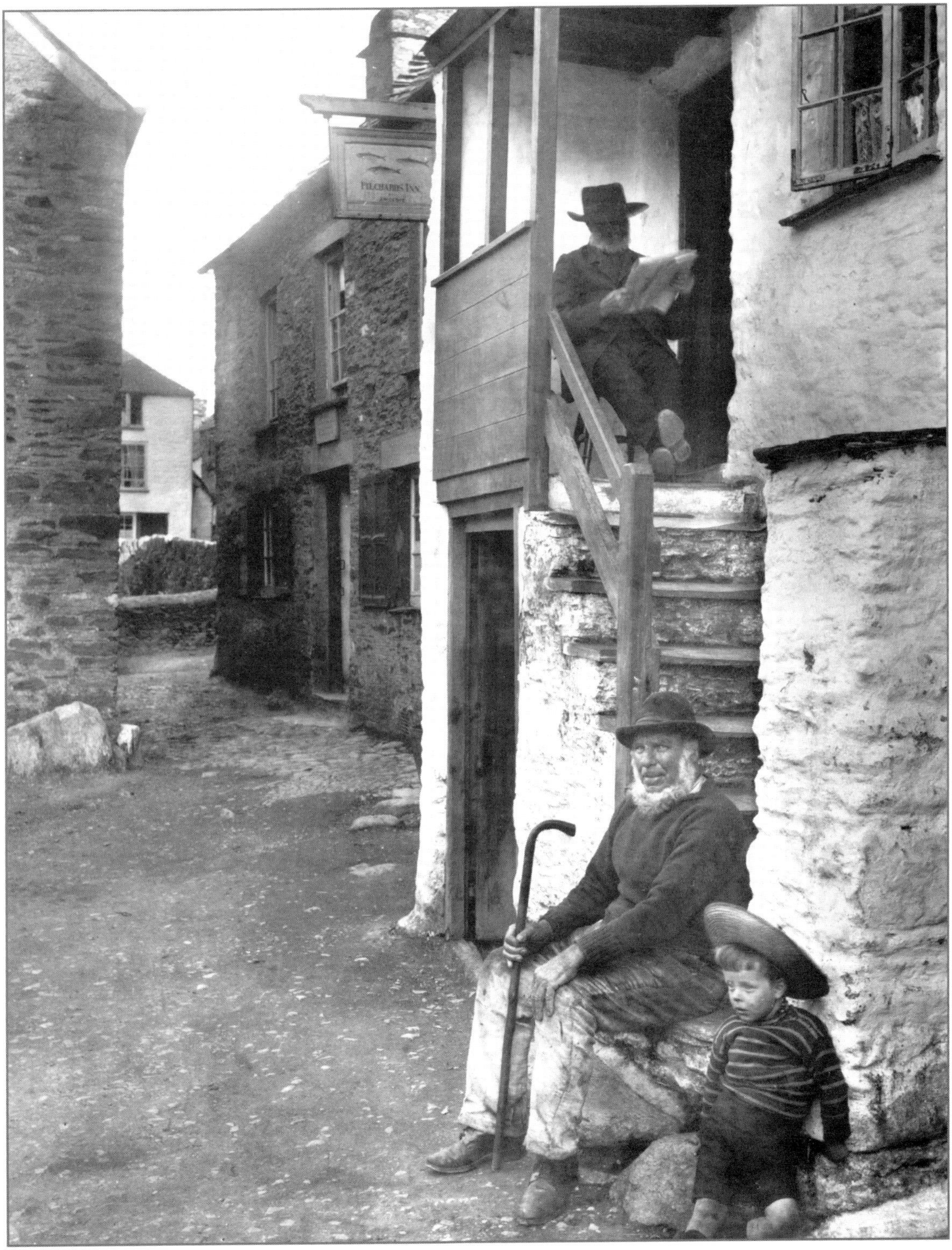

Polperro, The Pilchards Inn 1907 59269
The older generation, one with his newspaper, wait for opening time at this aptly-named pub down by the fishing harbour.

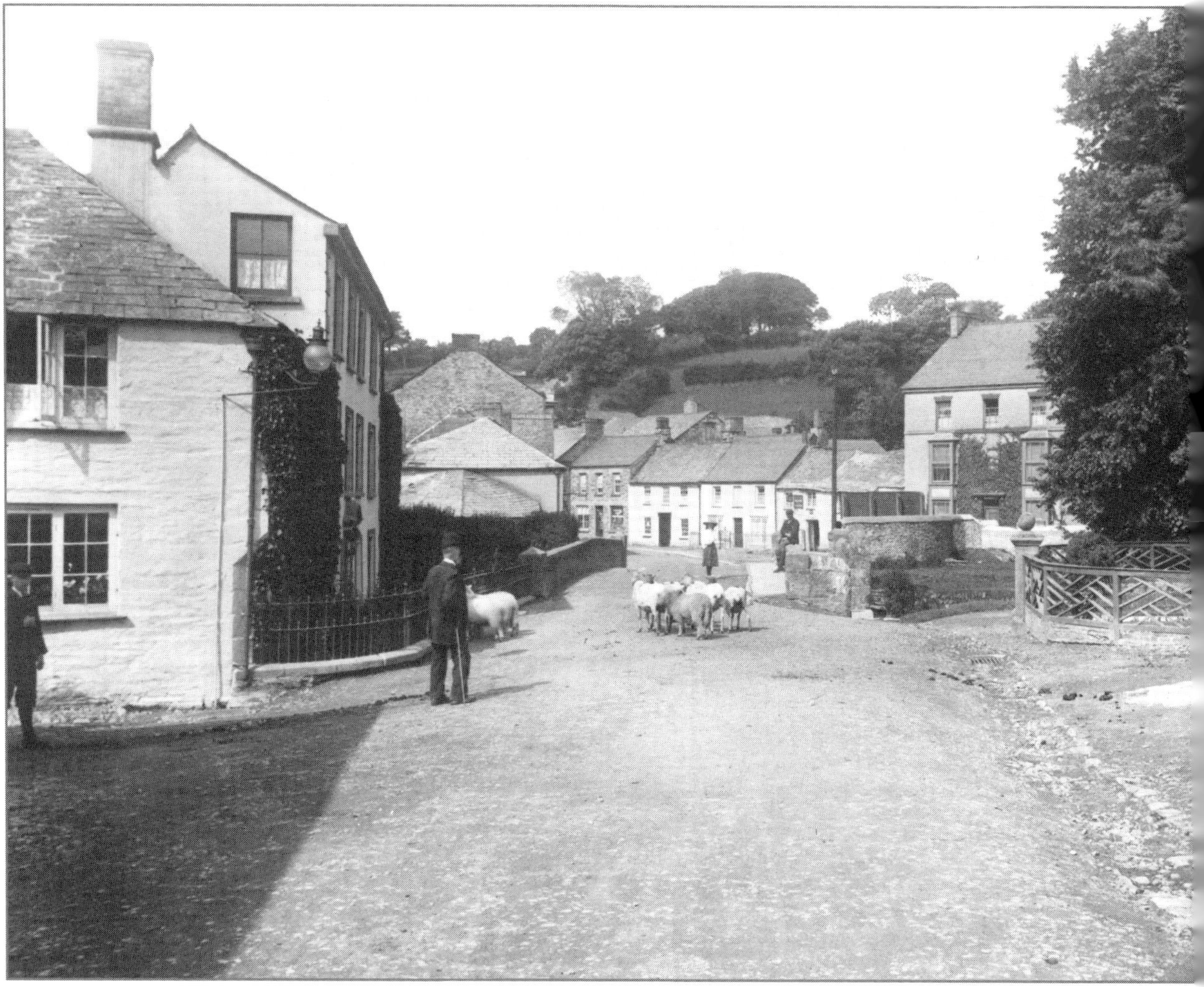

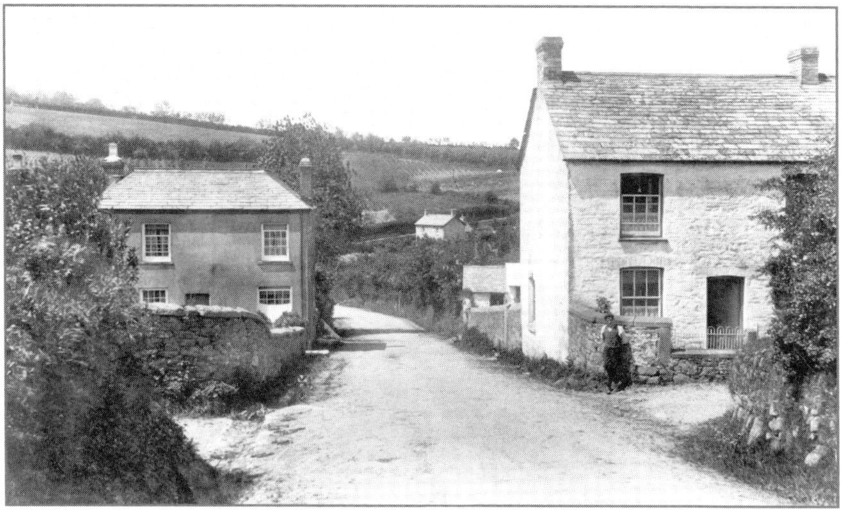

Downgate, The Village 1908 59718
A quiet hamlet on the north side of Kit Hill near Callington. Such a scene, but with an improved road and without the figure by the wall, would still be familiar today in many rural parts of Cornwall.

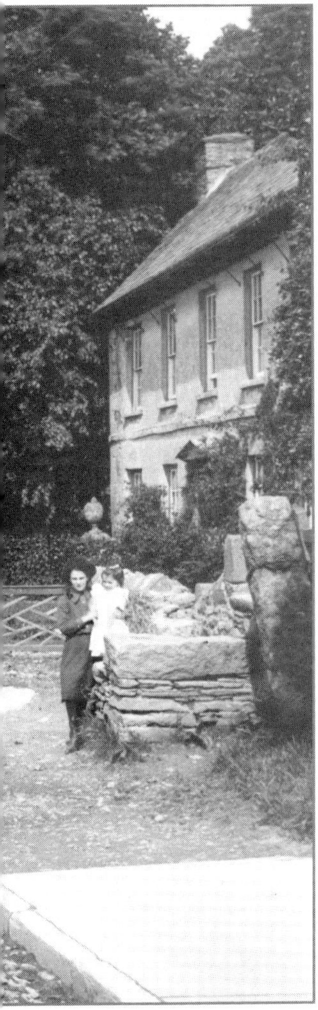

◄ **Camelford The Bridge 1906** 56160

A few sheep wandering in the road are watched over by a lad sitting on the bridge parapet in this view looking west along what is now the busy A39 through the village. The bridge, of course, is over the River Camel.

▼ **Stratton, The Village 1910** 62400

A corner of the village near the church with Ching and Sons' wine merchants, general shop and post office. The 'Western Morning News' is advertised for sale, and the newspaper headlines include a fire in Exeter and the announcement that Lemberg is this year's Derby winner.

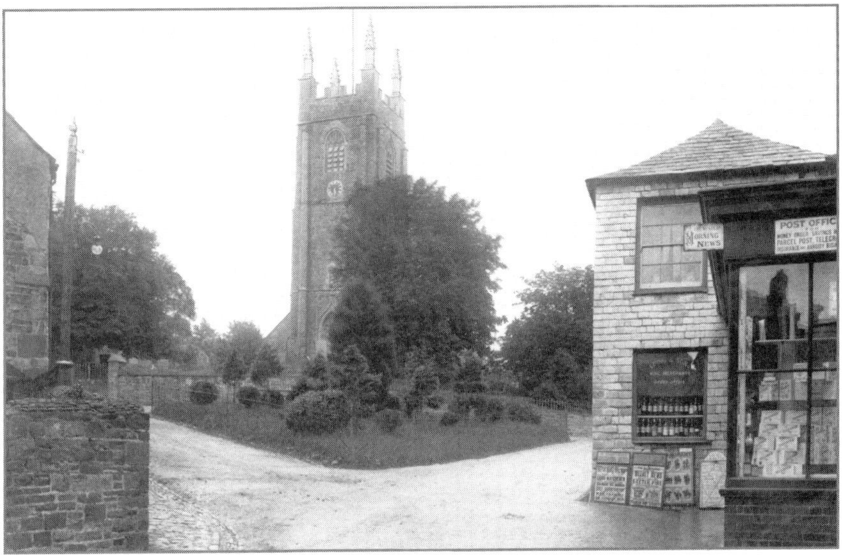

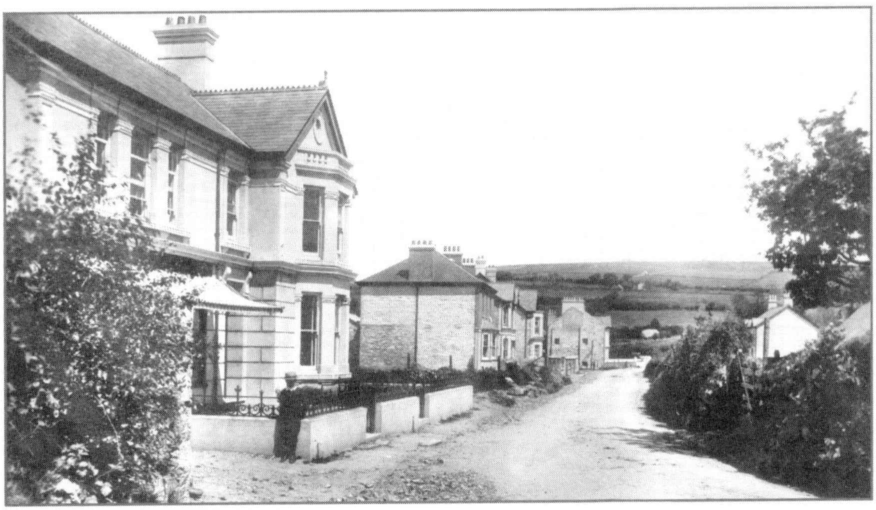

◄ **Kelly Bray, The Village 1908** 59721

An architect-designed villa on the left has probably recently been built in this settlement, which is just north of Callington and at the terminus of the railway branch line from Plymouth.

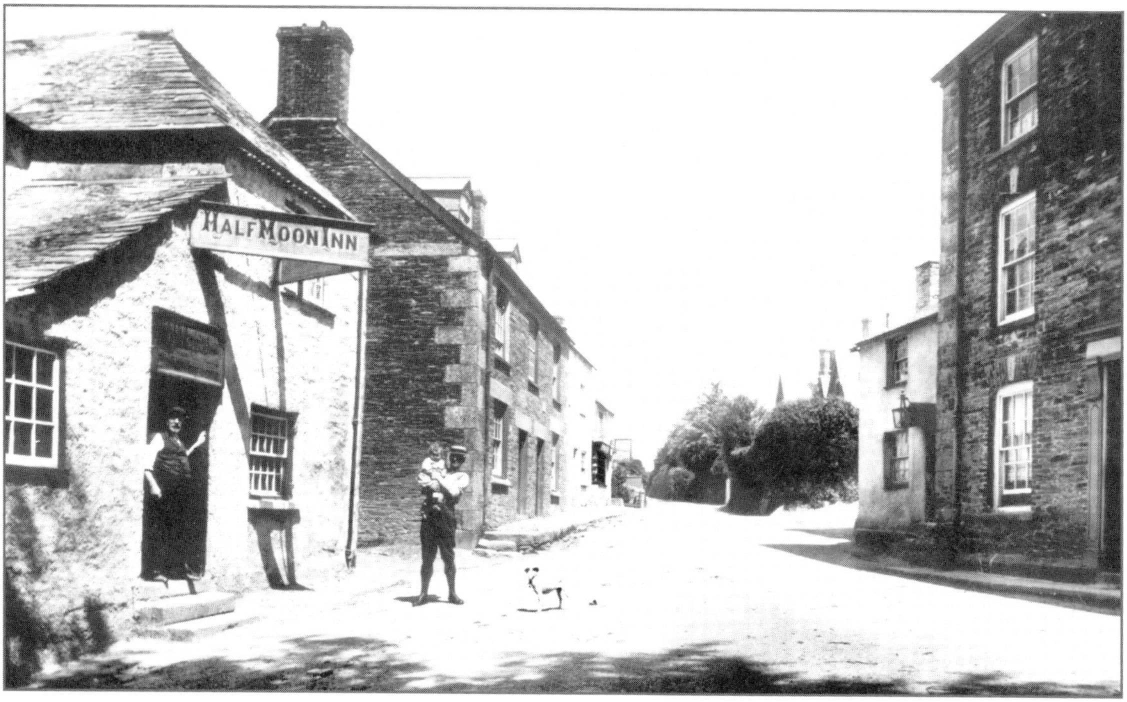

Stoke Climsland, The Village 1908 59716
Two men, a young child and a dog outside the Half Moon Inn provide the only sign of life in the village centre.

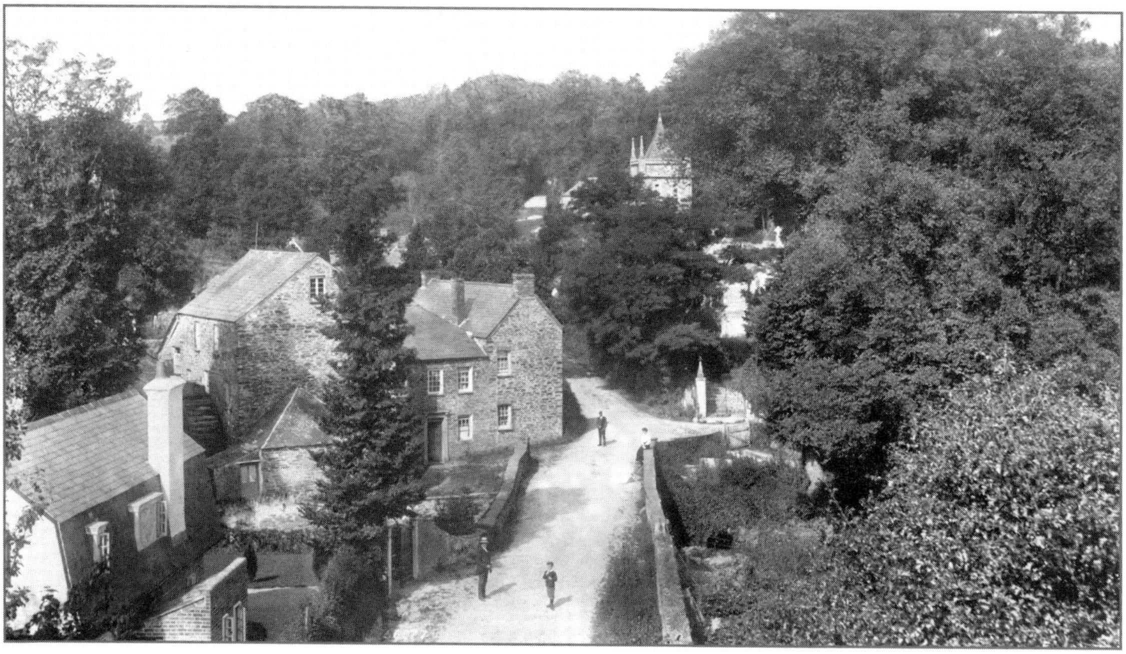

Little Petherick, The Village 1906 56277
The village lies at the head of a small creek off the Camel estuary; this narrow lane has become the main road between Wadebridge and Padstow. The pinnacled tower and pyramid roof of St Petrock's church is seen through the trees, and the village mill and its waterwheel are on the left.

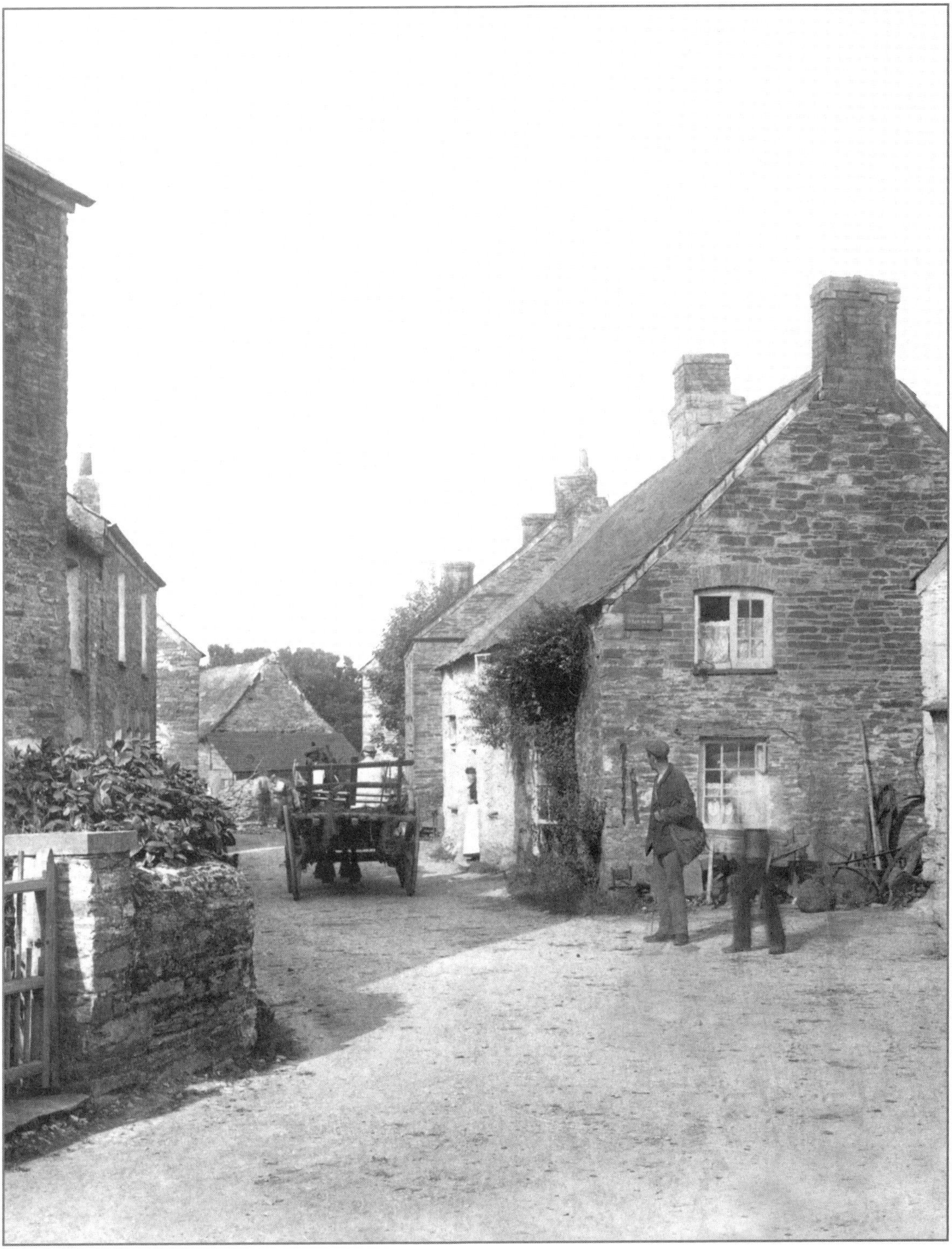

St Issey, The Village 1906 56276
A lone farm wagon trundles between the houses in a village built of local slate. Only some chimneys and window surrounds are finished in brick.

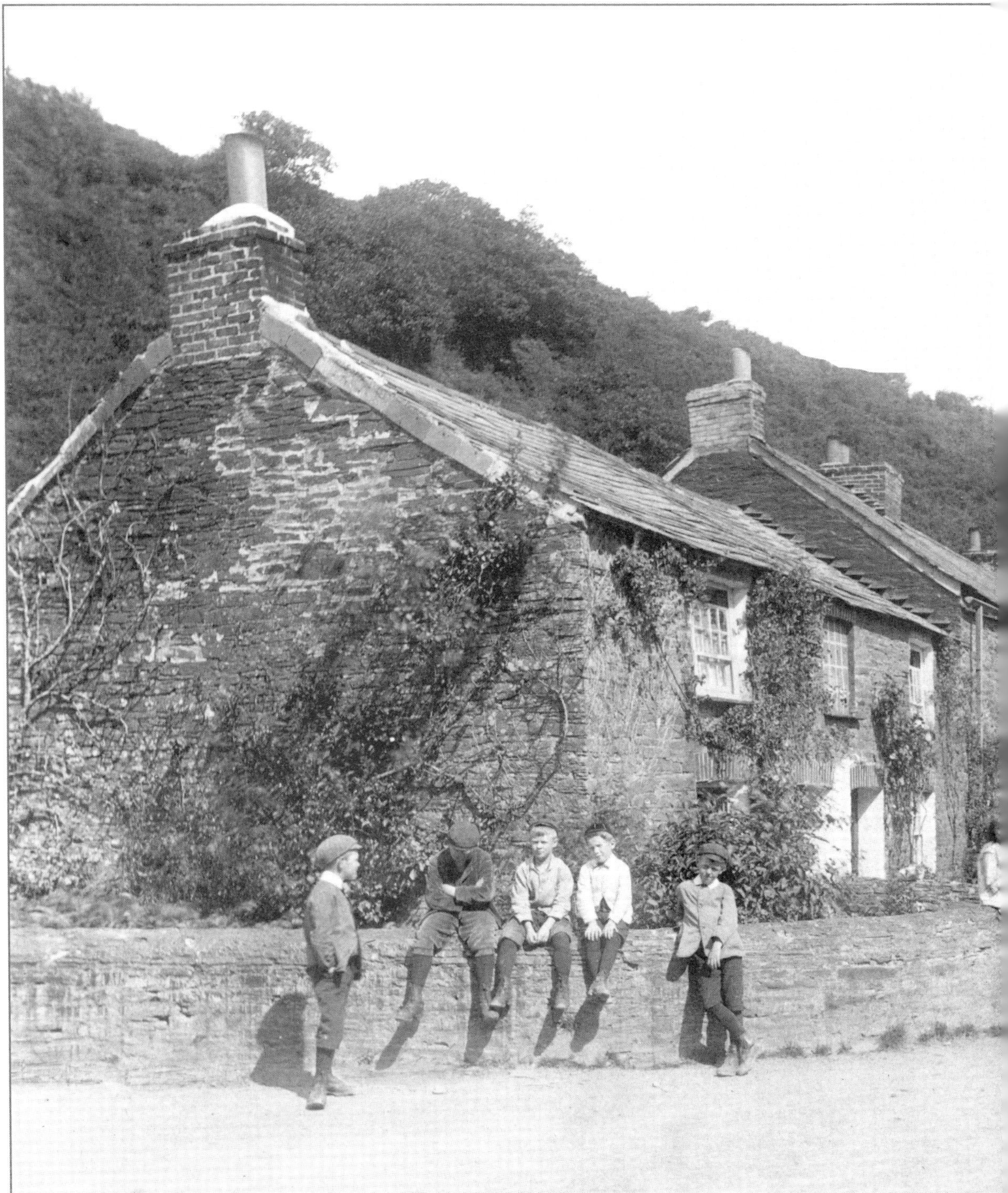

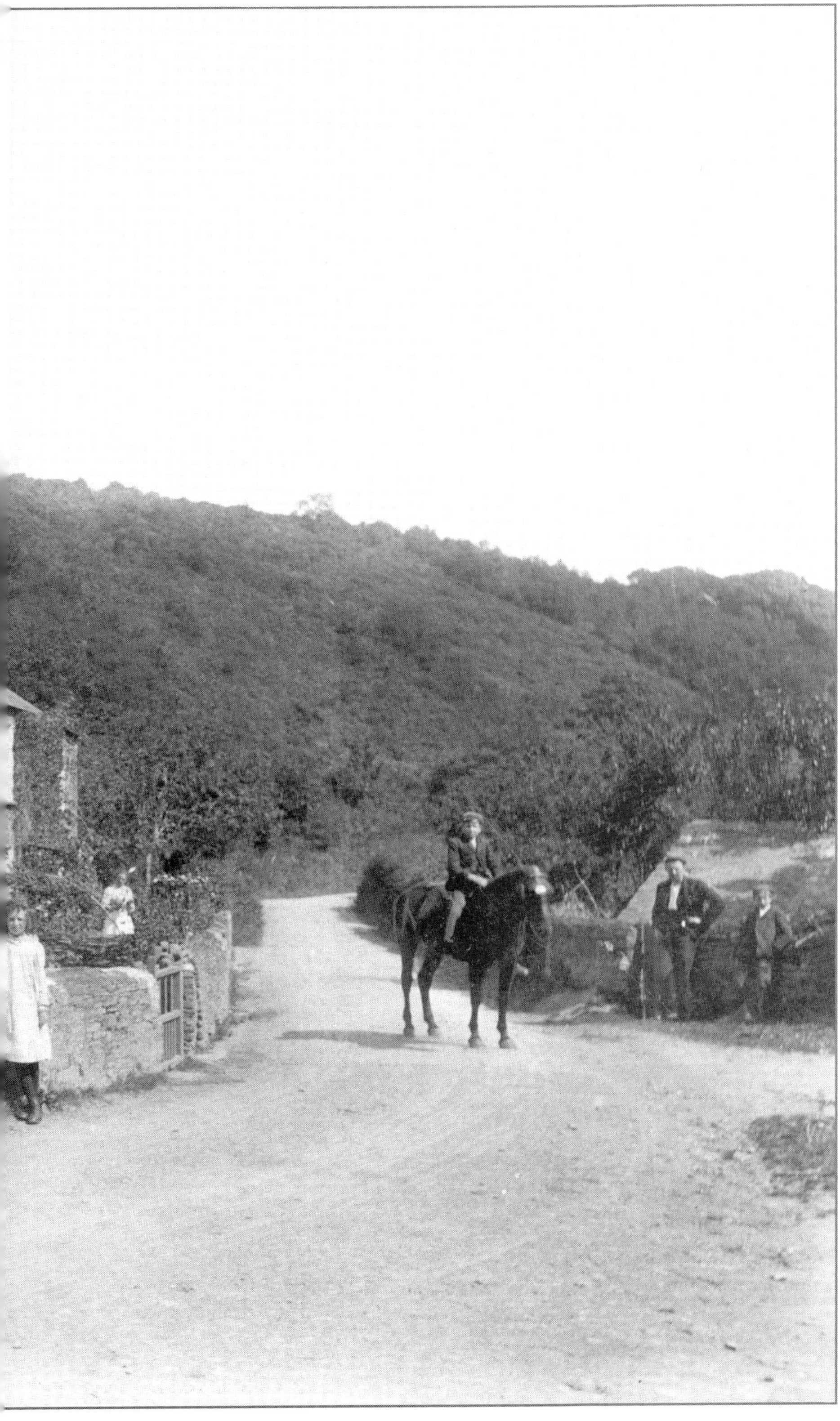

Wadebridge Polmorla Village 1906 56261
We must be seeing almost the entire population of this hamlet, as we look towards Wadebridge. Two boys on the left seem to be deliberately avoiding the camera.

▼ **St Columb Major, The Village 1894** 33543
This is a pretty view looking up into the town. The photographer appears to have stepped into a garden and asked the inhabitants of the house to come out and pose.

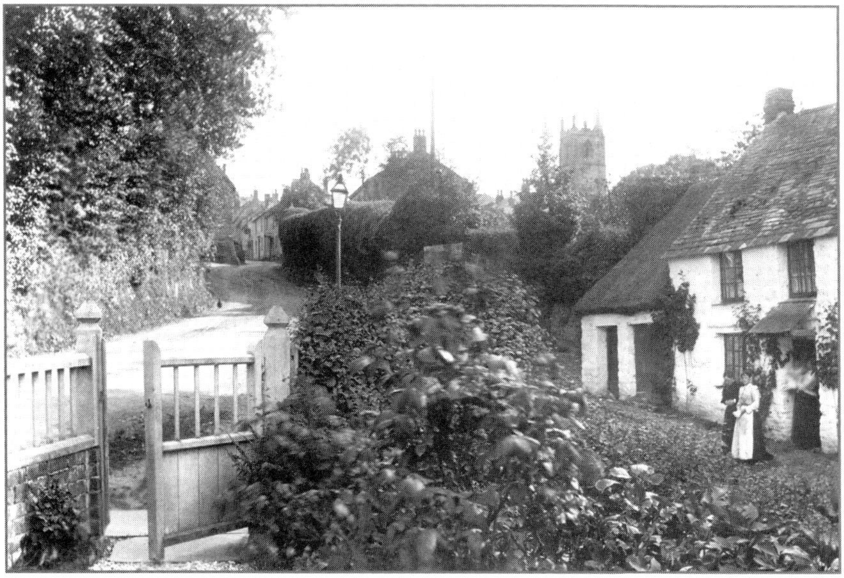

▼ **Truro, The Church and Cottages at St Clement 1890** 23949
This is a most attractive hamlet of thatched cottages not far from Truro. Its church is on an ancient site, for a Dark Age inscribed stone was found here. The way from St Clement to the Tresillian River, a branch of the Truro River estuary, lies to the right of the cottage.

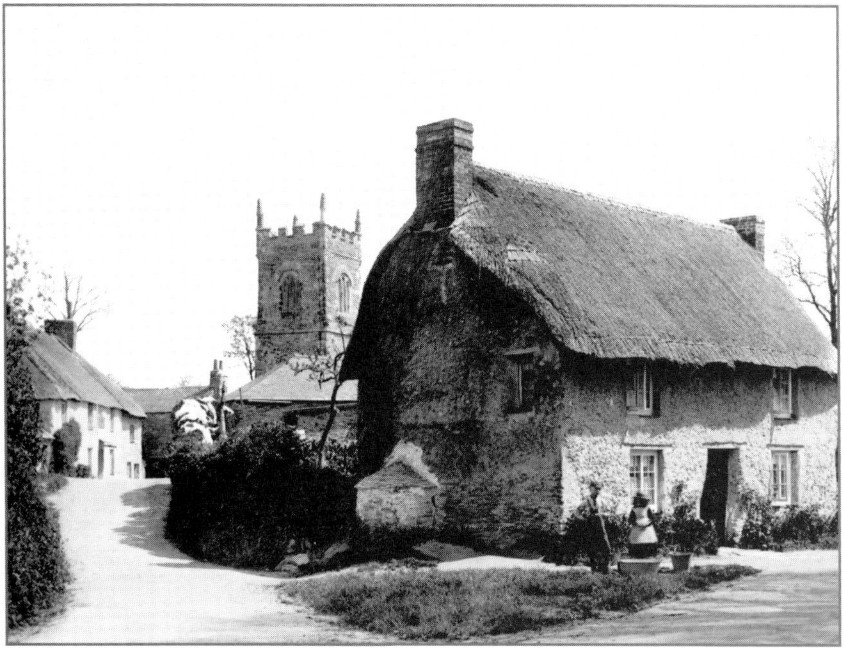

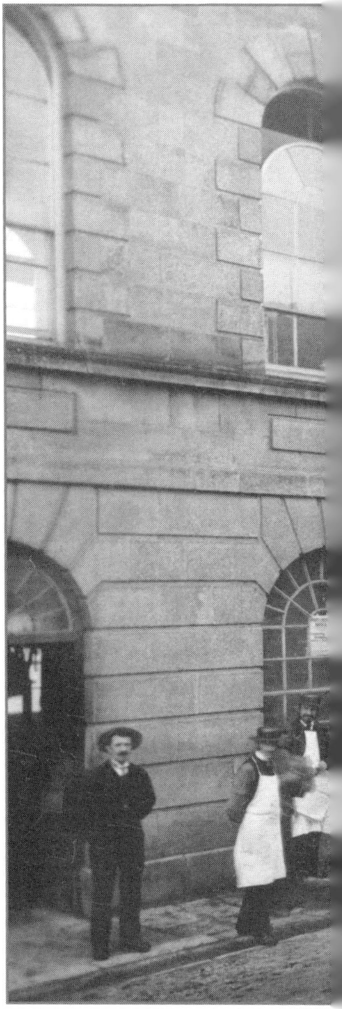

▲ **St Columb Major, The King's Arms 1888** 21196
Fore Street is exceptionally narrow at this point, where the King's Arms with its slate-hung upper floor is rather lost in the middle distance. The Town Hall on the left has a meat market on the ground floor, and butchers have come out to pose for the photograph.

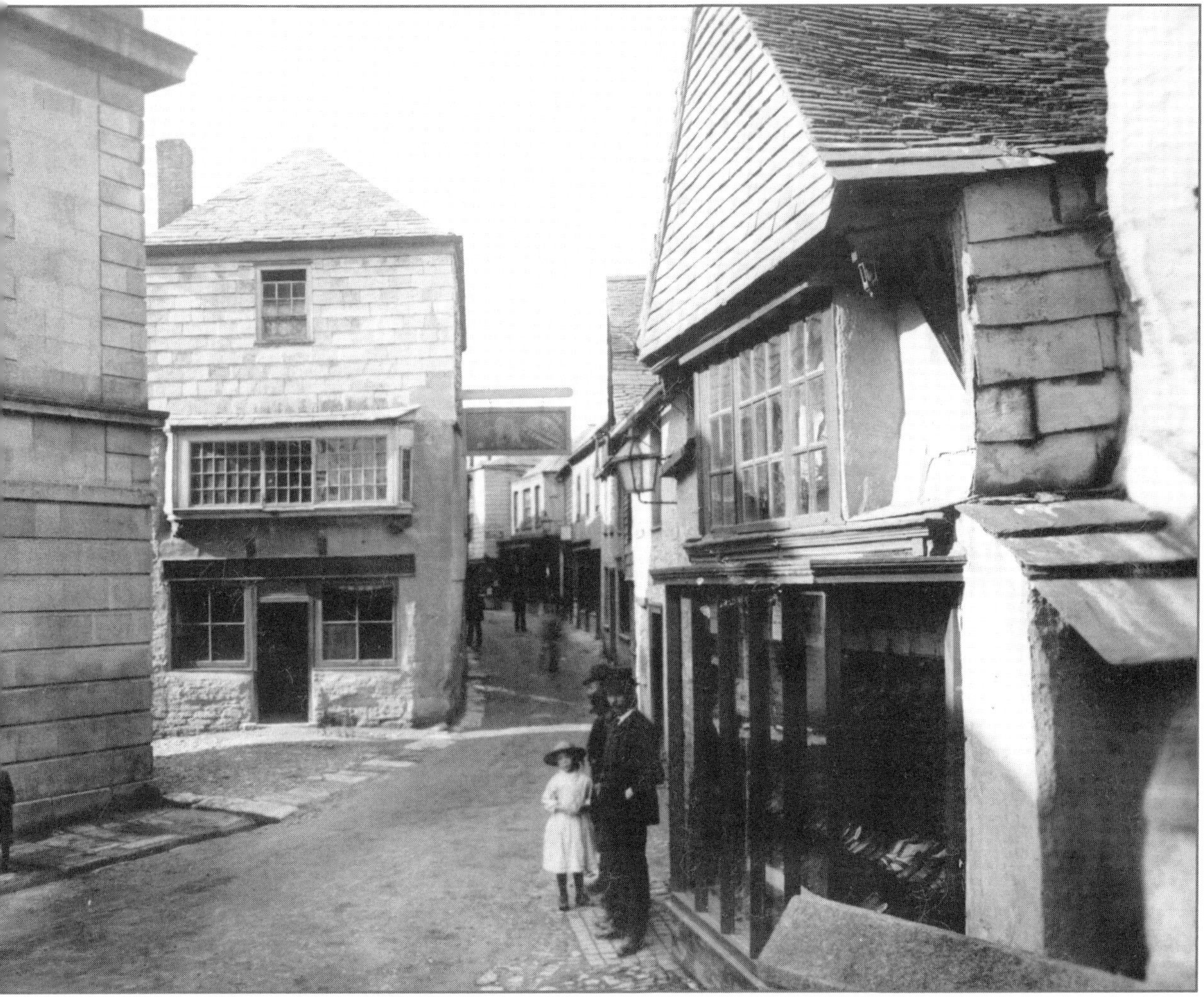

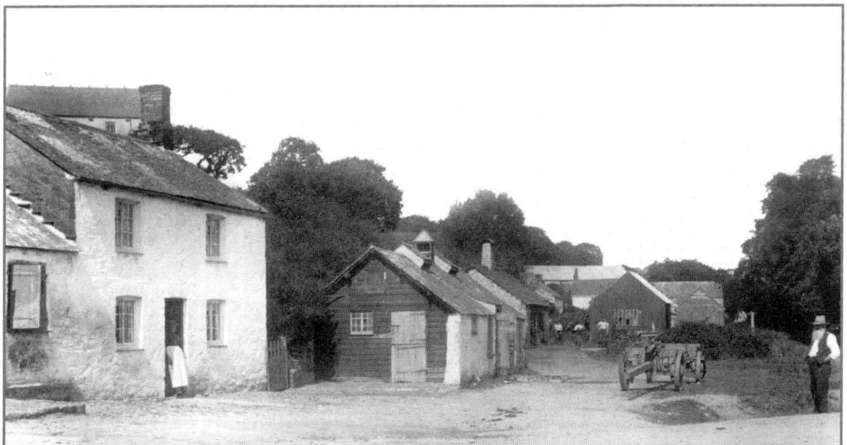

◄ **Gweek, The Village Green 1904** 53045
Situated at the very head of the tidal Helford River, Gweek was an important port for distributing goods to and from Helston and the surrounding district. Note the wagon for carrying timber in front of the works. The old quay is just behind the camera.

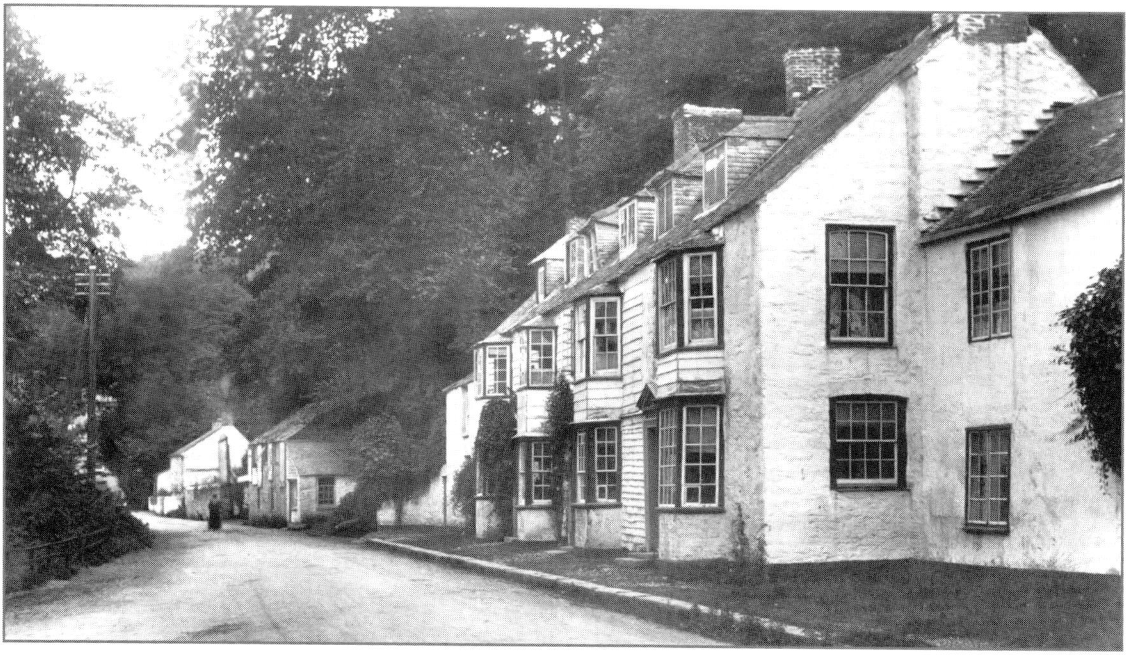

Perran Wharf, The Village 1904 53048
The bay windows make this a striking block alongside the main road from Truro to Falmouth. There was a major iron foundry here until 1879: the Williams Perran Foundry imported raw materials and exported goods such as steam engines from the wharf on the creek.

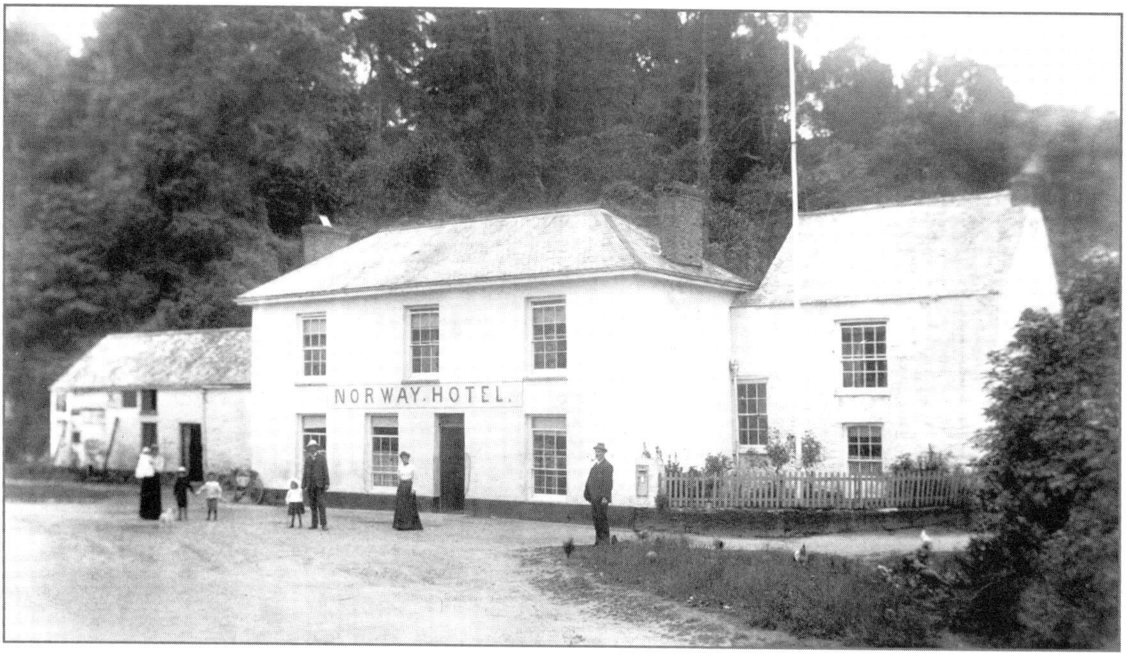

Perran Wharf, The Norway Hotel 1904 53049
This well-known house takes its name from the Scandinavian ships that came up to Perran Wharf to discharge timber for the tin and copper mines many years ago. The creek has long since silted up, and the hotel is now the Norway Inn, incorporating the old stables, left, into the restaurant.

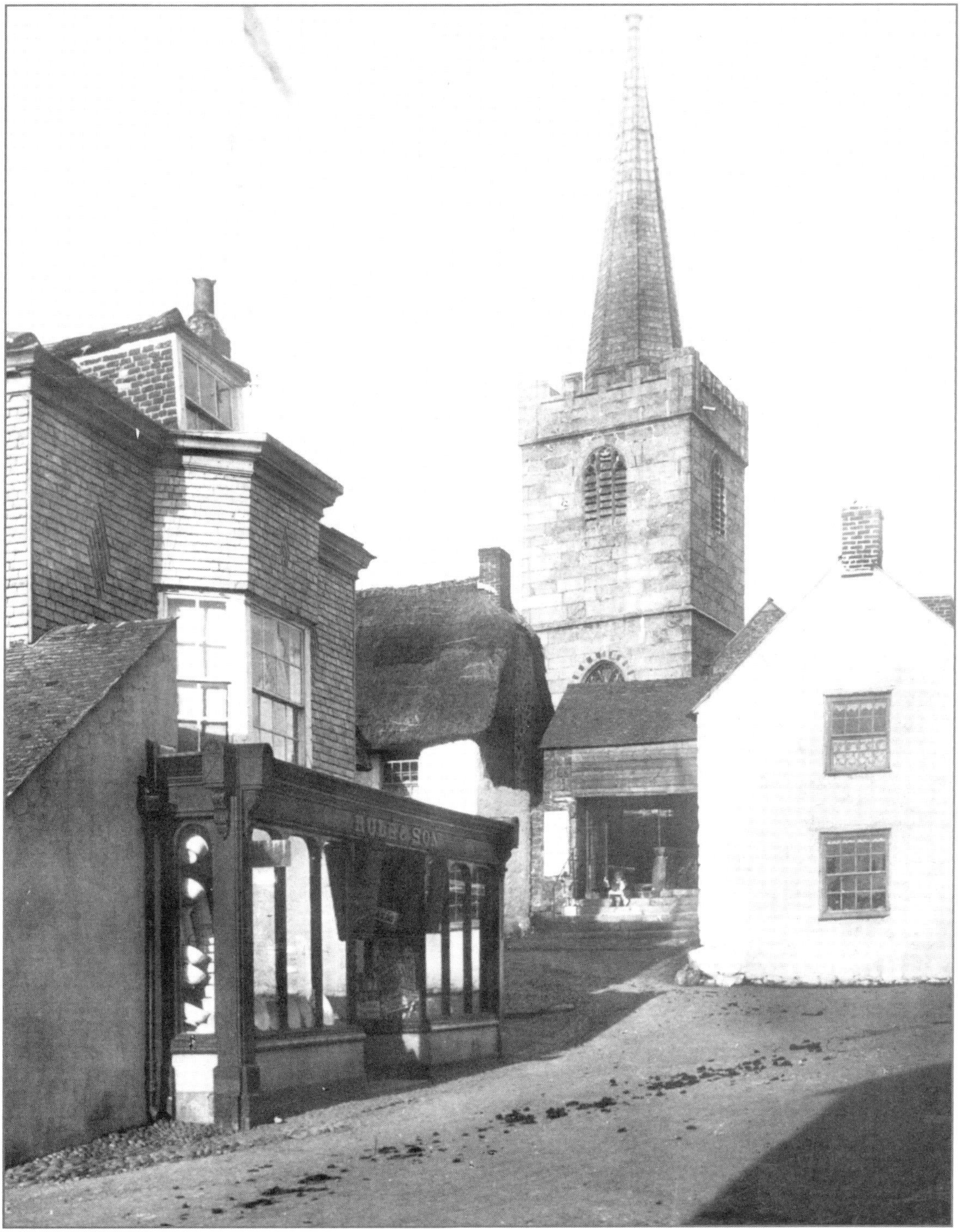

St Keverne, The Church and the Village 1904 53038

This village scene is overlooked by the tower and spire of the church, the whole about 100 feet high and providing a landmark for sailors off the Lizard peninsula. Rule and Son have a fine shop frontage. Edwin Rule was described at the time as a grocer, draper and egg and butter dealer. Note the thatched roof near the church.

▼ **Mullion, The Old Inn 1904** 52268
Here is an unusual mix: the older thatched inn is attached to a three-storey Victorian block at Churchtown in the village.

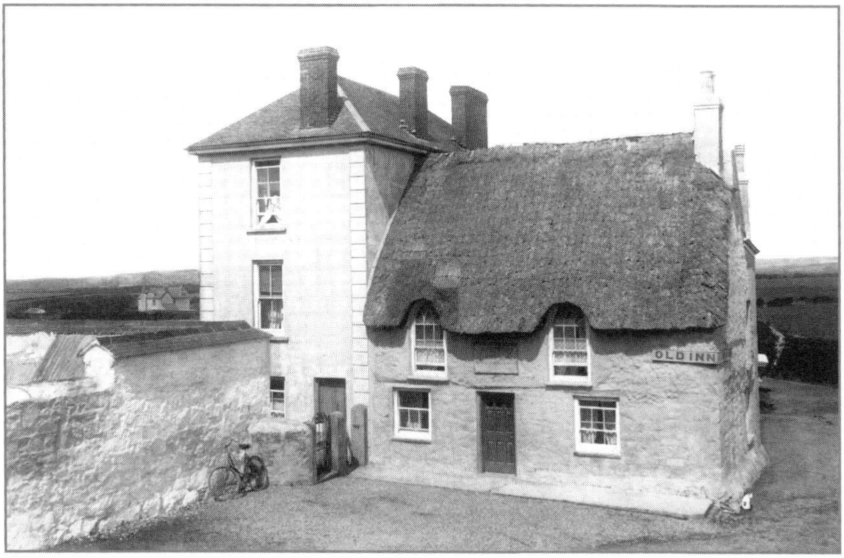

▼ **Gulval, The Village and the Church c1900** G185001
Thatched cottage roofs are unusual in Cornwall, particularly this far west, and this one has seen several repairs. The 16th-century granite church tower is behind. Gulval is still a separate village, even though it is only a mile outside Penzance.

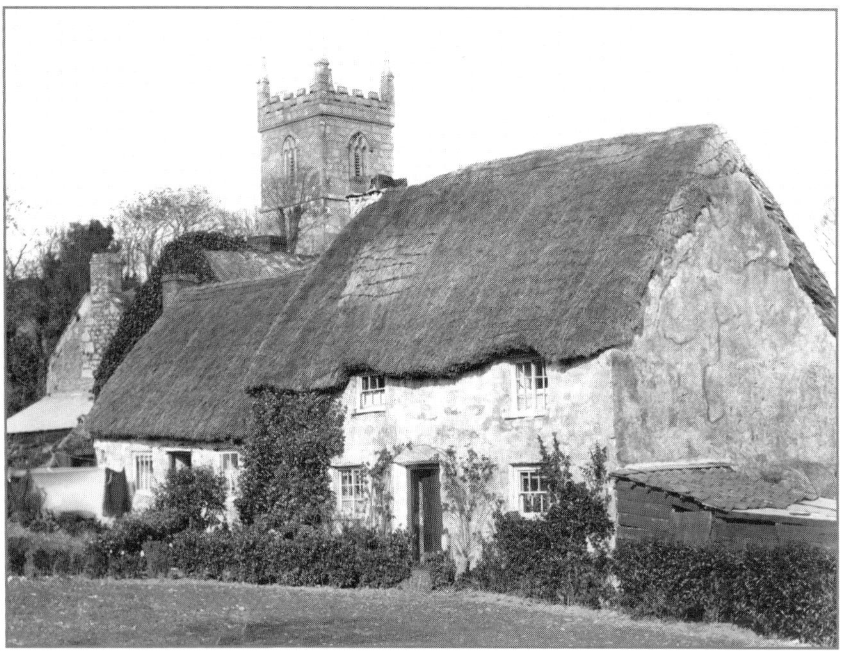

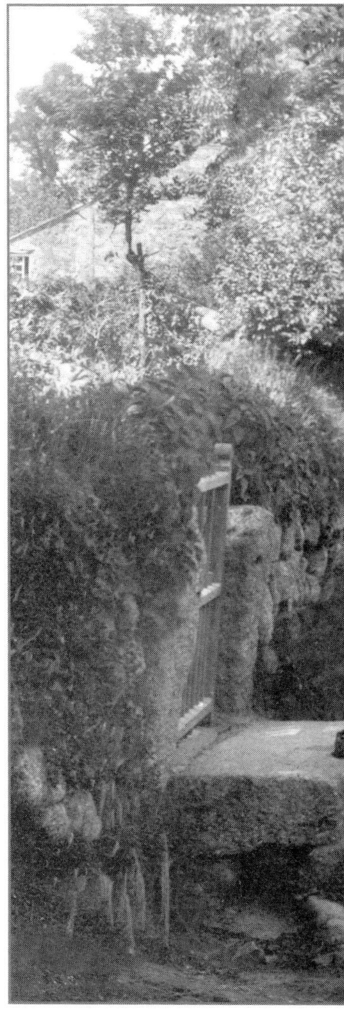

▲ **Lelant, Church Lane 1892** 29876
Granite cottages and walled gardens line this quiet lane leading invitingly to the church tower beyond. A lucky wee lad on a granite step has managed to get into the picture.

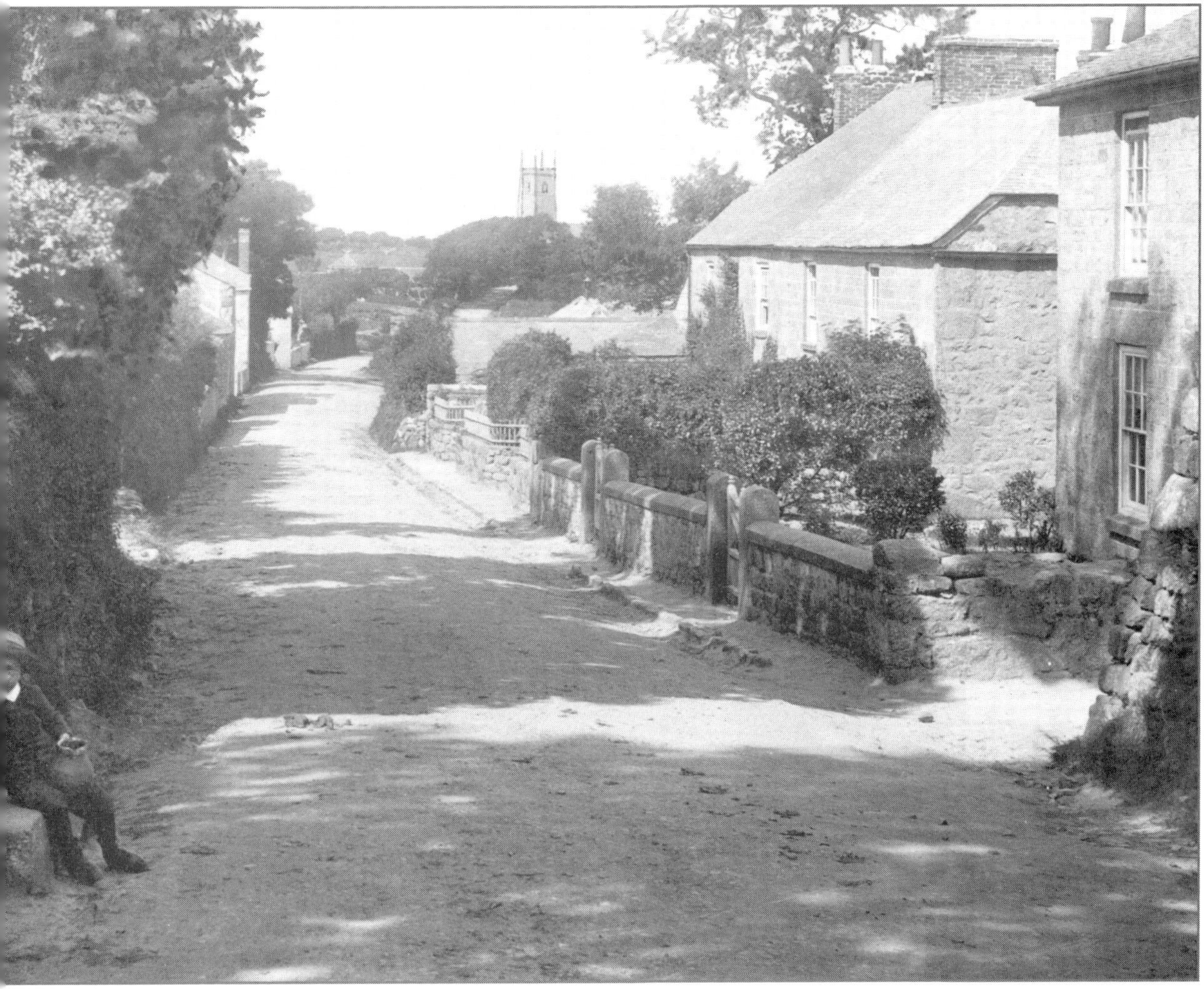

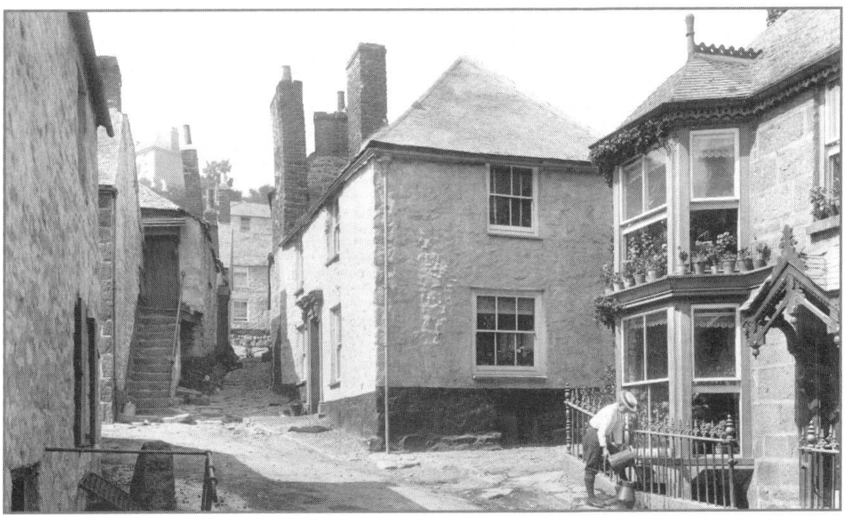

◄ **Newlyn, Fishermen's Houses 1903** 49958
Here we see a corner in the old part of the fishing village, with a Victorian granite house added on the right. Flower pots are all around the upper bay window ledge. Note the tall leaning brick chimneys behind.

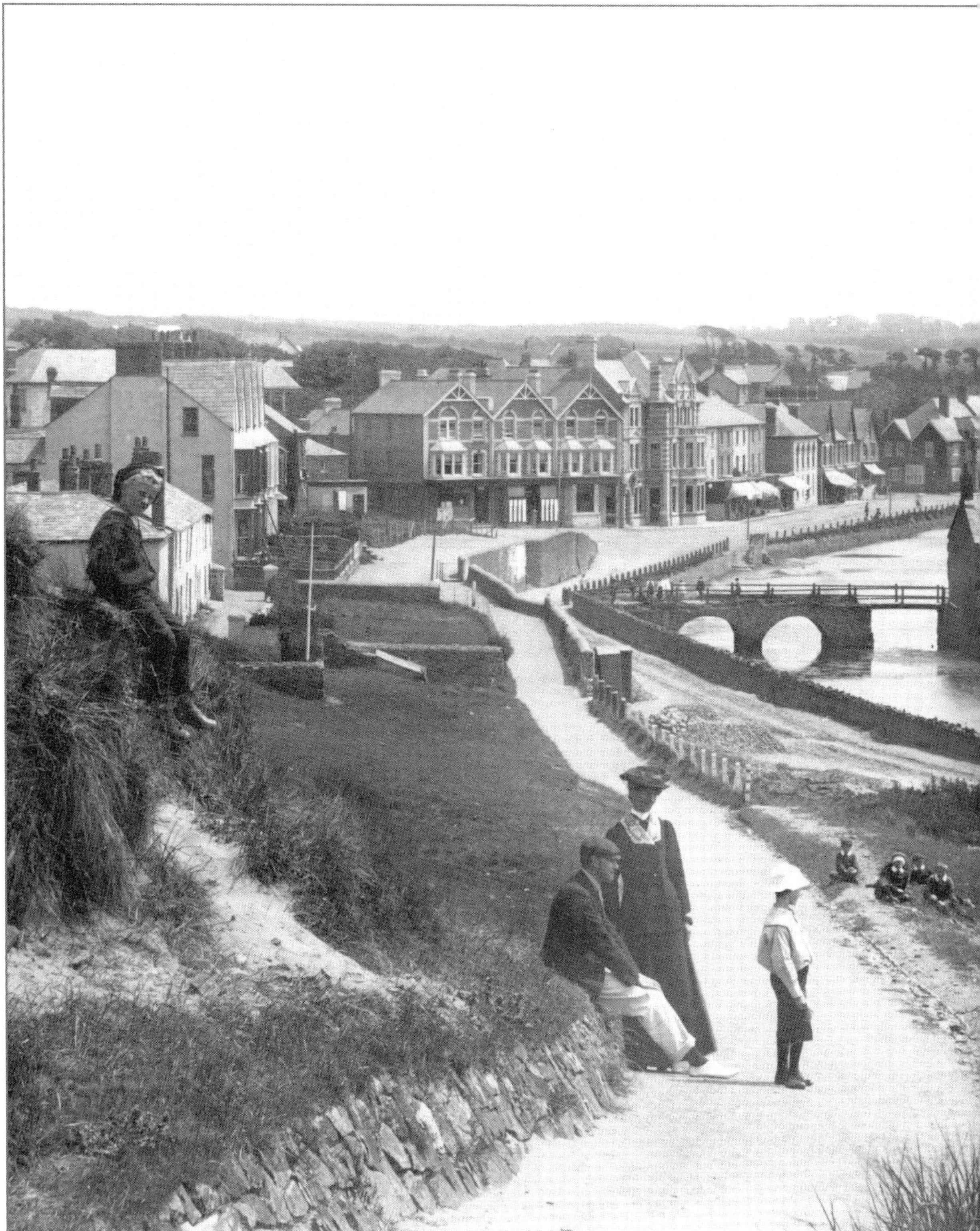

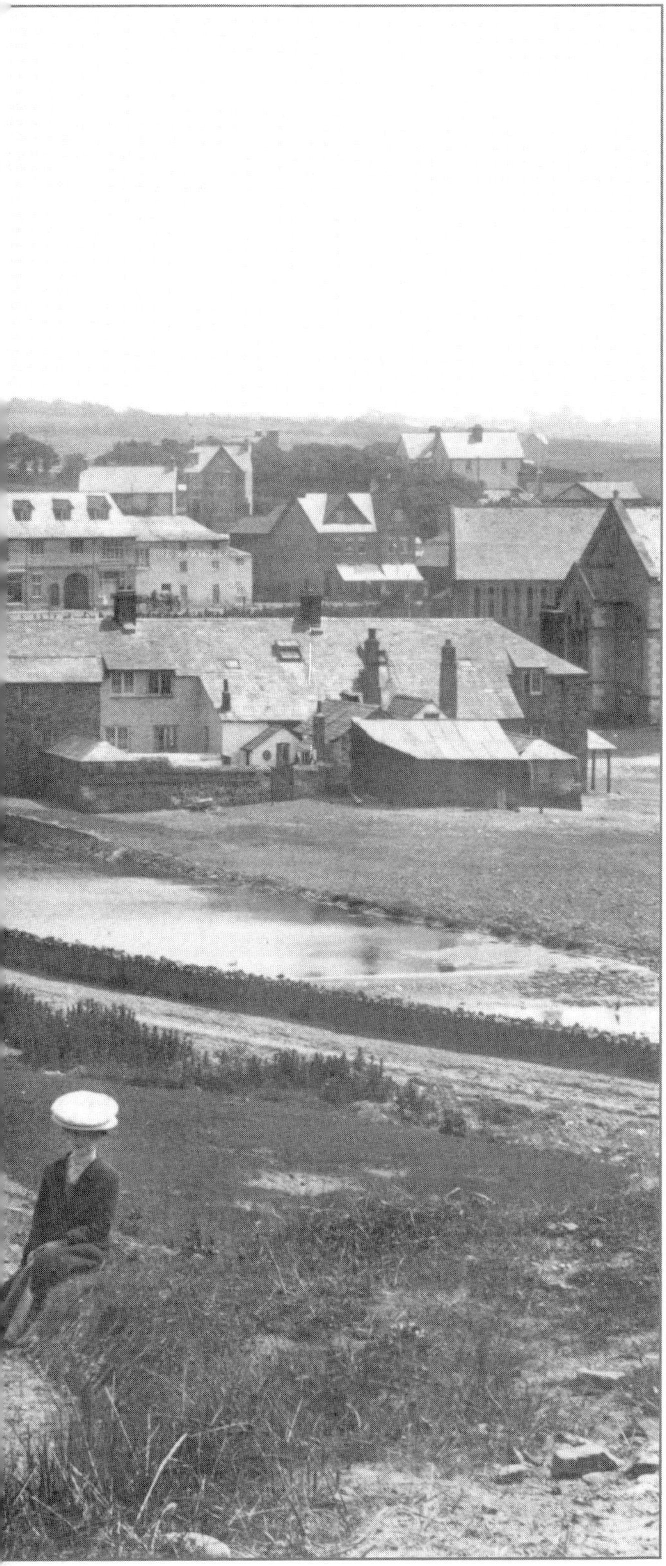

East Cornwall Towns

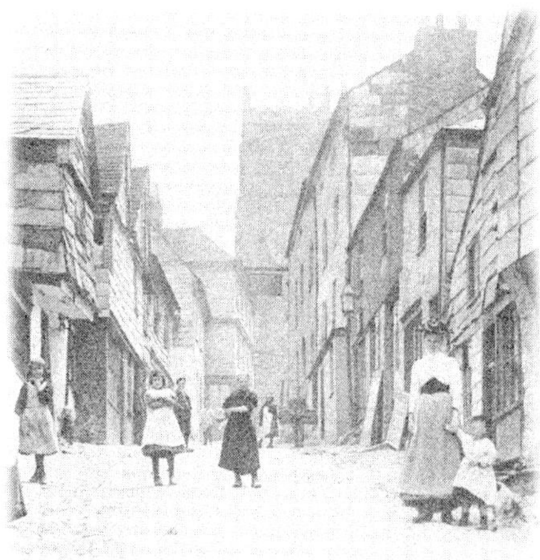

Bude, The Strand 1906 56076
Taken just a few years after photograph No 45876, this view shows Granville Terrace (left) and the Strand curving away beside the Neet beyond. The missing stone arch of Nanny Moore's Bridge marks the site of a mill.

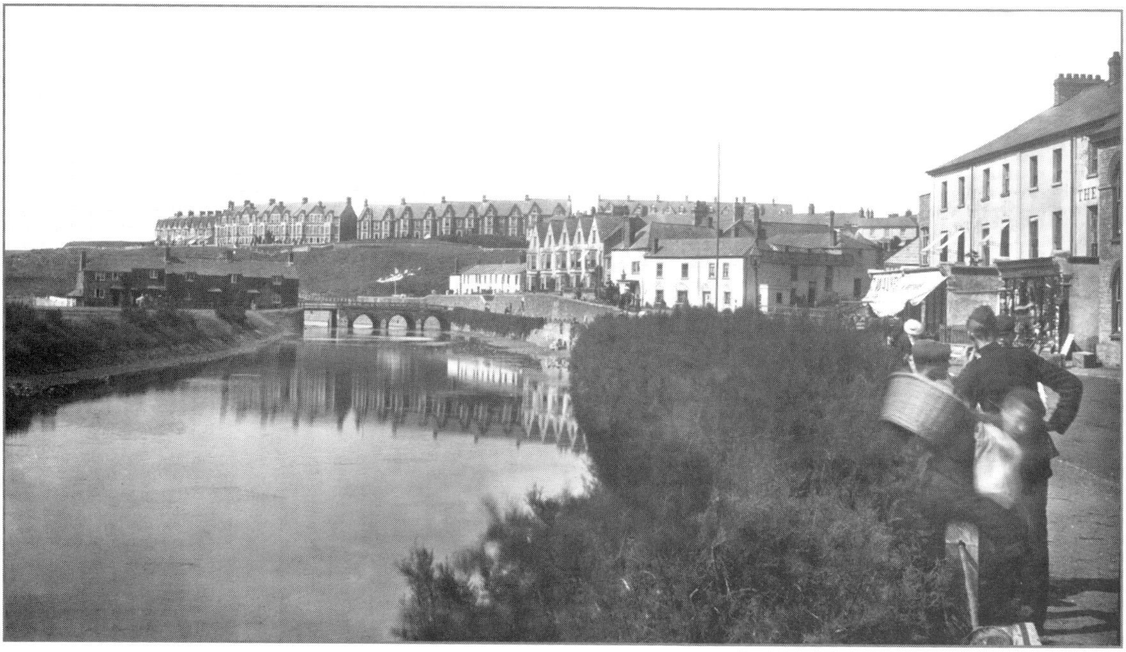

Bude, The Strand 1900 45876
We are looking north-west from the end of the Strand towards the terraces of Summerleaze Crescent on the skyline. Granville Terrace is just to the right of the bridge across the River Neet. Note the delivery basket in the foreground.

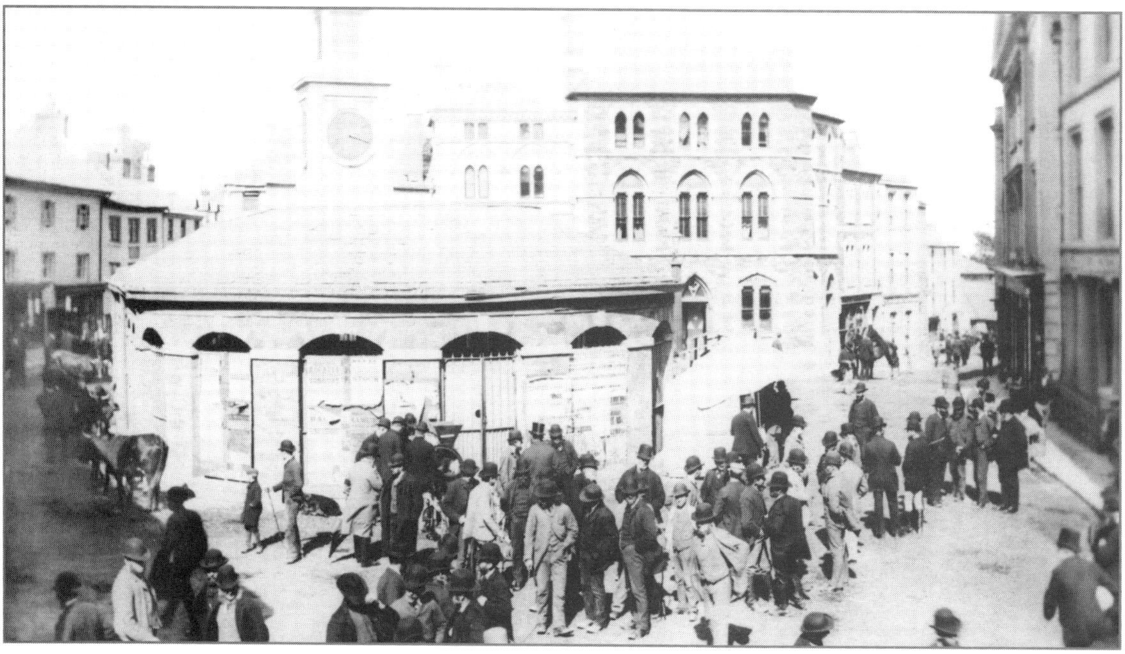

Launceston, Market Place 1890 23761
Bowler-hatted farmers go about their business in the centre of town around the Butter and Poultry Market Hall. A few cattle can be seen on the left. Posters advertise farm stock sales and the Torquay regatta, no doubt enticing travellers onto the railway.

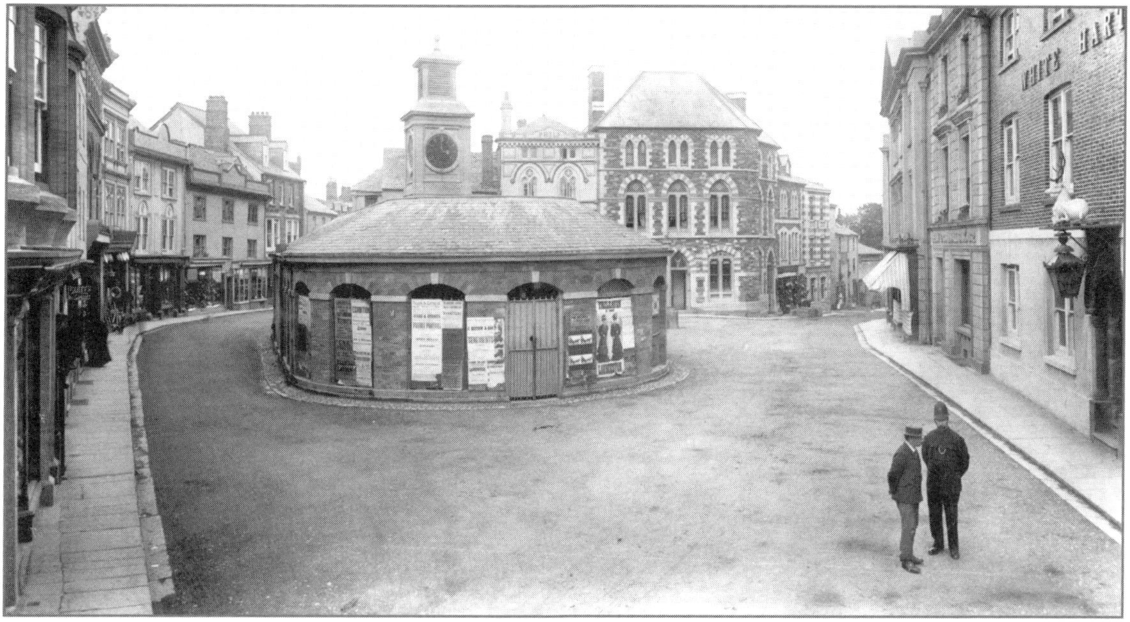

Launceston, Market Place 1906 56132
This is almost the same view as No 23761, but the Market Place is now deserted save for a solitary policeman speaking to a citizen. The Market Hall has more posters, including Great Western Railway excursions to Weymouth, Reading and London. The White Hart Hotel, seen on the right, is still there, but the market has been replaced by a large war memorial.

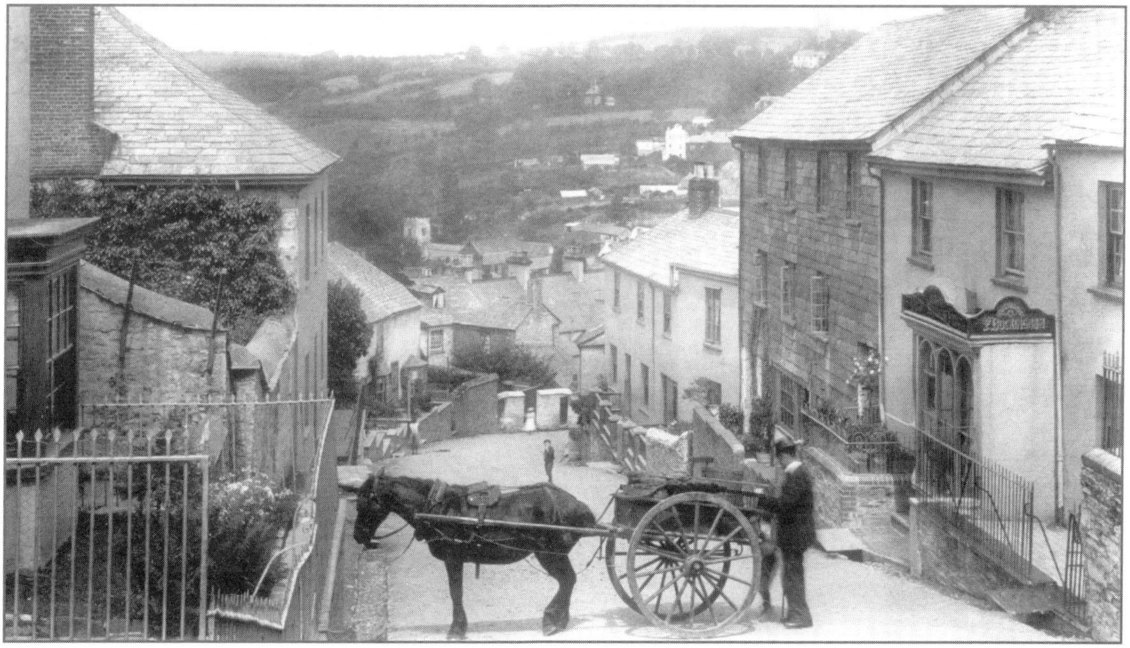

Launceston, St Thomas Hill 1906 56136
Here we see the best way to park on a steep hill - sideways! We are looking down this attractive street to the St Thomas and Newport part of Launceston, where the old church tower is just visible. The pinnacled tower of St Stephen's church stands on the hill to the right.

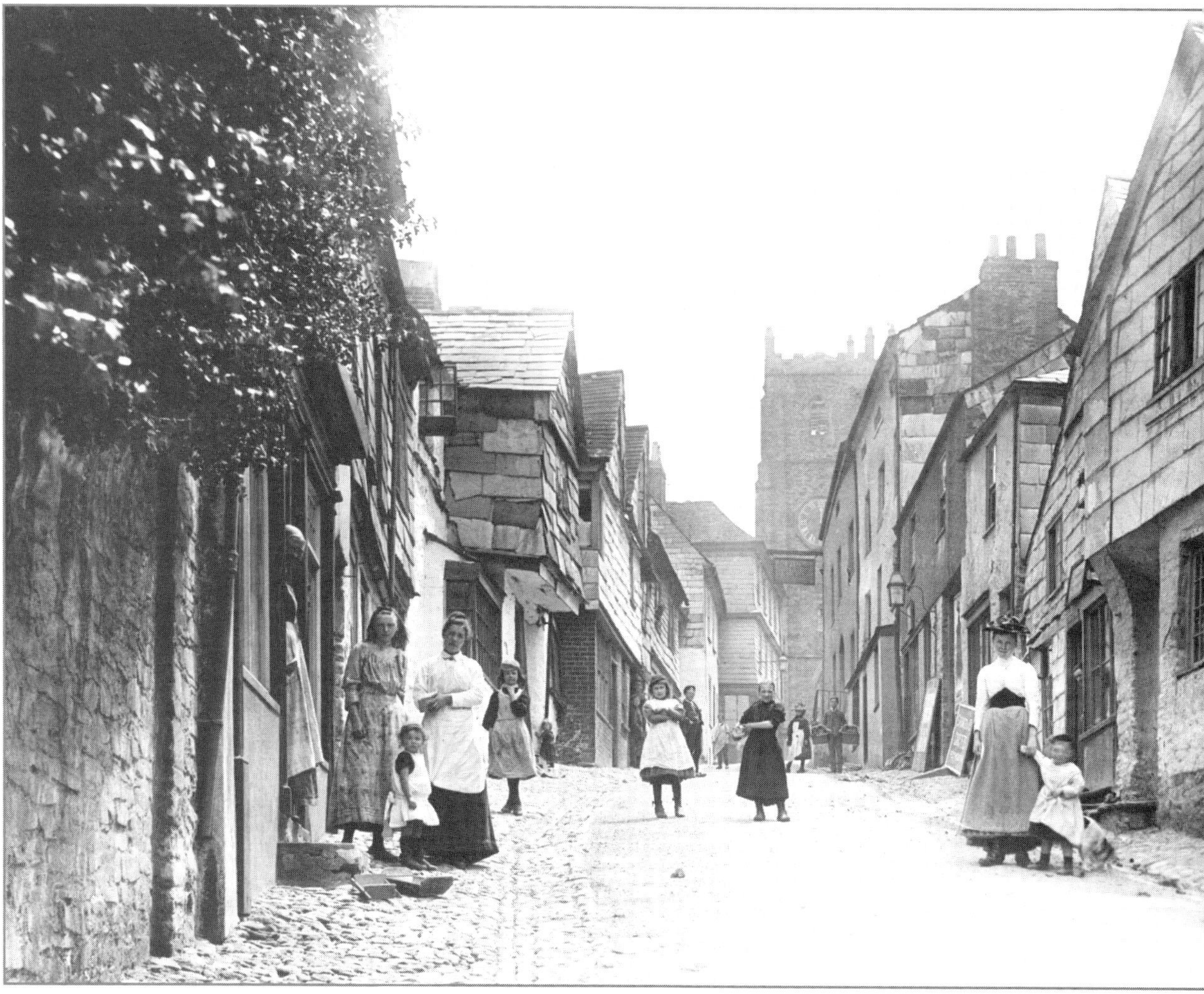

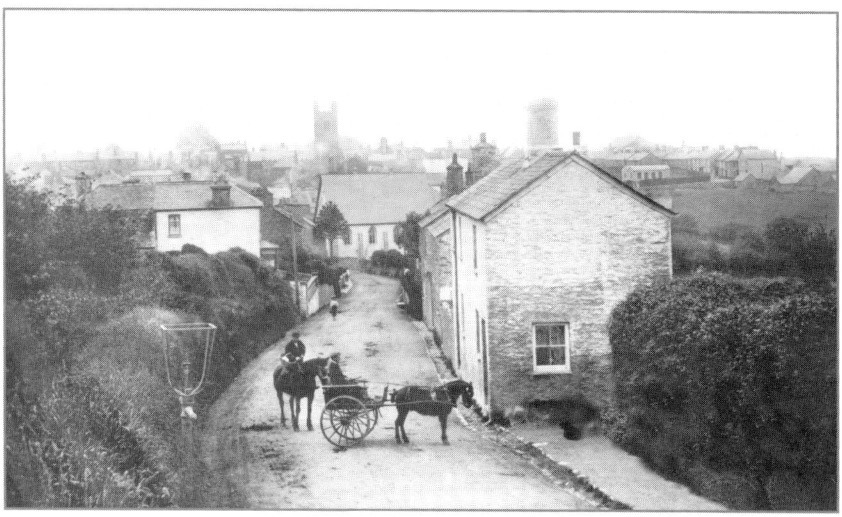

Callington, From the North 1908 59726
This is a picturesque view of the approach to the town along Launceston Road. The pony and trap has time to pose across the road without hindering other traffic. Note the gas street lamp, left foreground.

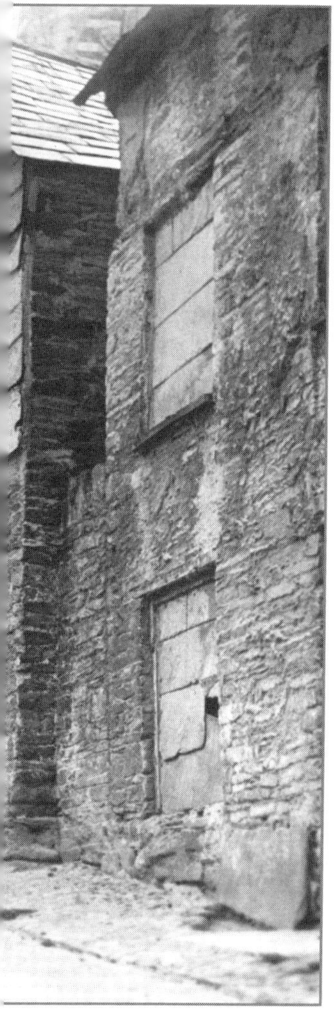

◄ **Launceston, Northgate Street 1893** 32166
Women, their daughters and a delivery boy stand for the camera where the street climbs to St Mary Magdalene Church. We see good examples of slate-hung houses; these slates are large, and they have even been used to board up the windows of the disused house on the right. The Jubilee Inn's sign is just below the church clock.

▼ **Callington, Fore Street 1893** 32343
Everyone is posing for the camera right through the town centre, and in the road too. Note the elderly bearded gentleman on the left, and the shopkeeper in his apron on the right. This is summer: awnings give shade to the shops on one side of the street, and one of the boys holds a cricket bat.

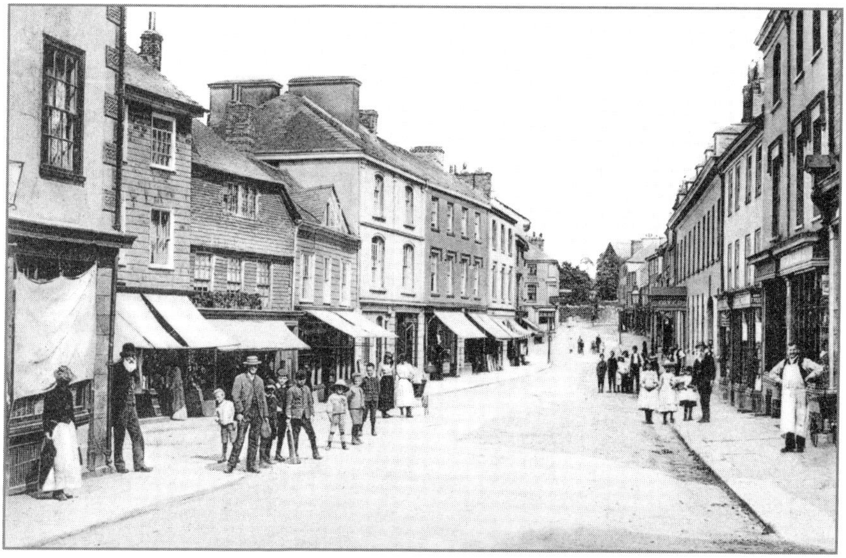

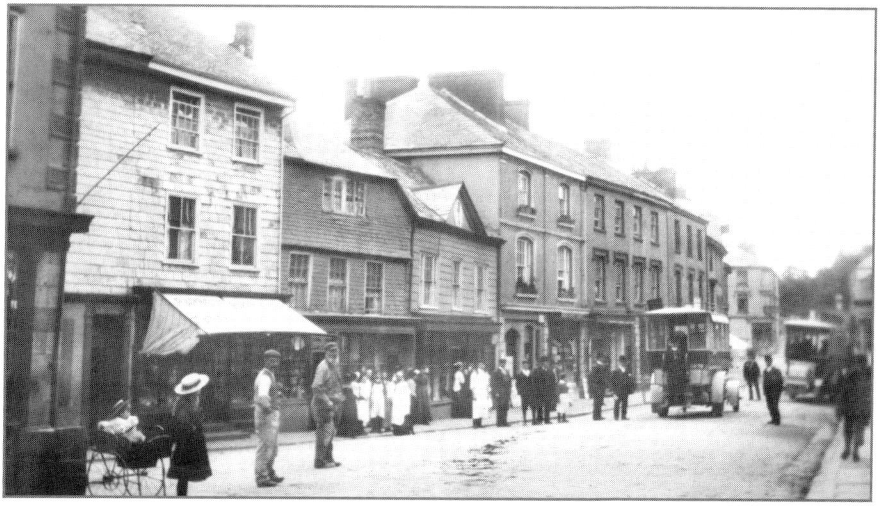

◄ **Callington, Fore Street 1904** 51824
Less than a decade after photograph No 32343, the focus of attention is the motor bus in the street. In contrast, note the girl and large-wheeled pram on the left.

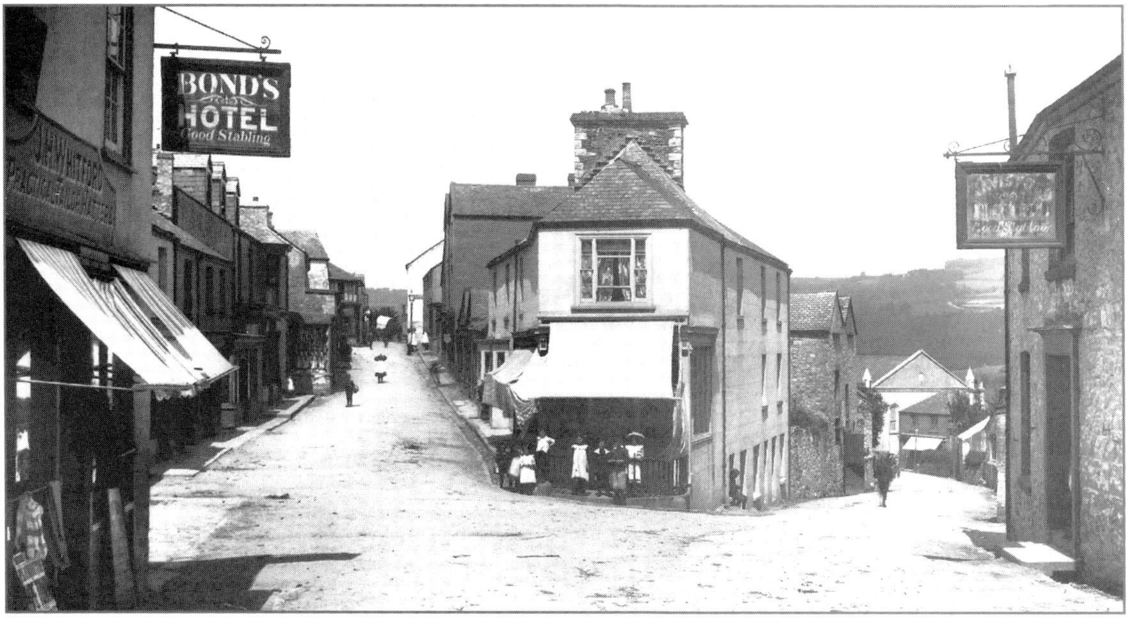

Gunnislake, Commercial Street 1908 59709
There were busier days here before the mines closed around the turn of the century. To the right, Newbridge Hill descends to the Tamar crossing into Devon, with a large chapel on the bend. Bond's Hotel advertises good stabling, with John Henry Whitford's grocer's shop in front, in contrast to the Tavistock Hotel's rather faded sign on the right.

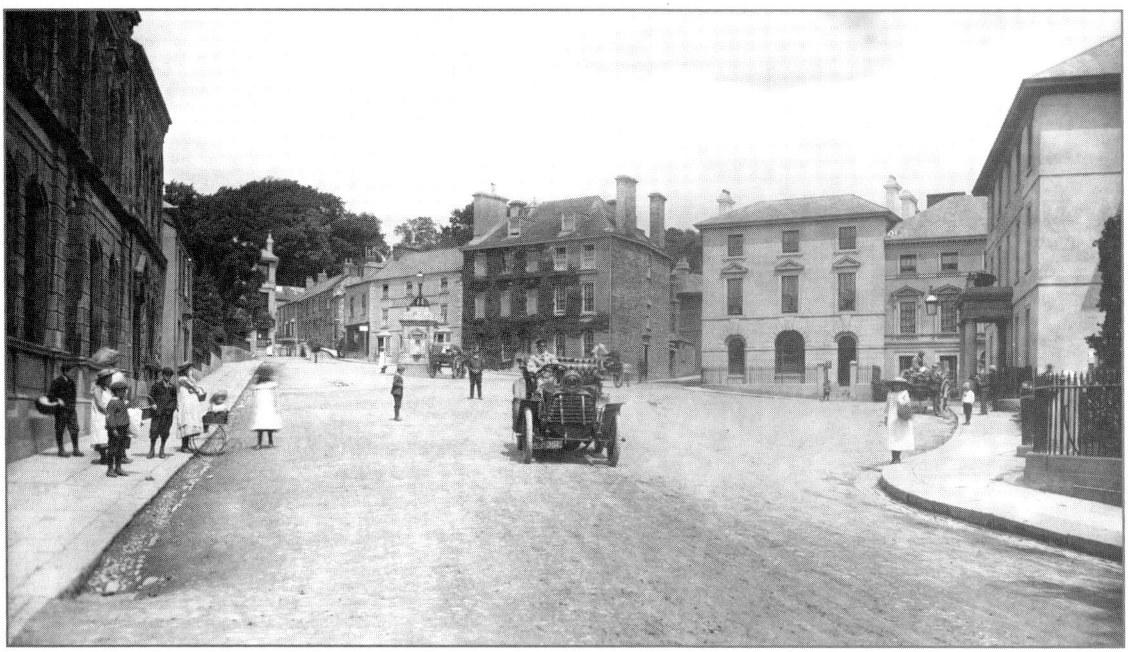

Liskeard, The Parade 1906 56297
An early motor car is driven proudly down the middle of the road in Liskeard's centre. All these buildings survive, such as Webb's Hotel and the East Cornwall Bank (now Barclays) on the right, although half of the house behind the car has been demolished to widen the road.

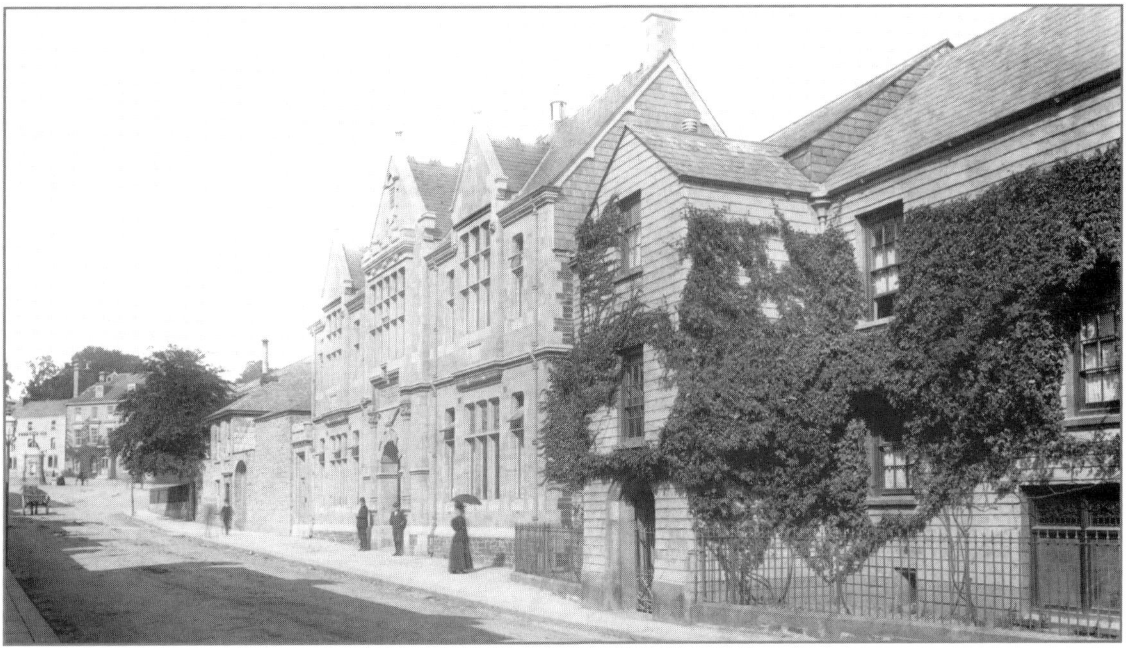

Liskeard, The Library and Stuart House 1900 45896
We are looking along Barras Street towards the Parade in the background. The Passmore Edwards Free Library, centre, was opened in 1896. On the right is the slate-hung Stuart House, where Charles I stayed several nights in 1644.

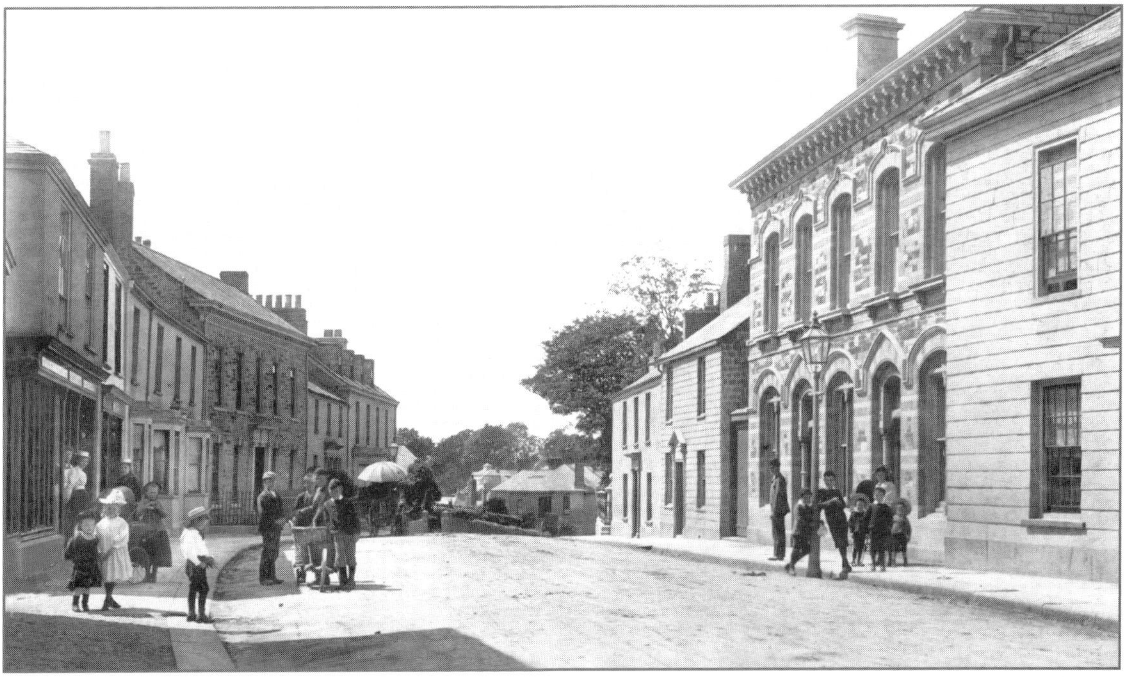

Liskeard, Dean Street 1893 32349
Again, this scene has hardly changed. A building has architectural pretensions on the right, in front of which the gas lamp post, with leaning boys, appears to be standing in the gutter and not on the pavement.

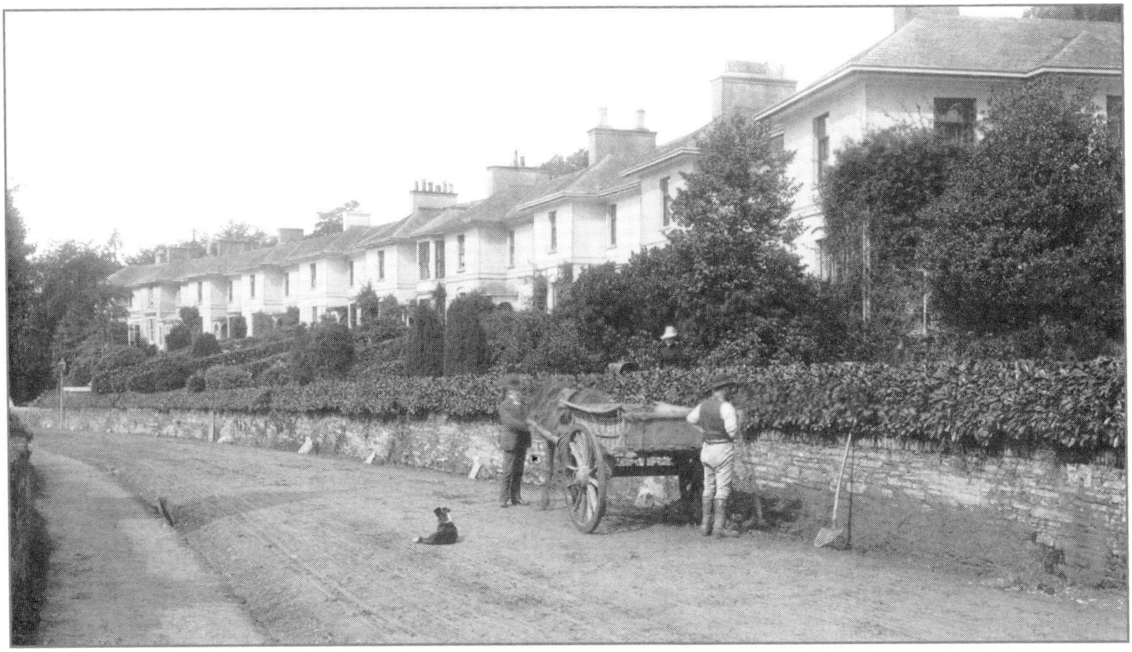

Liskeard, Dean Terrace 1890 24466
This smart terrace of houses stands just down the hill from picture No 32349, on the western approach to the town. The nature of the road surface is very clear, with the roadmen at work in the days before the use of tarmacadam. The dog awaits traffic from the Bodmin direction.

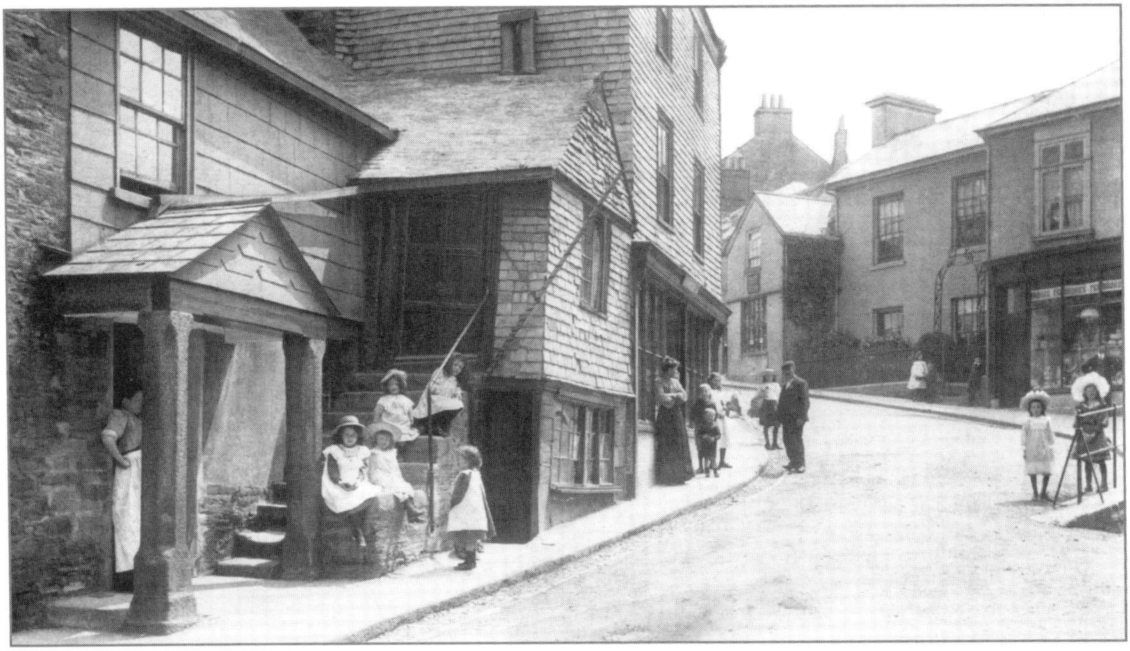

Liskeard, Church Street 1906 56305
We see here a corner just below the church. The houses use much finer slates than those seen in Launceston. The house with the porch is one of the oldest in town. Note the little girls with their summer bonnets, and the barber's pole, centre.

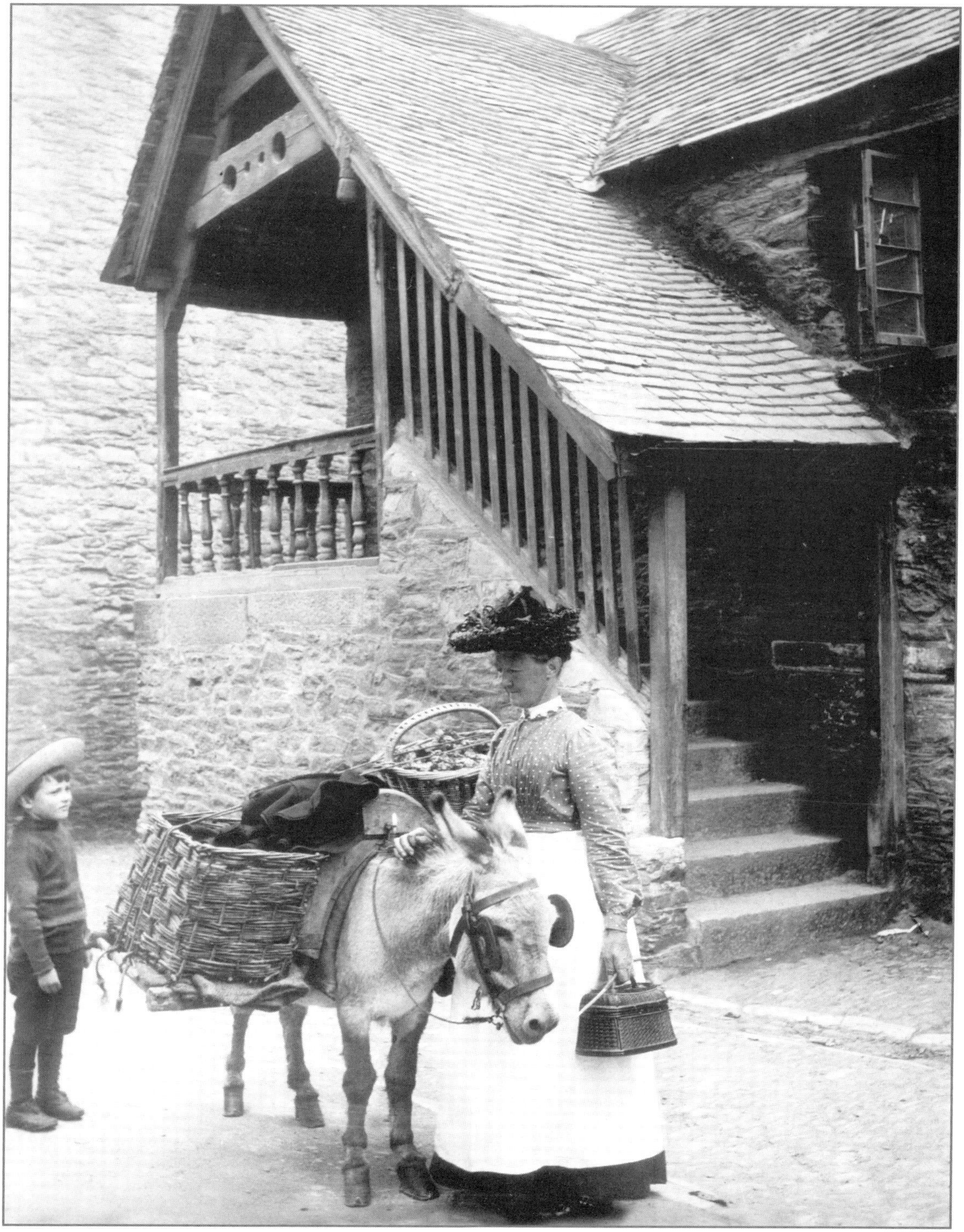

Looe, The Guildhall 1906 56396
A lady in traditional dress poses with her pannier donkey in Higher Market Street, East Looe, outside the old 16th-century guildhall. The outer stair to the top floor is protected by an extension of the roof, and the old stocks or pillory are set in the gable. A new stone guildhall was built in 1877.

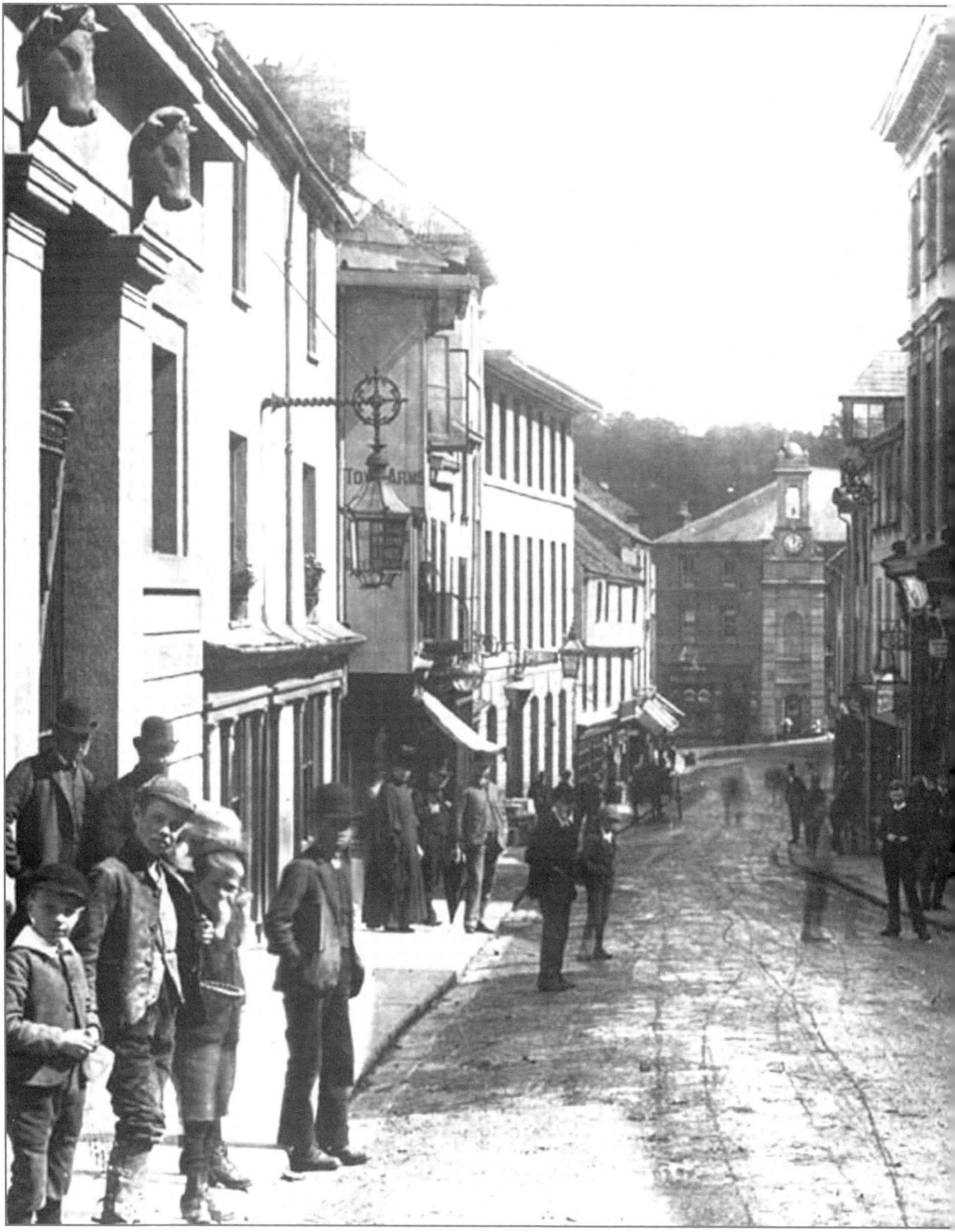

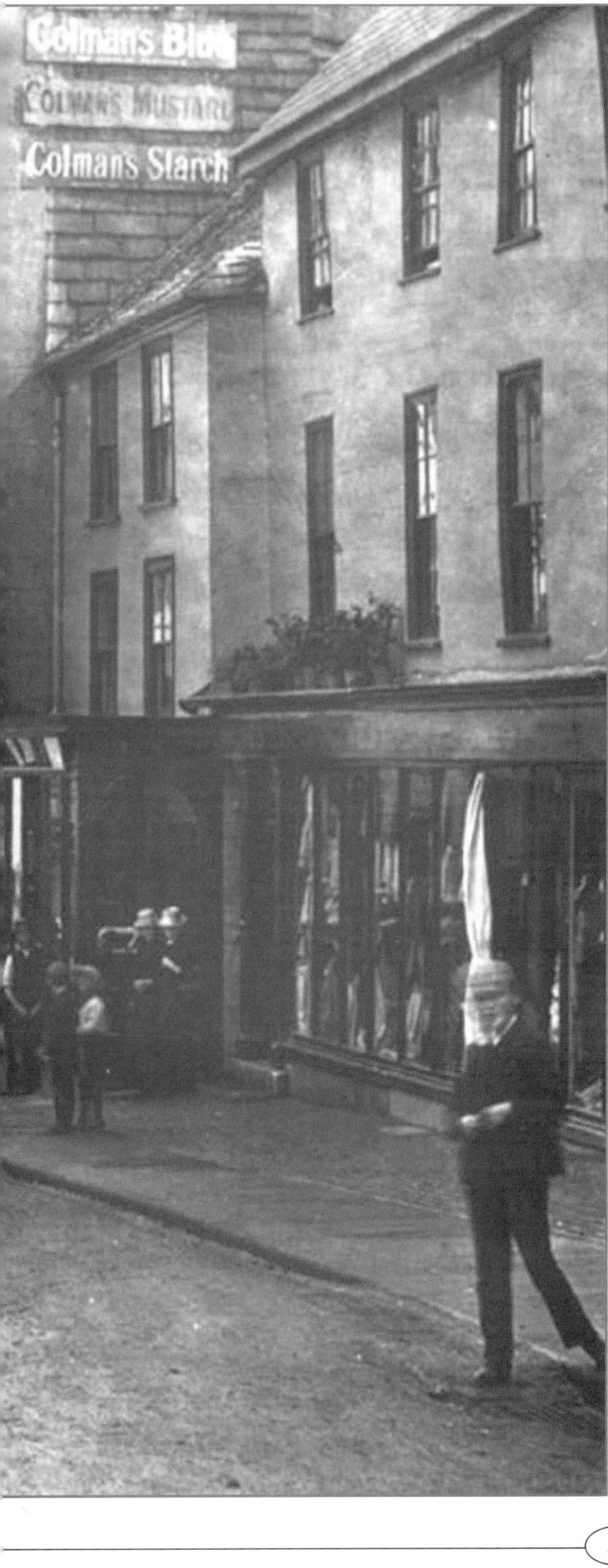

Mid Cornwall Towns

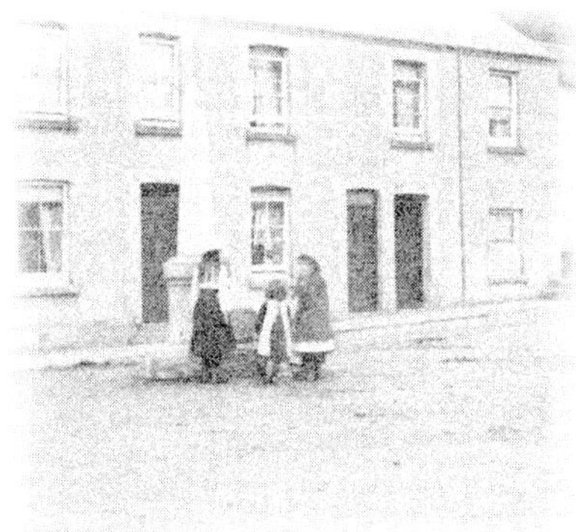

Bodmin, Fore Street 1890 24482
Lads of all ages pose in groups for the camera in this traffic-free scene, with the turret clock at the lower end of the street. Two ox heads above granite pillars on the left indicate the Market House entrance, erected in 1840 for meat, poultry and butter. Three advertisements proclaim Colmans products high on the shop building on the right.

Bodmin, Fore Street 1901 47769
This photograph was taken at the top of this main thoroughfare where it levels out and widens into Bore Street. The large building on the right is for the assembly rooms of the Methodist church, the steps of which are just visible in the foreground.

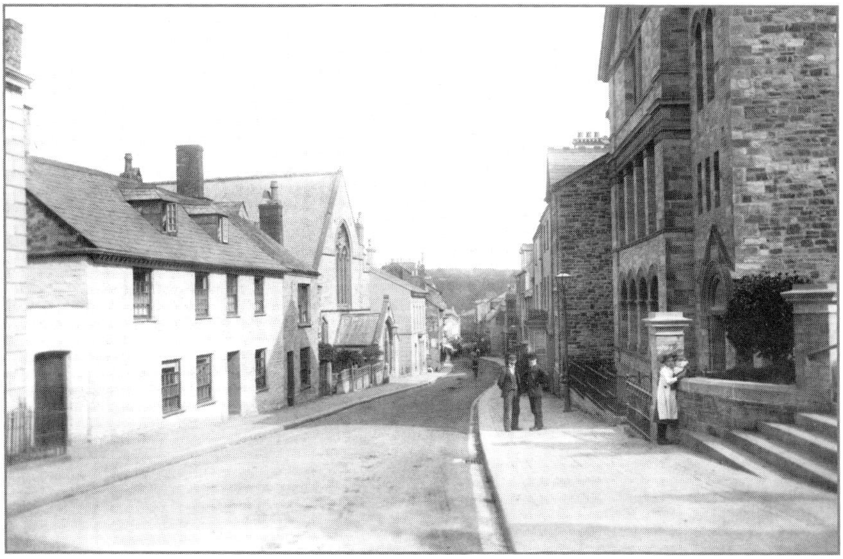

Bodmin, The Asylum 1901 47775
The County Lunatic Asylum was first built a little to the west of the town in 1820 to the design of the Plymouth architect John Foulstone. Later additions were made five times before the end of the century. Patients relax in the grounds under the shade of tall elm trees.

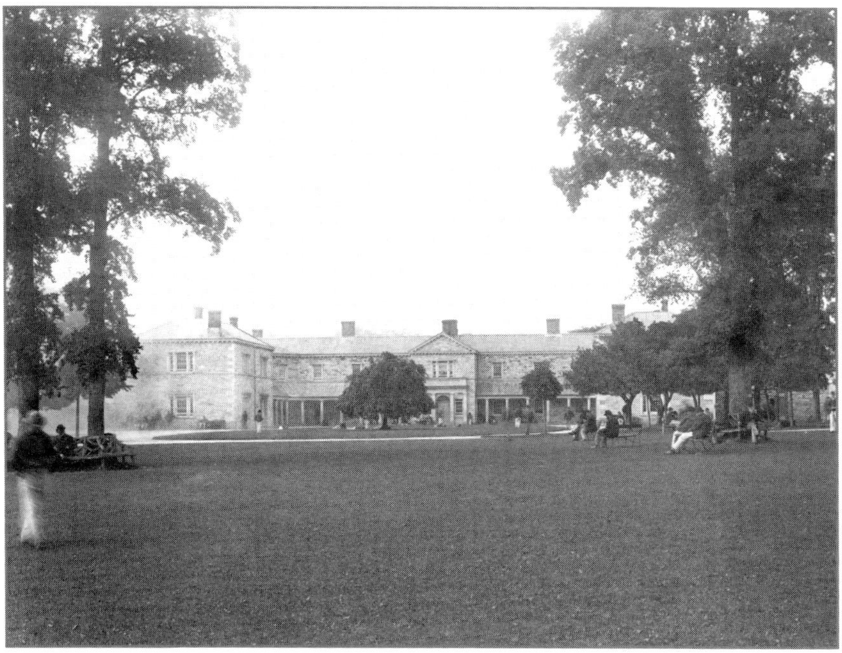

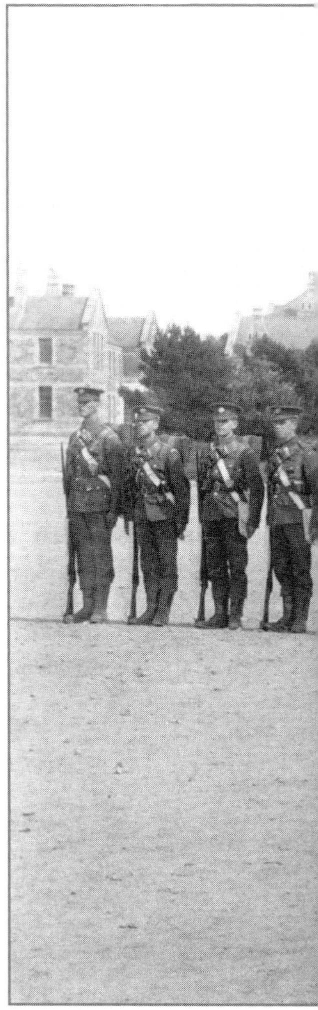

Bodmin, The Barracks 1906 56286
Disciplined soldiers stand to attention on the enclosed parade ground of the Duke of Cornwall Light Infantry barracks, off the Lostwithiel Road.

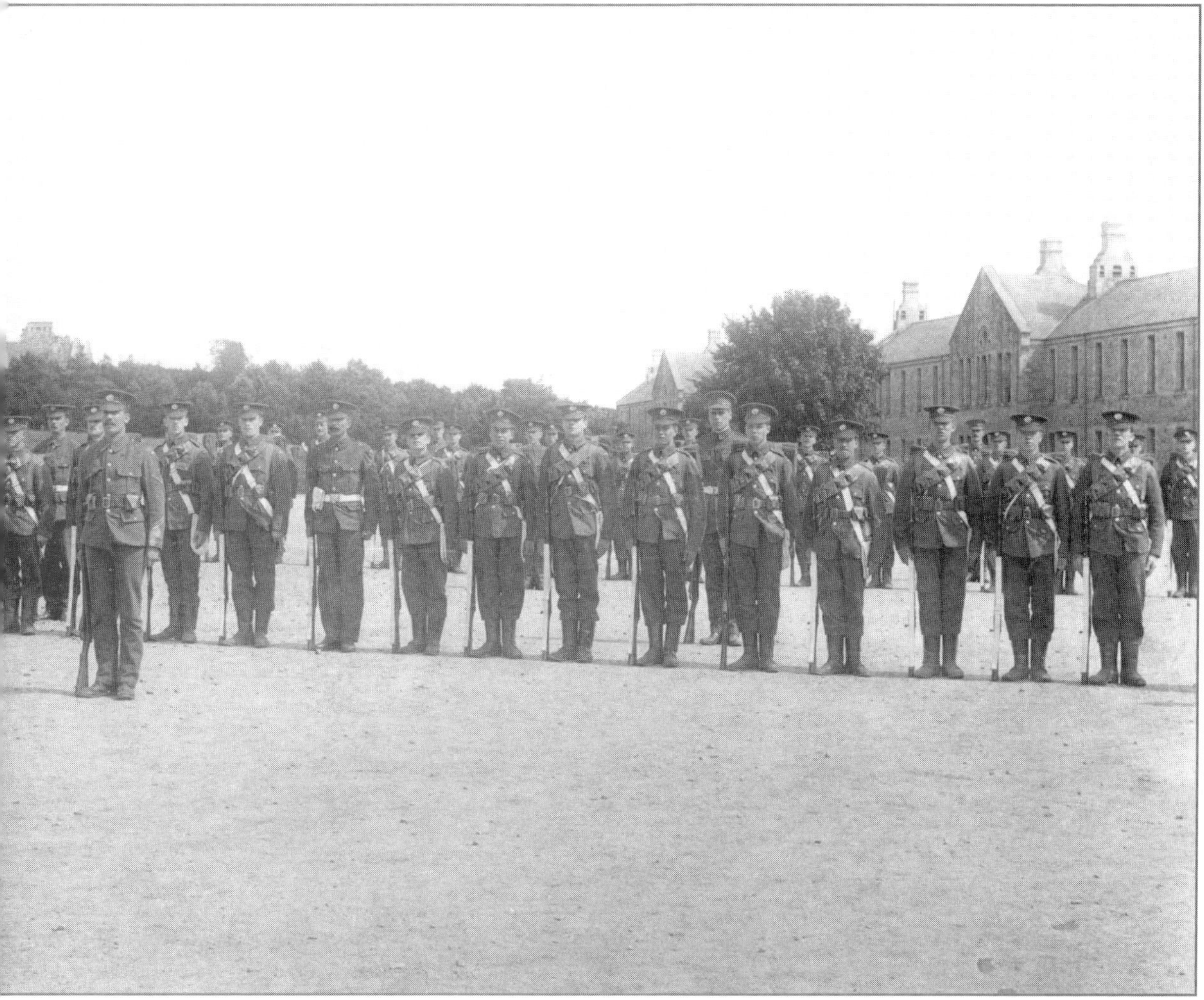

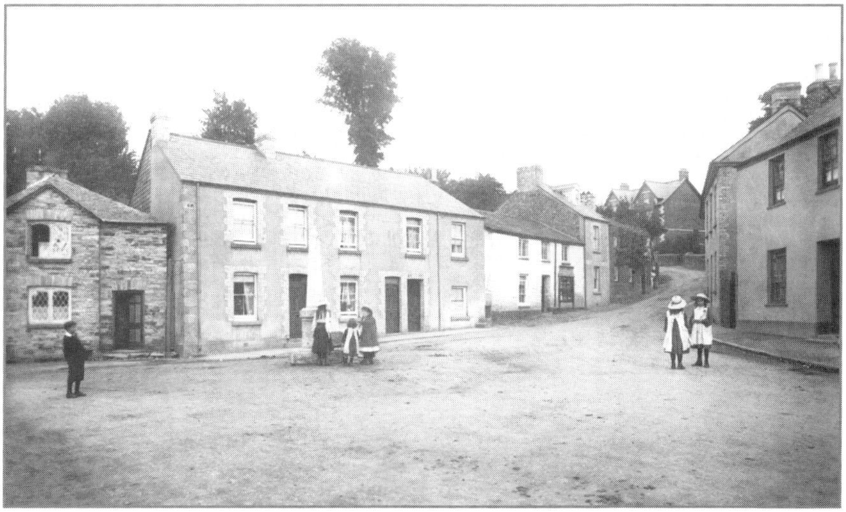

Lostwithiel, Bridgend 1906 56423

The humbler quarter of town is on the east side of the bridge over the Fowey, where the old road climbs out towards Liskeard. This is long before the by-pass was built, but nevertheless the children are free to play by the memorial in the street, as there is so little traffic.

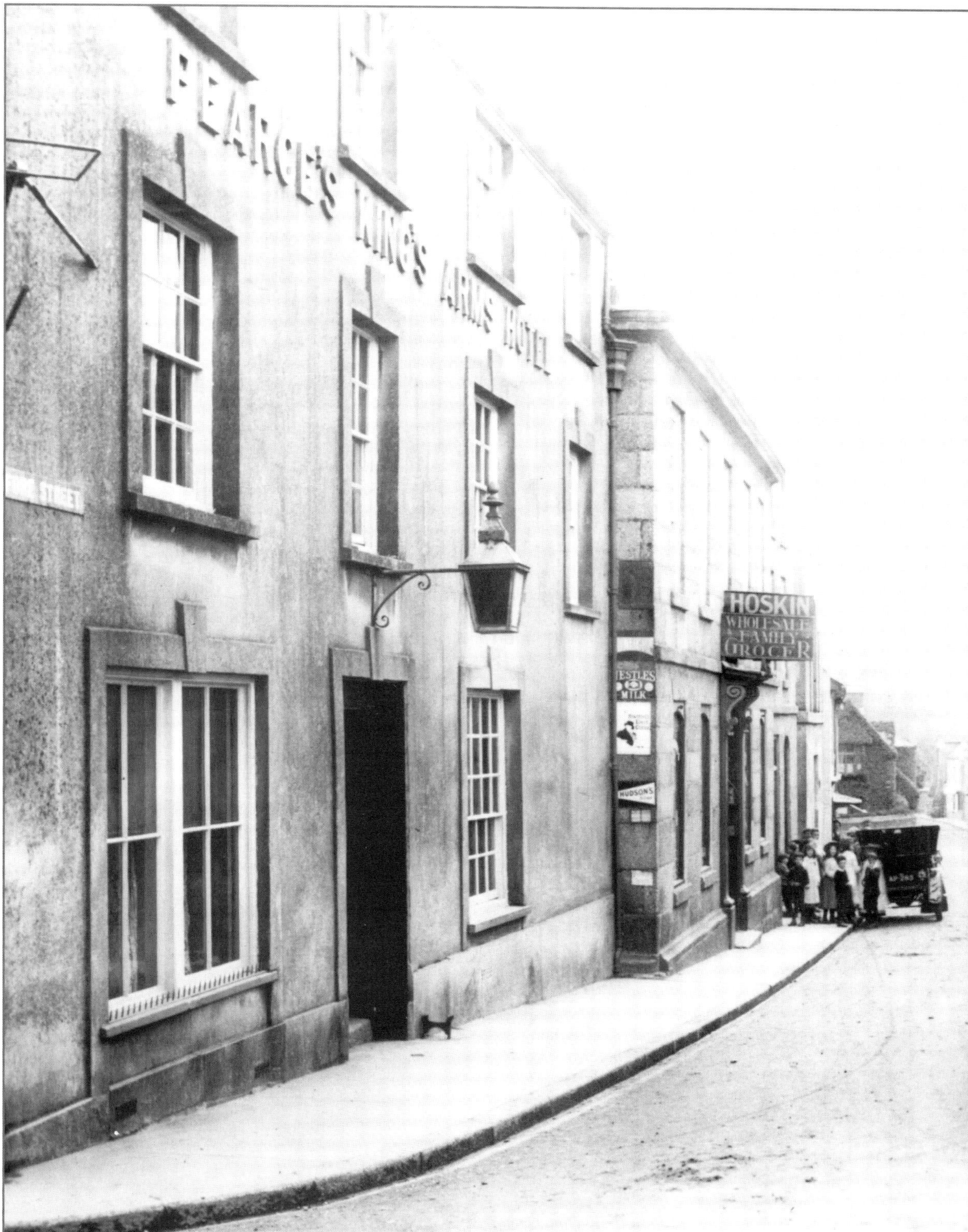
PEARCE'S KING'S ARMS HOTEL
HOSKIN
WHOLESALE
FAMILY
GROCER
NESTLES
MILK
HUDSON'S

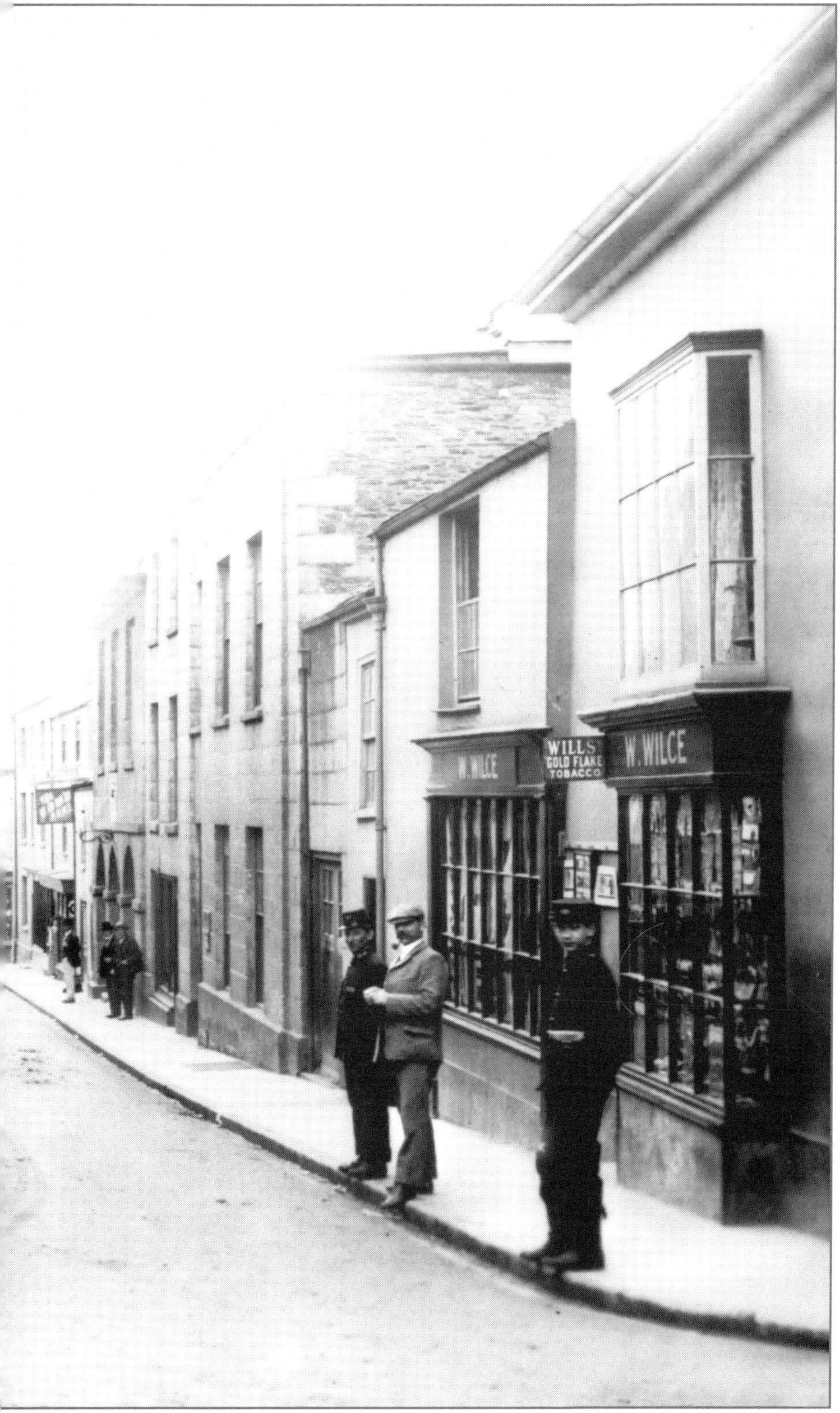

Lostwithiel, Fore Street 1906 56419
A small group of children seems to be attracted by an early motor car, while a Hovis delivery cart waits just past the Town Arms. William Wilce's drapery and fancy repository is on the right, and Thomas Hoskin's family grocers on the left next to the King's Arms Hotel. There are two postmen on the right, for the post office is nearby.

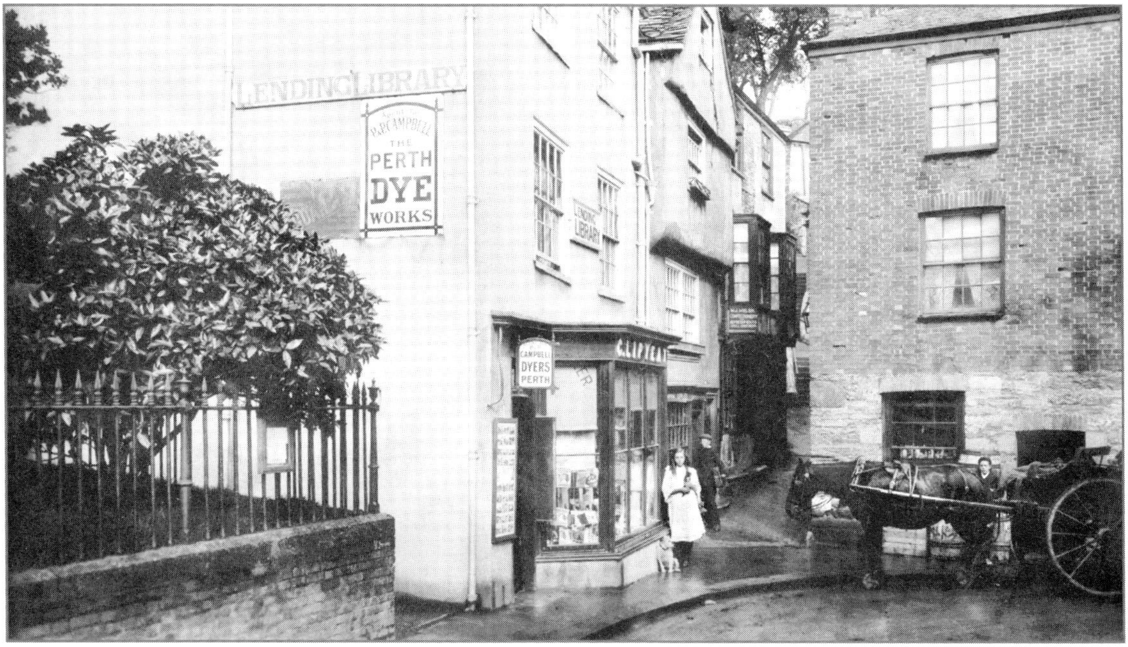

Fowey, South Street 1908 60919
The churchyard rails are on the left in this scene in the heart of the old town. The nearest shop is a lending library and agent for Campbell's Perth dyes; the display of postcards for sale is perhaps a selection of Frith's. The narrow alley between the houses leads off to Bull Hill.

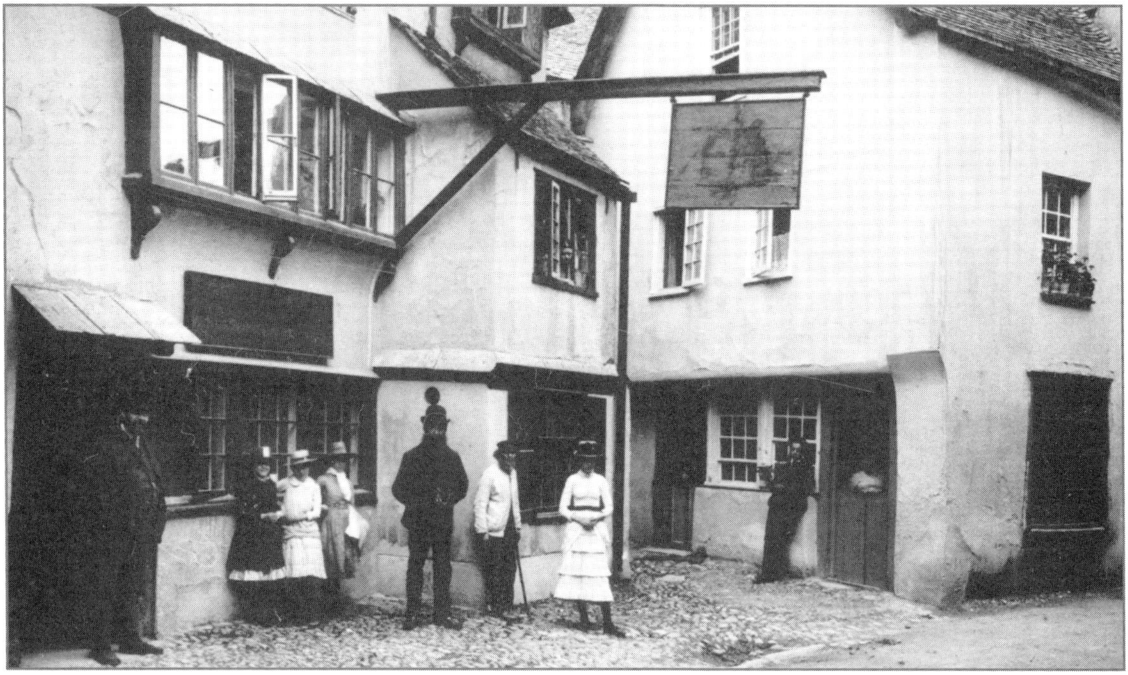

Fowey, The Lugger Inn 1888 21252
This old inn in Fore Street dates from 1633 and is among the oldest houses in Fowey. It is set back behind a small cobbled forecourt, so that the inn sign has been deliberately extended out to be noticed by passers-by.

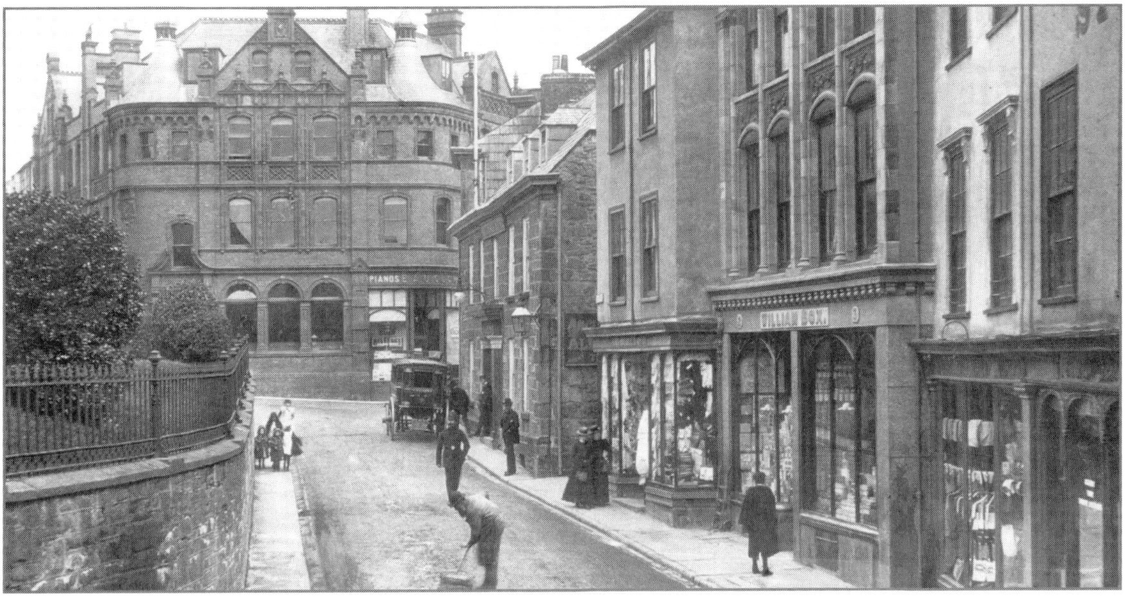

St Austell, Church Street 1898 41389A
A street cleaner works below the church wall, while a boy seems interested in William Box's grocery, wine and spirit shop; two ladies approach Russell and Co's drapery shop next door. Facing the end of the street beyond the White Hart, the huge block reflects the confidence and wealth generated in the town by the china clay industry. Newly built in red bricks is Coode, Shilson and Co's St Austell Bank (now National Westminster); it was commonly known as 'the red bank'.

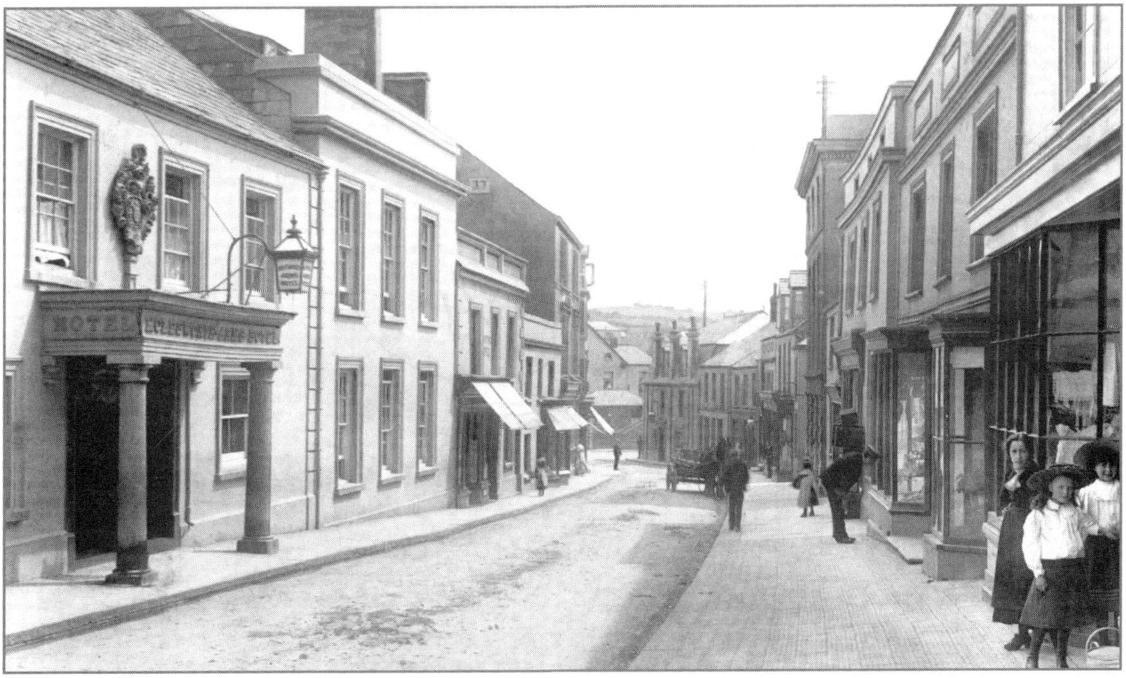

Wadebridge, Molesworth Street 1903 49943
The Molesworth Arms Hotel, well placed on the principal street climbing through the town from the bridge, was said to be 'conveniently arranged and well conducted', and offered an 'omnibus to meet all trains'.

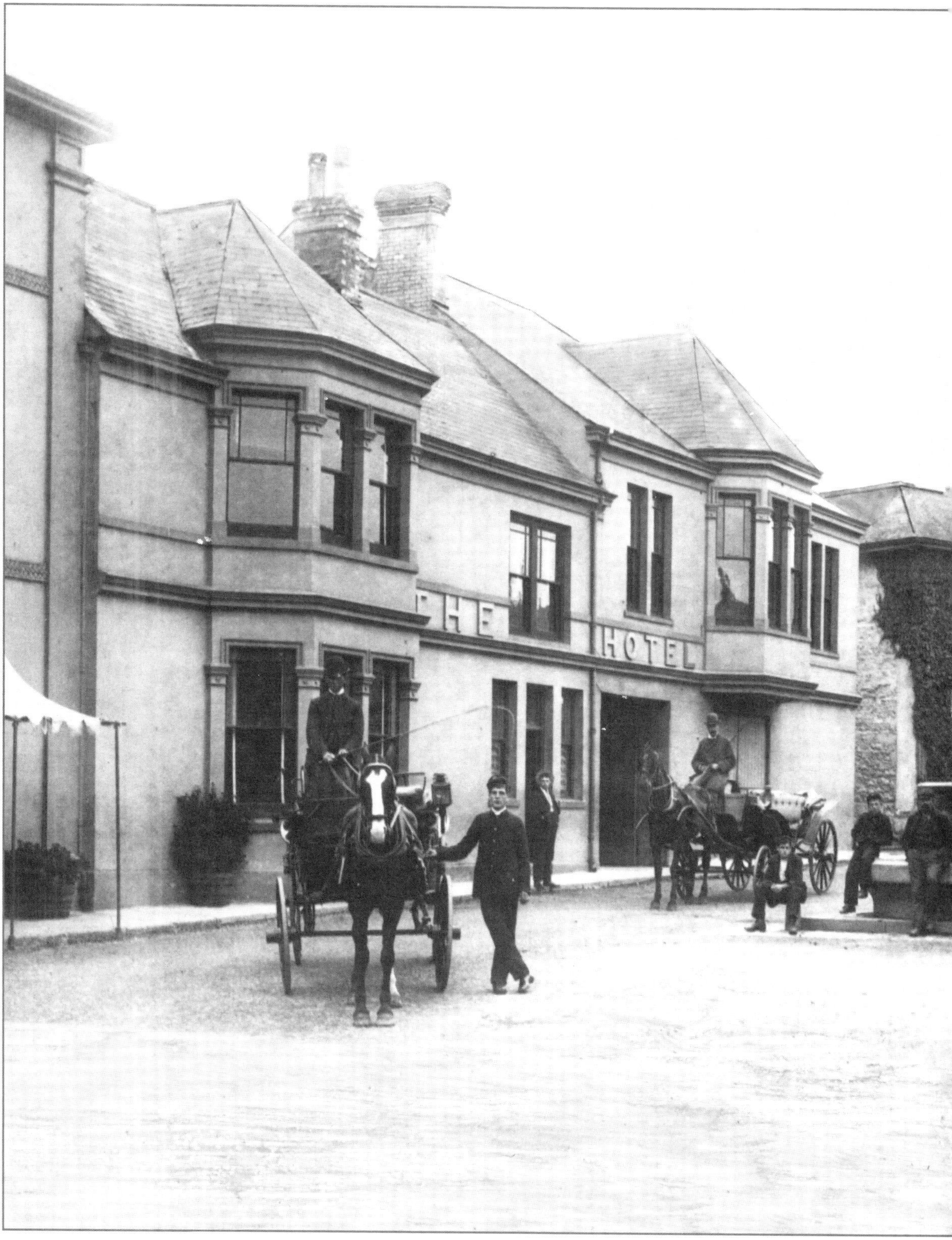
THE
HOTEL

West Cornwall Towns

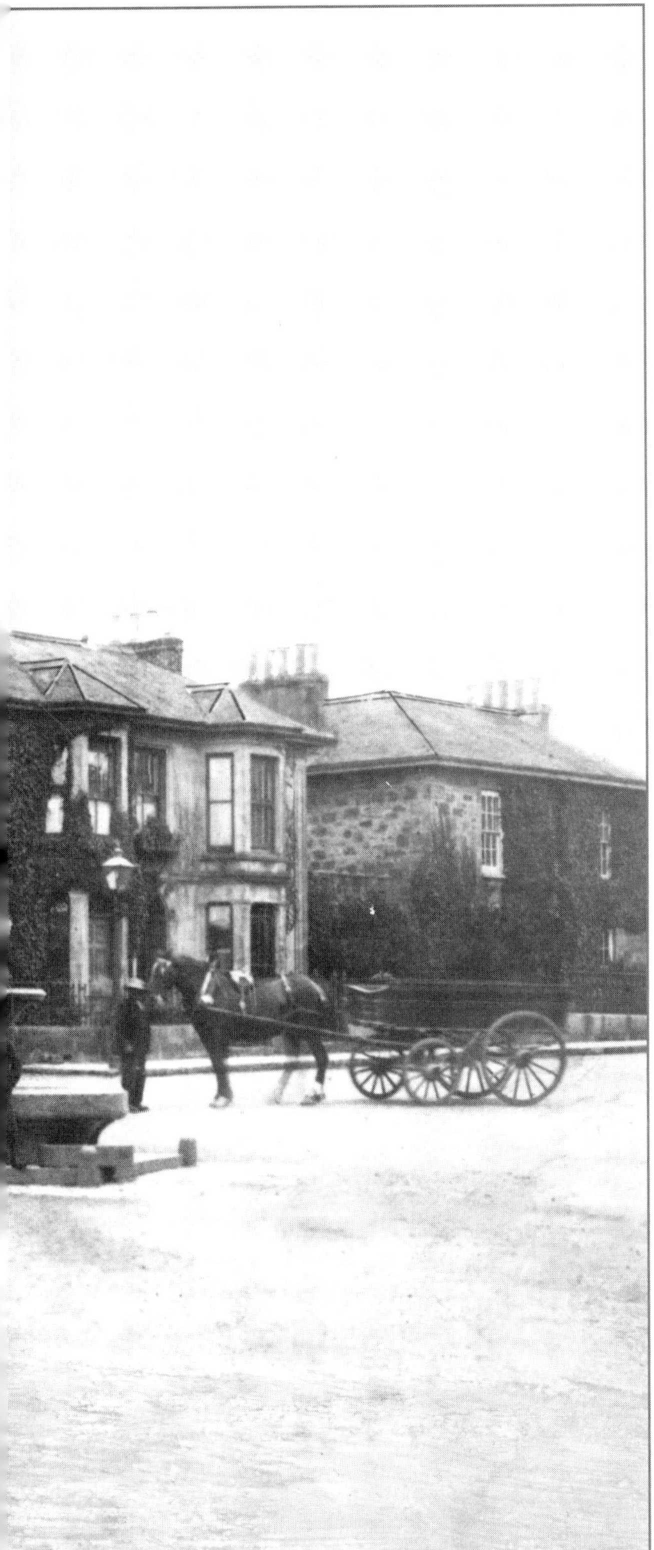

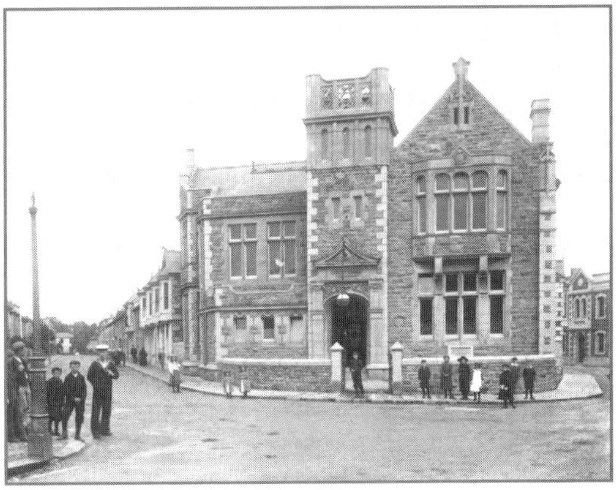

▲ **Camborne, The Free Library 1902** 49116
Built at a cost of £2,000 on the junction of Basset Street (left) with Trevenson Street, the Passmore Edwards Free Library was opened on 23 May 1895 and boasted 5,400 volumes. A statue of Richard Trevithick, the Cornish engineering genius, now stands outside the building. The benefactor John Passmore Edwards also financed the library at Liskeard, seen on page 55.

◄ **Camborne, Commercial Square 1902** 49112
Transport for guests is lined up outside the Commercial Hotel, advertised at the time as being 'lighted by electricity; families, tourists and commercial, billiards and posting'.

▼ **Redruth, Fore Street 1898** 41620
The main shopping street climbs towards the town clock. This view is dominated by Tower House, the premises of John Evans & Co, outfitters. Hats, jackets, mackintoshes, overcoats, umbrellas and leggings are advertised in the windows, and to further tempt gentlemen shoppers, one sign reads: 'The Apparel Oft Proclaims the Man'. Opposite, a barber's pole advertises a humbler shop.

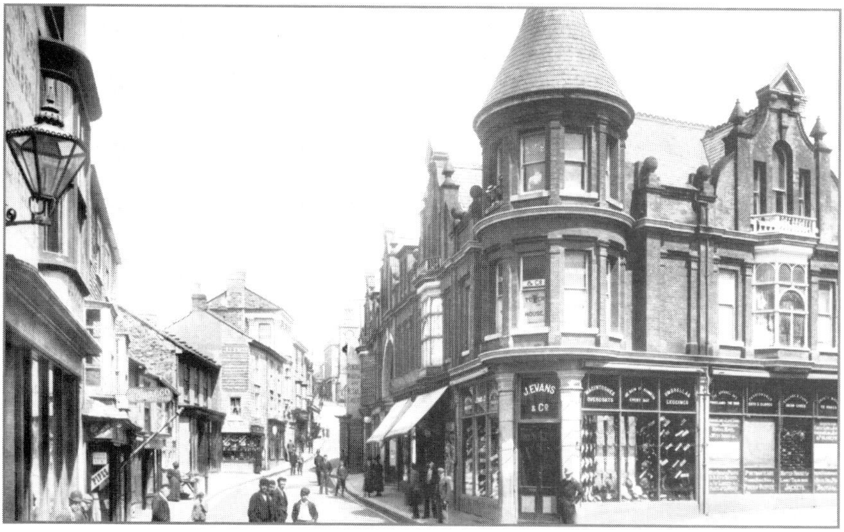

▼ **Penryn, Market Street 1890** 27648
This scene is dominated by the granite clock tower, which was erected in 1839. Behind it is the Town Hall of 1825, containing council chambers, a market hall and a police station. The horse-drawn coach is perhaps waiting for custom from the Elephant and Castle Hotel opposite.

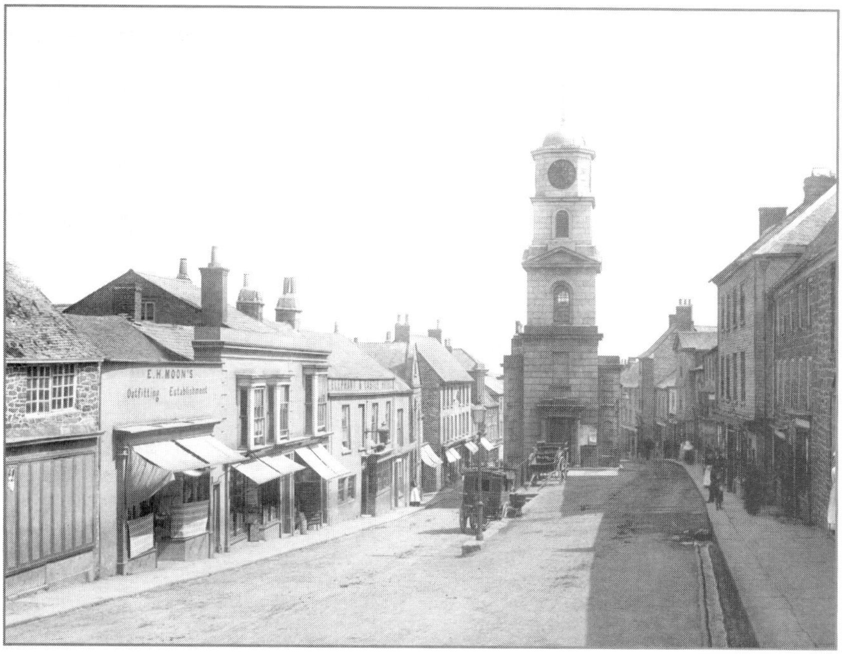

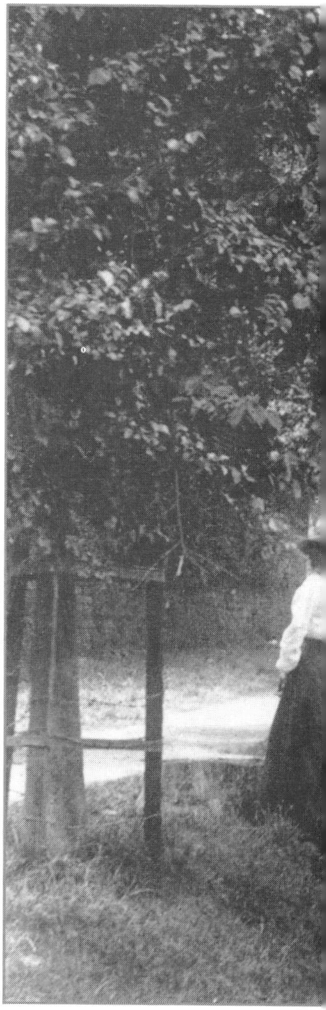

▲ **Falmouth, Arwenack Avenue 1904** 52229A
A good selection of early Edwardian costume can be seen in this well-wooded avenue. New trees have been planted between their older cousins, and a gas lamp struggles to be seen on the right.

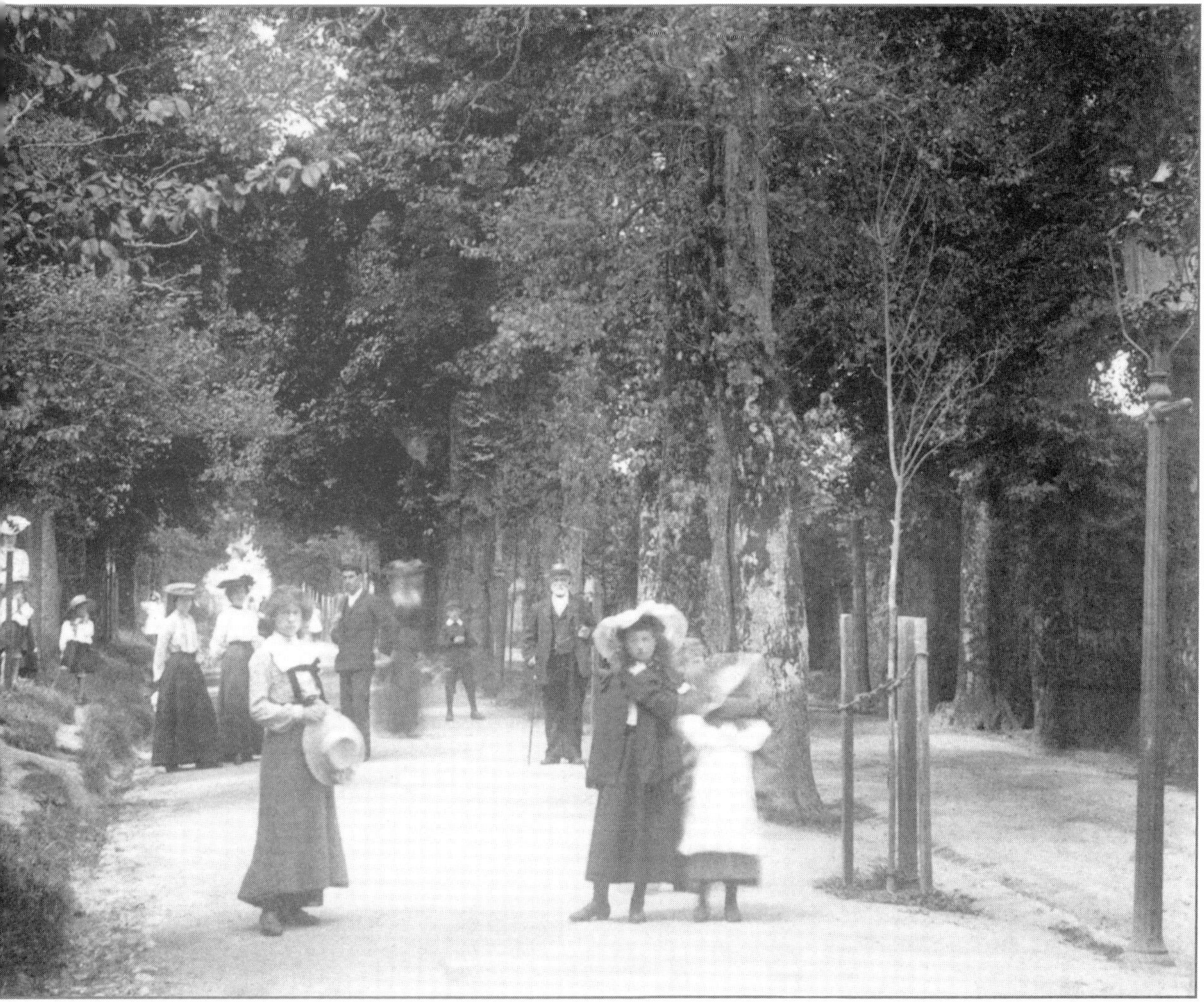

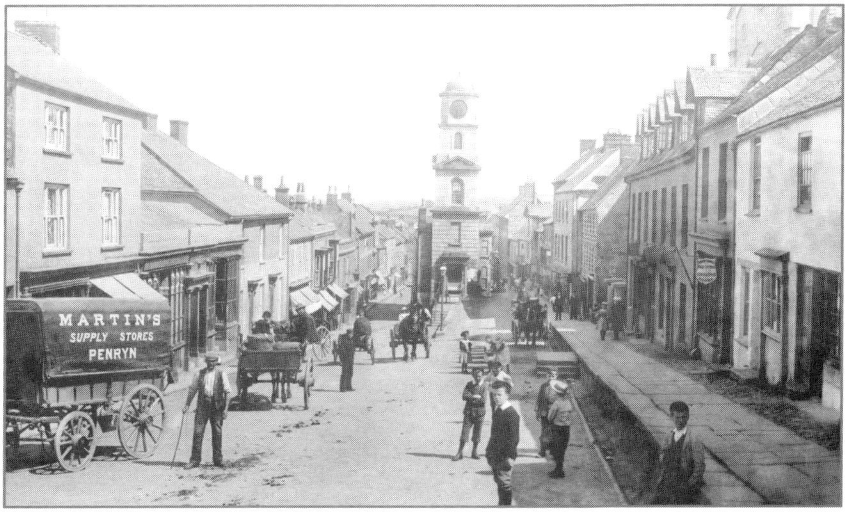

◄ **Penryn, Market Street 1897** 39496
There is lots of activity here, with delivery carts and wagons and pedestrians willing to pose for the camera. The small shop along the raised pavement on the right advertises 'Thomas's hair cutting and shaving rooms'. This photograph was taken a little further up the street from No 27648; Moon's outfitters, seen in the earlier photograph, has been given a second storey.

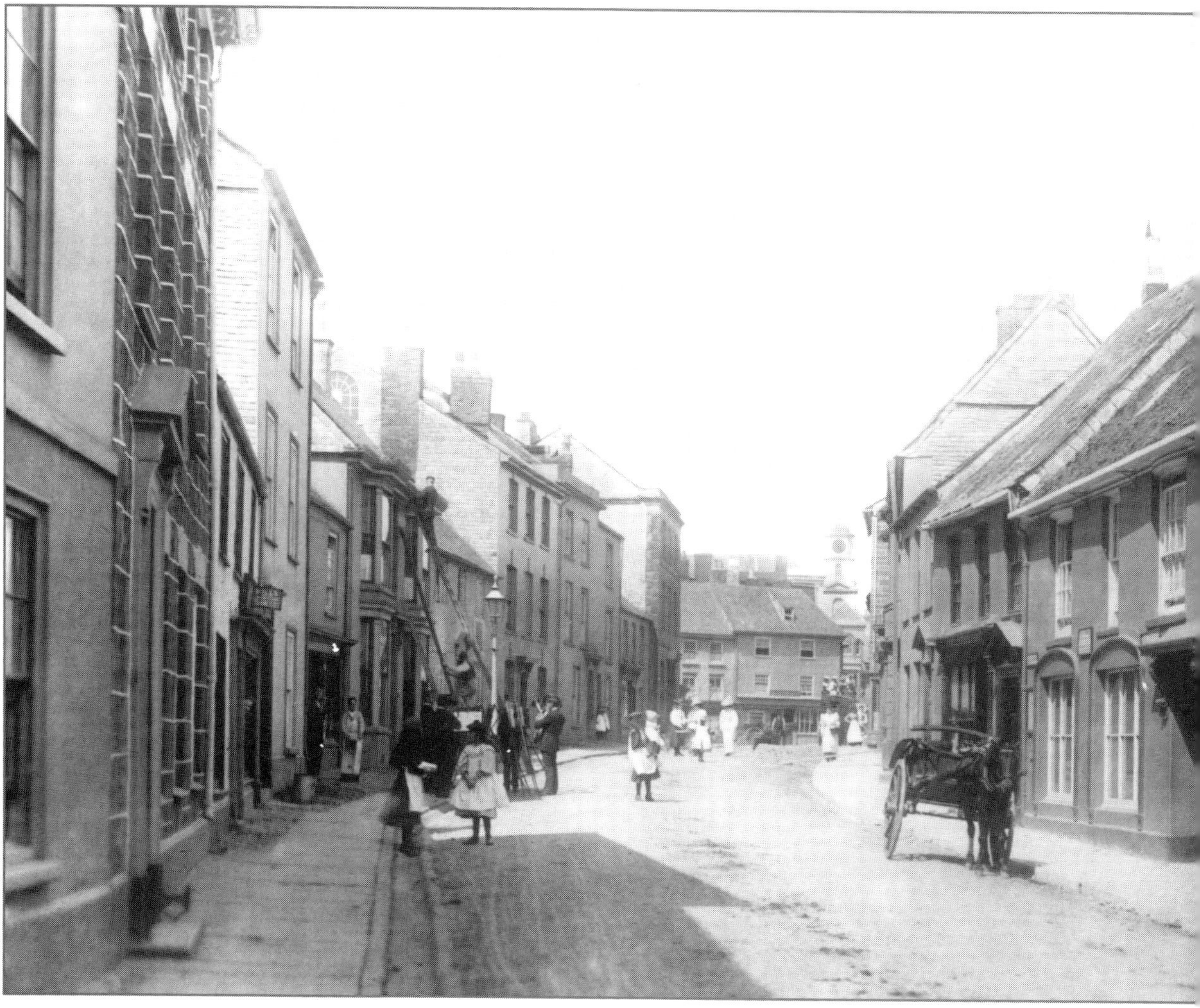

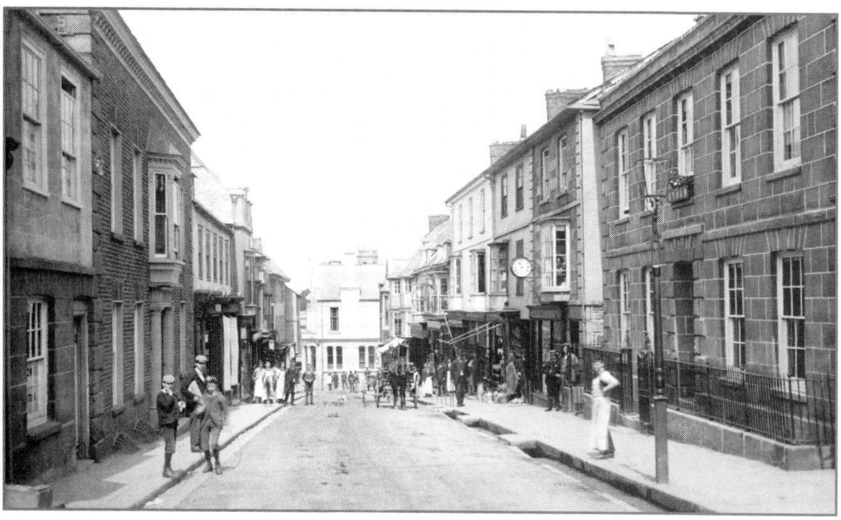

◄ **Helston, Meneage Street 1895** 36187
In one of Helston's principal streets, we see on the right a characteristic gutter channel with running water. Wares are displayed outside the shops, and shopkeepers, with their aprons, are among the crowd, and a boy stands with a hoop on the left. At the street's end is the Cornish Bank.

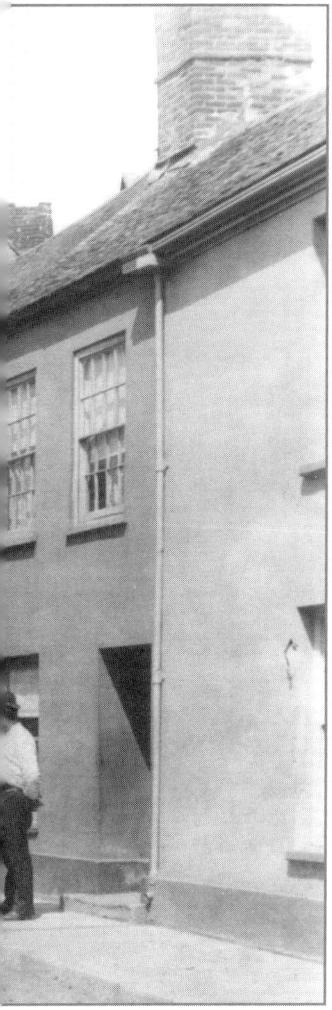

Penryn, Broad Street 1897 39499

We are further down into the town and looking back up towards the clock tower, which is just visible. A house on the left is being decorated or renovated by men on ladders, while a man with a euphonium and other players serenade them below.

Helston, The Monument 1890 24502

This fine Gothic archway was erected by subscription to the memory of Humphrey Millett Grylls in 1834; it is built in granite ashlar with four tall octagonal pillars. It is still a major landmark, and stands at the foot of Coinagehall Street with a view of open countryside behind.

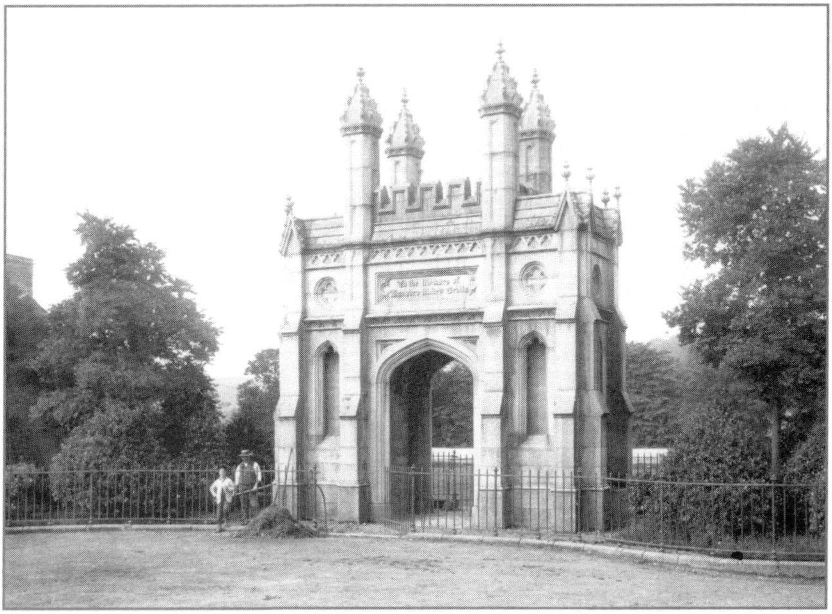

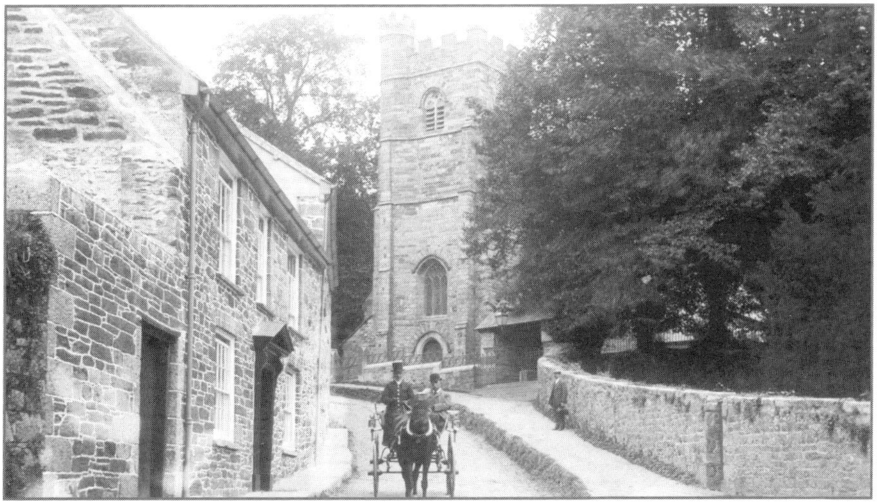

Penryn, The Church 1904 53052

A liveried driver negotiates a light carriage down the narrow lane beside the church in this well-composed picture. The church is actually at St Gluvias, just across the head of the Penryn River creek.

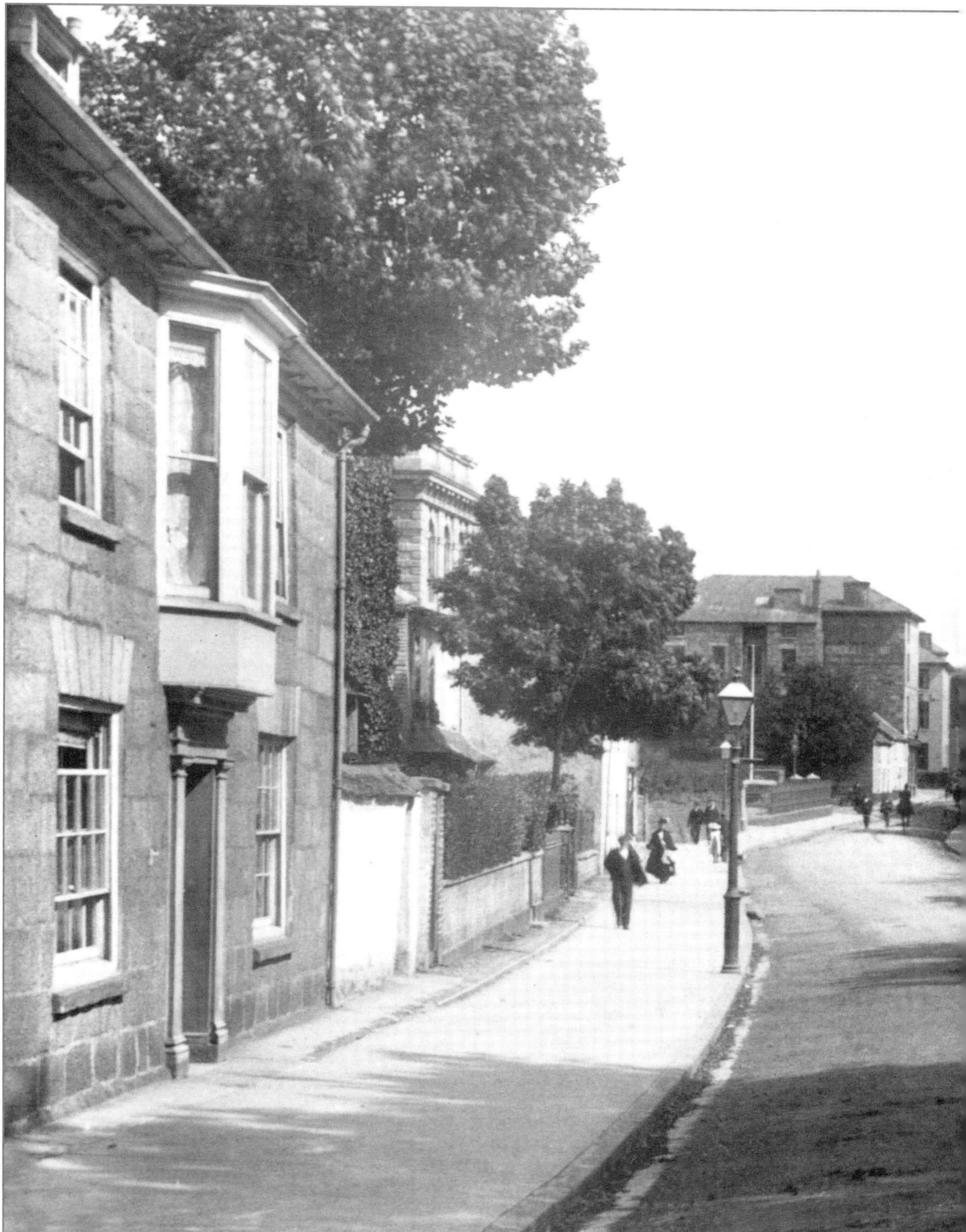

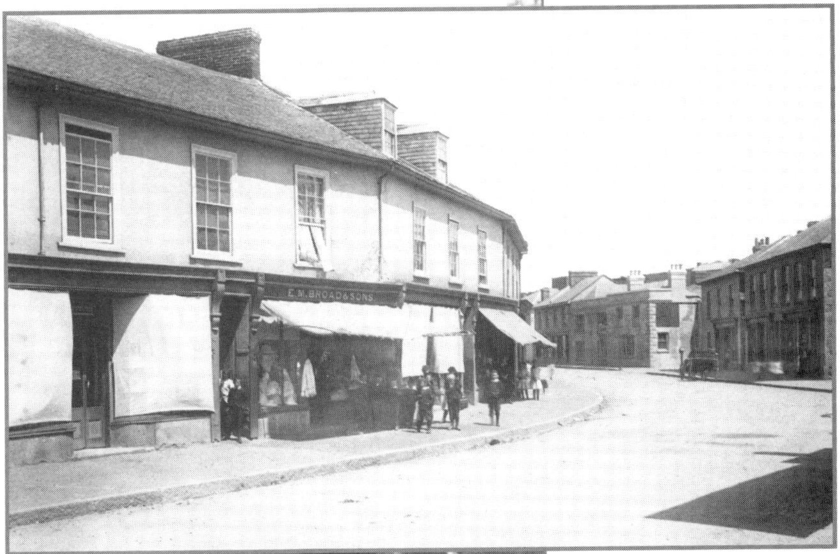

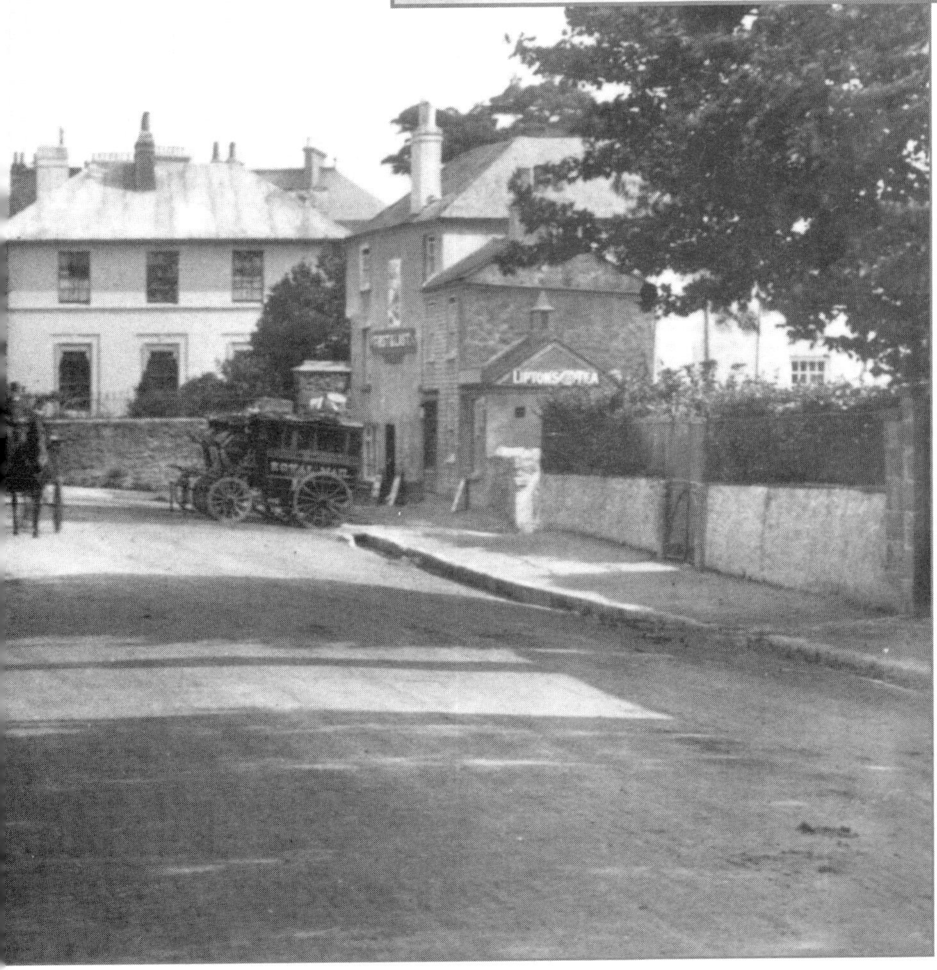

▲ **Hayle, Copperhouse 1892** 29881

Solid, if plain, buildings on both sides of Fore Street give this district of Hayle the look of a mining town. The name comes from the copper works, which closed in the early 19th century. In the foreground is Edwin Broad's draper's shop. Shades and awnings suggest that this is summer.

◀ **Penzance, Alverton Street 1908** 61233

We are looking east towards the town centre; the Market House dome is just visible at the end of the street. On the left, set back and partly hidden by a tree, are the Public Buildings and St John's Hall. A Royal Mail coach is outside the First and Last Inn, which is appropriately named, as this road leads out towards the Land's End.

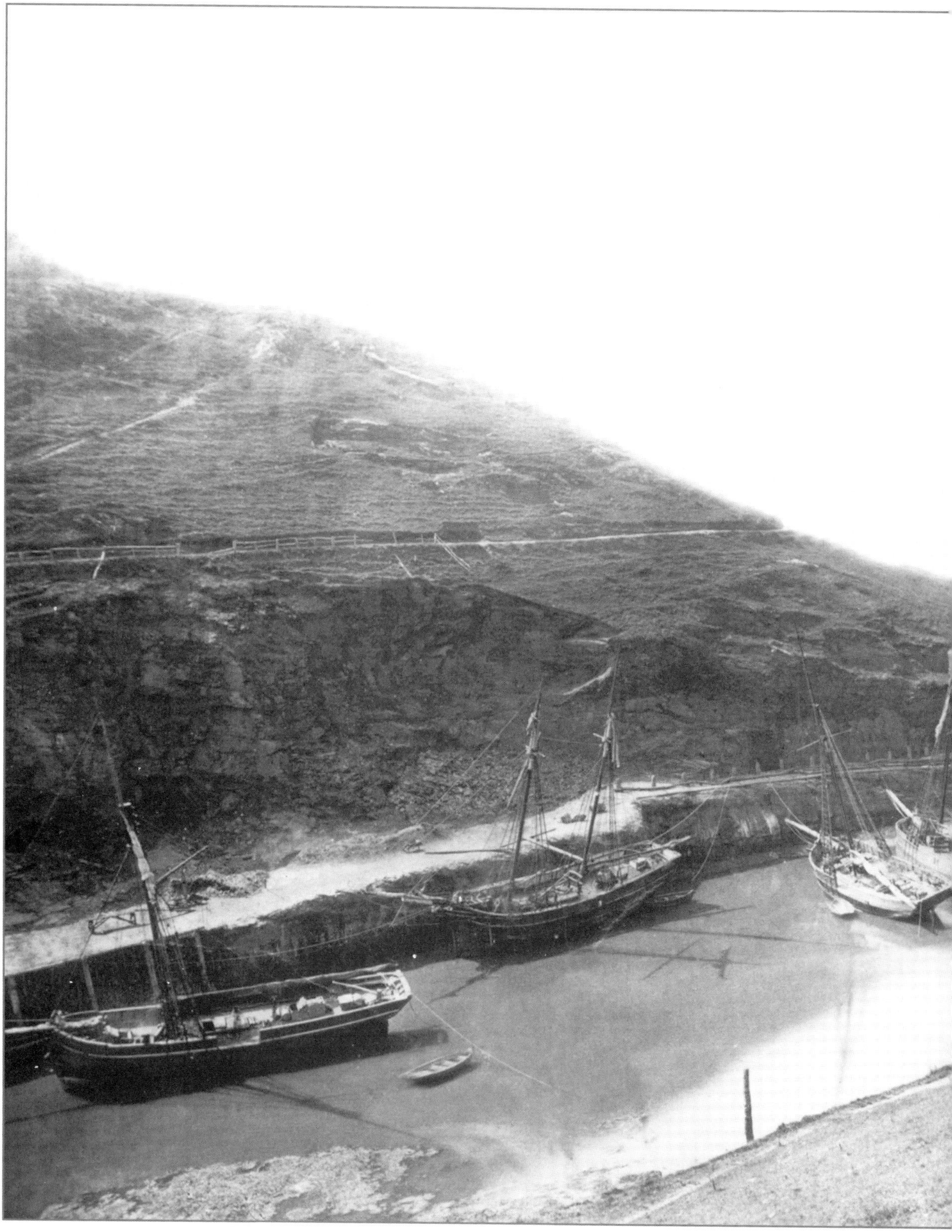

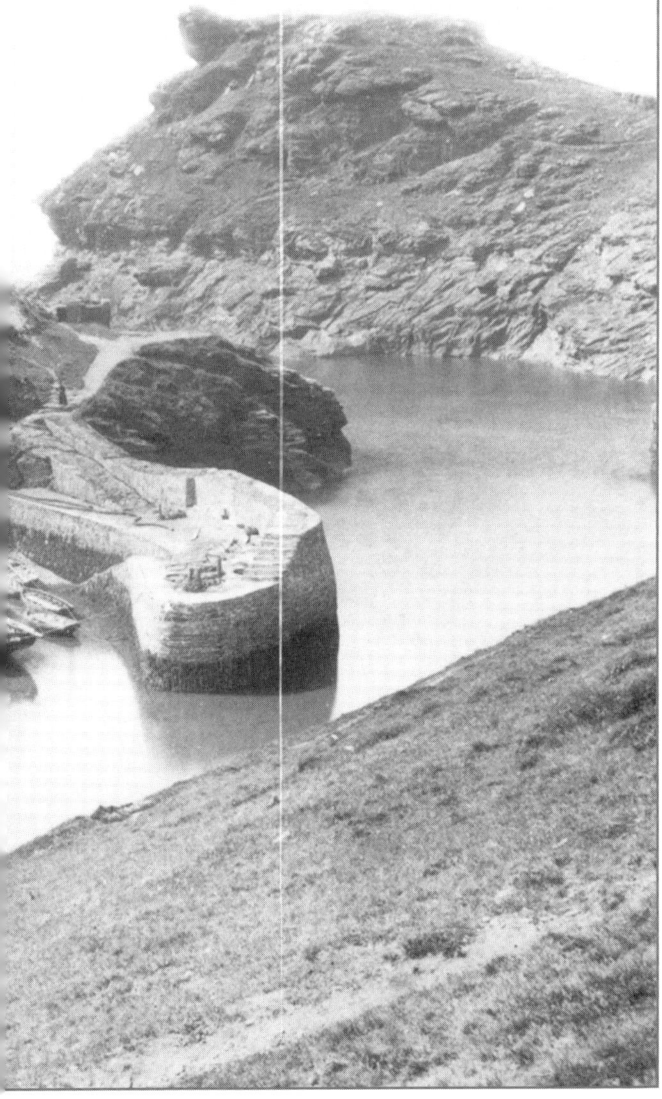

Trading Ports

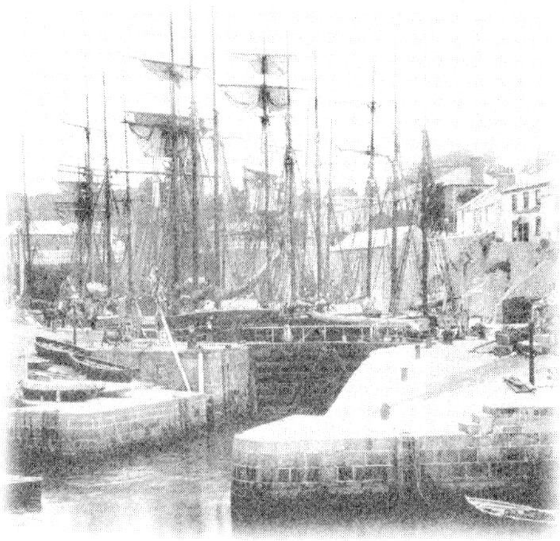

Boscastle, The Harbour and Profile Rock c1871 5964

The picturesque harbour gives good shelter, once vessels have negotiated a difficult entrance between high cliffs. This early photograph gives evidence that Boscastle was indeed a trading port, with a small schooner and smacks lying aground at half-tide. The main imports of lime and coal declined after the railway came to Camelford in 1893. The Profile Rock on the headland was said to resemble Queen Victoria's head!

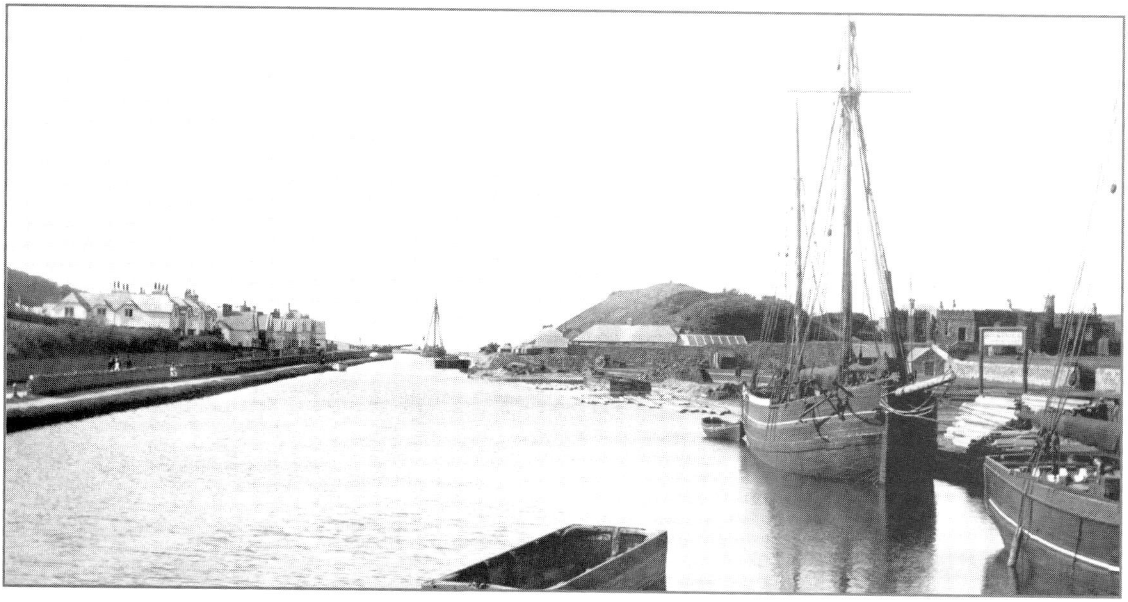

Bude, The Canal from the Bridge 1890 23780
The Bude Canal was opened in 1826 from this harbour basin, with a sea lock just visible in the distance. Shelly sea sand was carried inland for spreading on acid soils by tub boats: we can see one in the foreground. Two ketches lie alongside the quay of Hockin & Co, timber, slate, coal, salt, manure, grain and lime merchants. Note the timber on the quay and seasoning in the water. Between the ships is The Castle, built in 1850 for the inventor Sir Goldsworthy Gurney. The railway did not arrive until 1898.

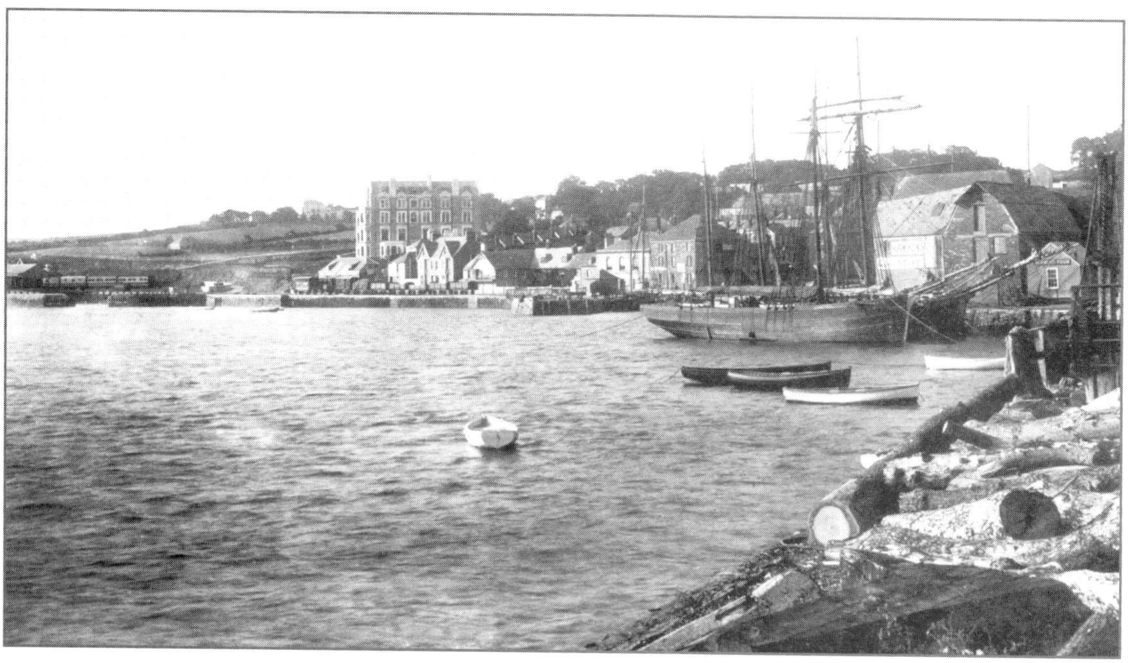

Padstow, General View 1901 47712
Two schooners are moored at the North Quay alongside John Hawken's coal store. In the background there is evidence of the railway that had arrived only two years before, with a line of trucks on the quay and carriages also visible. This was the furthest the London & South Western Railway ever got from Waterloo: 256 miles.

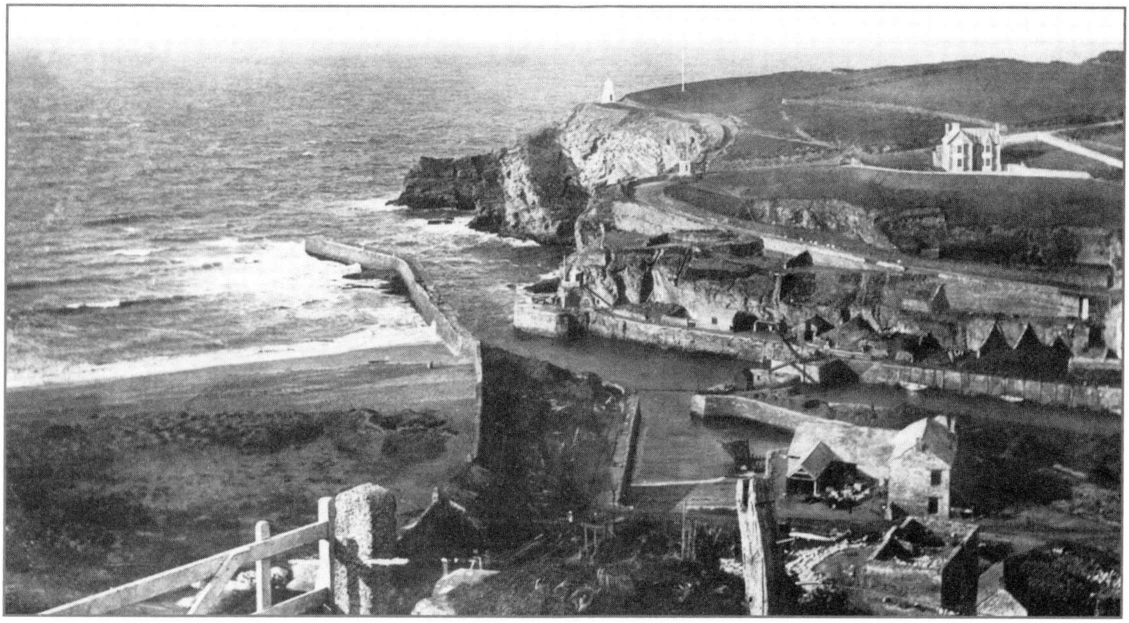

Portreath, General View 1890 23030
This was one of the most important mining ports in the 19th century; the harbour was often packed with sailing vessels bringing coal from South Wales and returning with copper ores. By 1890 the quays were quieter, with only a few imports of coal. This view shows the pier protecting the inner harbour from the Atlantic swell, and we can also see how the entrance is terribly narrow.

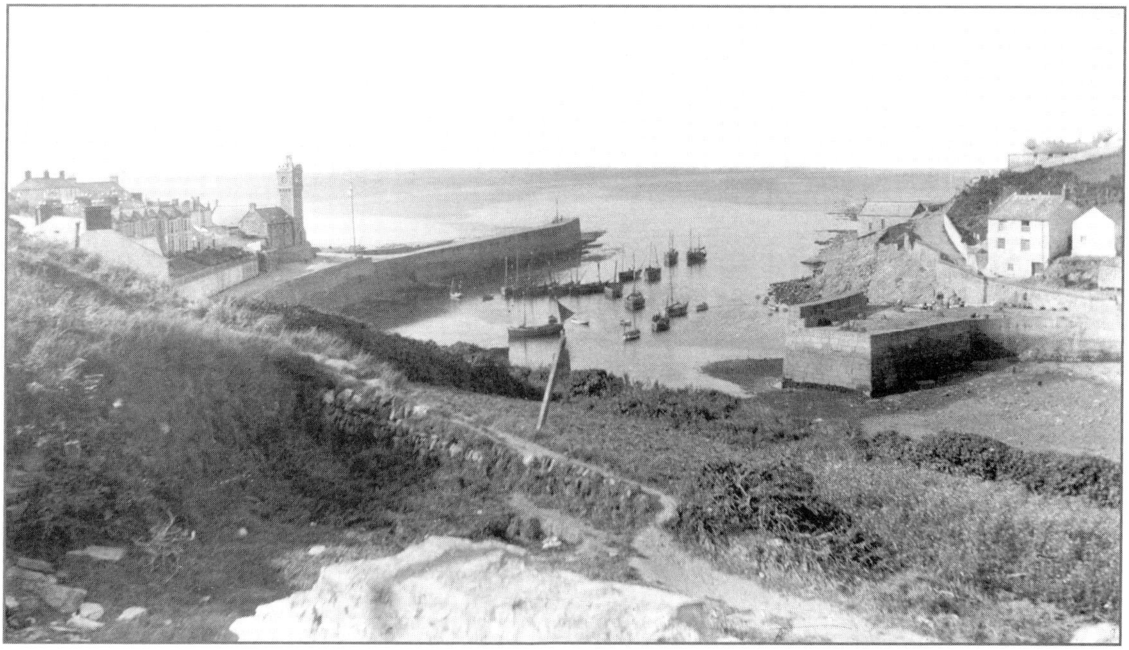

Porthleven, The Harbour Entrance 1890 24509A
The pier and harbour works were rebuilt after a storm in 1824, when Porthleven was developed as a trading port. Fishing was also carried on. Boats wait in the harbour entrance for the rising tide to take them into the inner harbour. The clock tower is conspicuous near the pier, and the new lifeboat house faces the sea on the right.

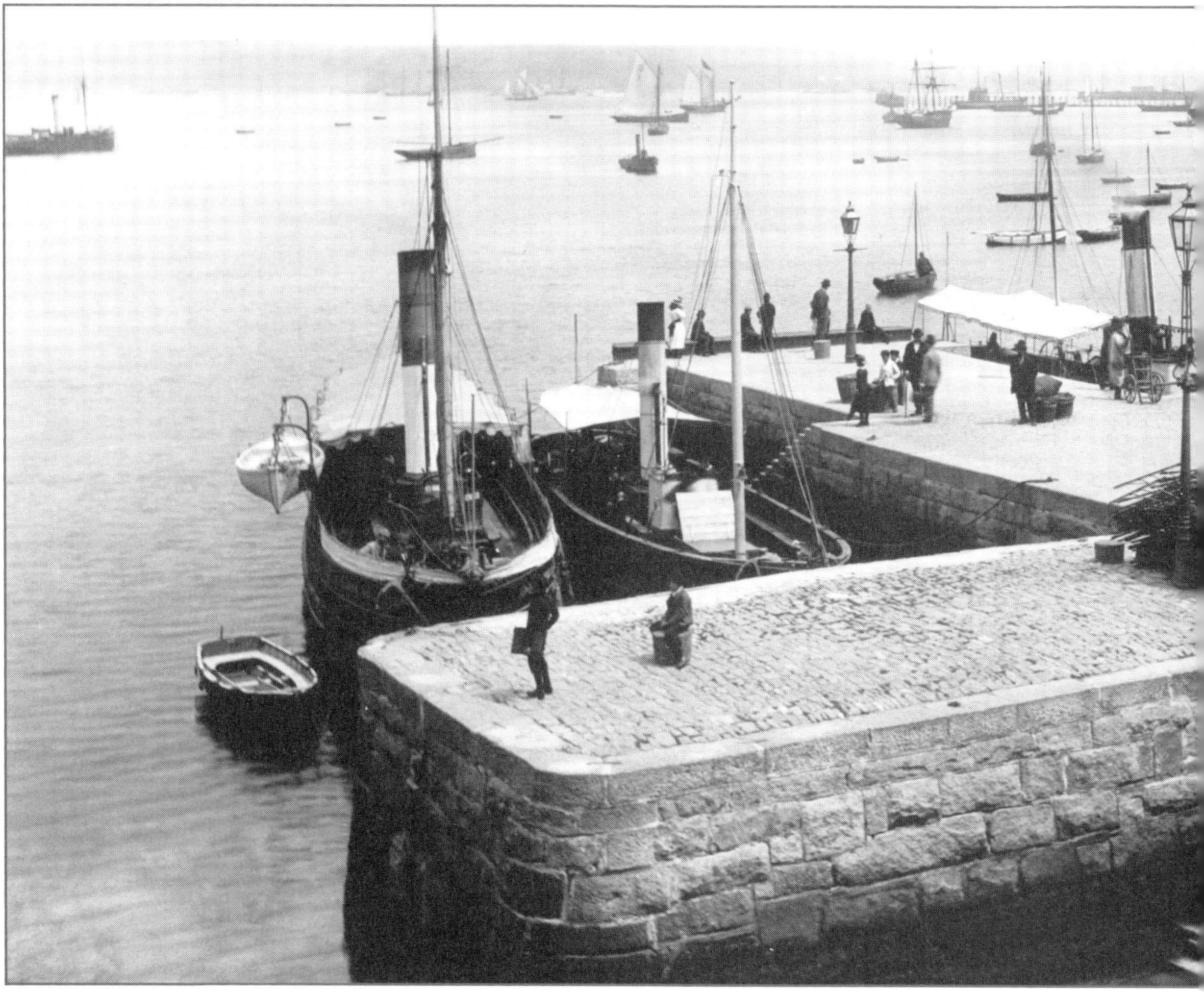

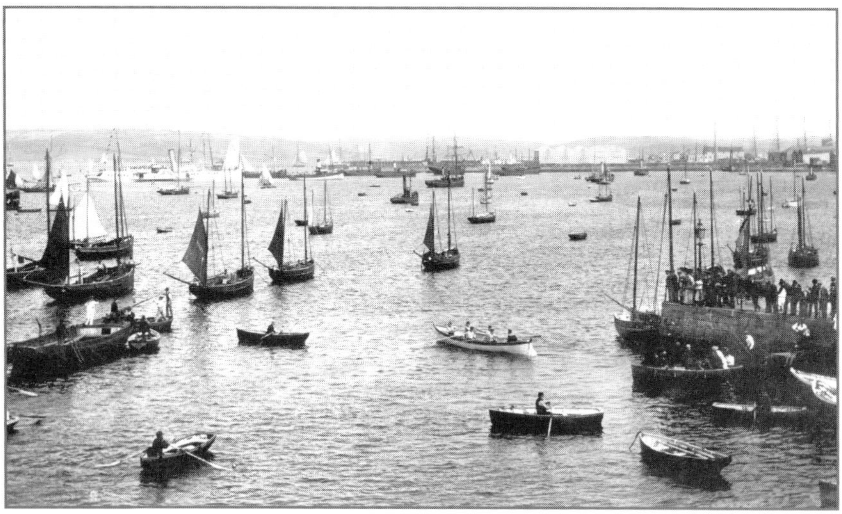

◄ **Falmouth**
The Harbour 1895

37047

Here we see a busy harbour scene, with fishing boats on the left and several sailing boats, along with a number of harbour tugs. The white paddle steamer is the 'Plymouth Belle', which ran for a year or two between Plymouth, Penzance and Torquay. Falmouth Docks are behind, with a four-masted sailing ship in one of the dry-docks on the right.

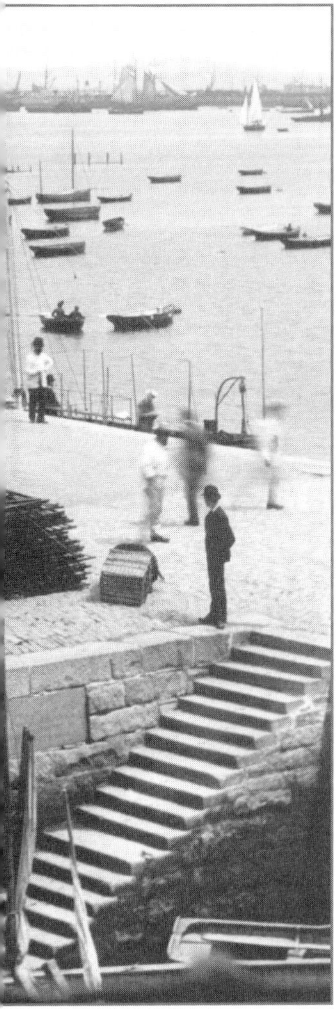

◄ **Falmouth, The Market Strand 1890** 24208
The three passenger steamers alongside the quay are, from left to right, the 'New Resolute', the 'Wotton' and probably the 'St Mawes Castle'. Market Strand Quay was later extended in 1905 to become the Prince of Wales Pier, which is still used for ferry services.

▼ **Penryn, From the River 1890** 27645
A trading ship is alongside the Town Quay. The industrial quarter of Penryn is behind the frontage quays almost at the head of the Penryn River.

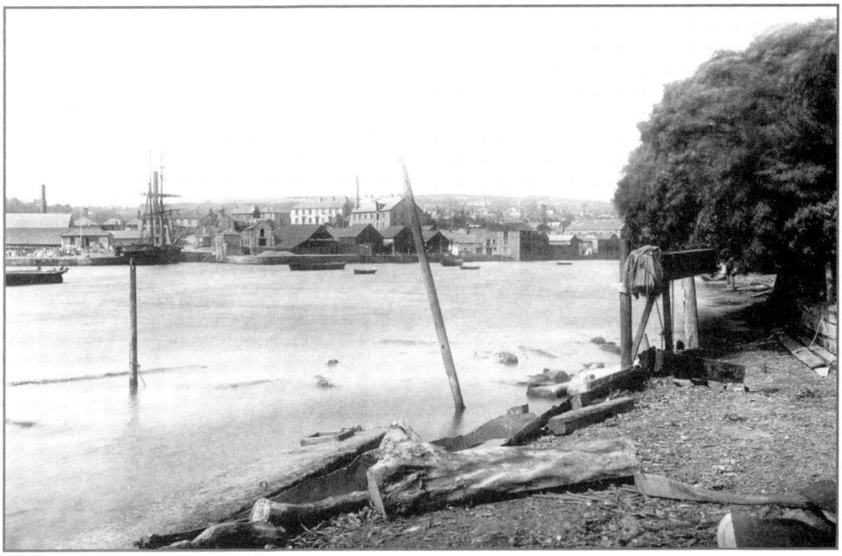

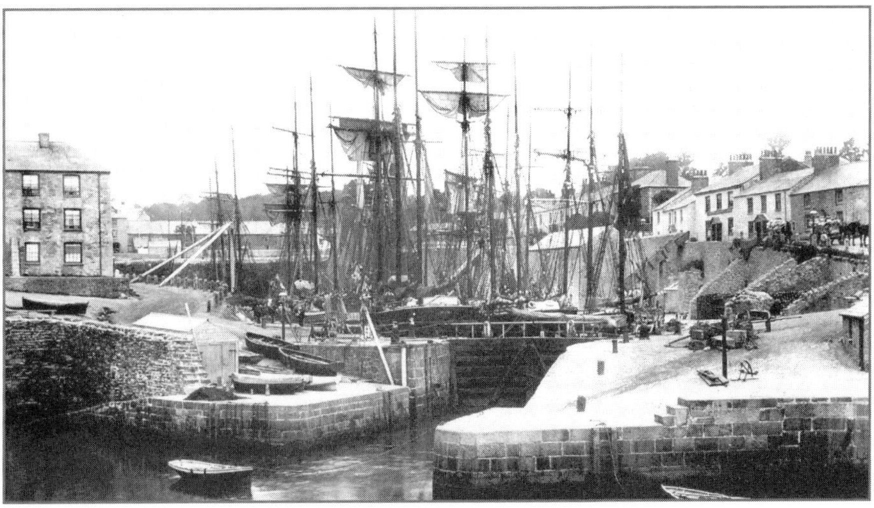

◄ **Charlestown, The Harbour 1904** 53050
Charlestown was developed by Sir Charles Rashleigh at the beginning of the 19th century for exporting china clay and other minerals. This view, taken from the outer pier, shows the lock gate and at least six three-masted sailing vessels in the floating basin. Apart from the shipping and the installation of a modern lock gate, this scene is little changed today.

▼ **Fowey, From Hall Walk 1893** 32537
Hall Walk on the Bodinnick side provides a fine view down the harbour to the open sea, with the town on the right. The deepwater estuary of the Fowey has long been an important haven, but especially since china clay exports were begun in the 19th century. A large sailing ship, and several smaller ones are waiting opposite the town for their turn to go up river and load clay.

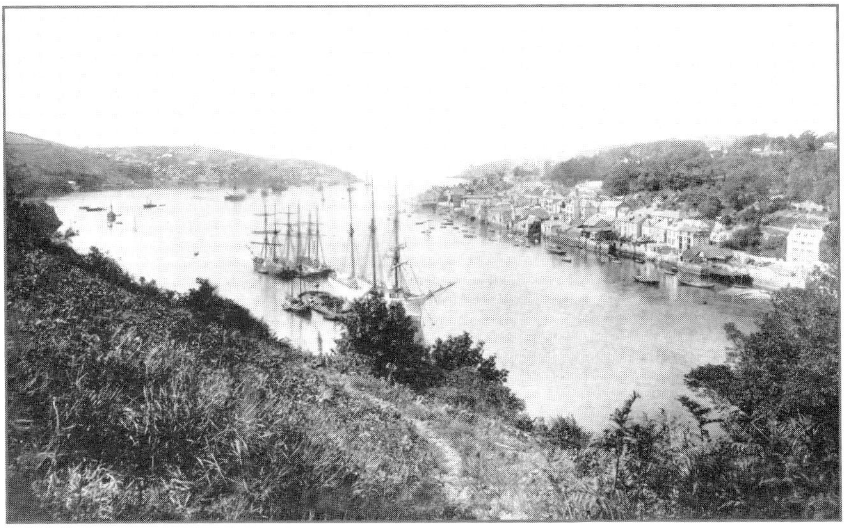

▼ **Looe, The Bridge 1888** 21296
A much earlier bridge was replaced by this one in 1853; at that time, the harbour was being improved for the export of copper ore and import of coal. Beyond is the long quay at East Looe, where ores were laid out before shipment. The harbour drains completely at low tide.

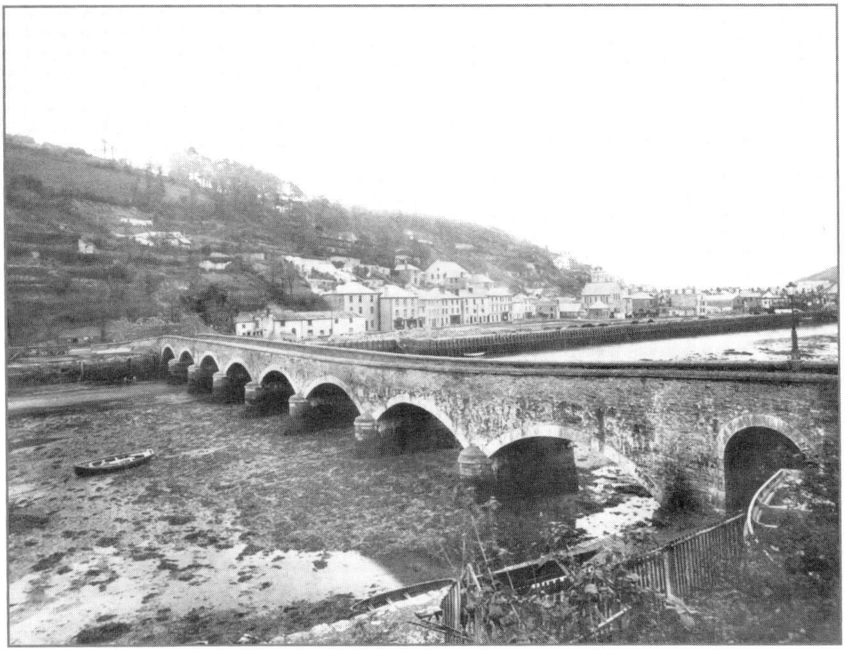

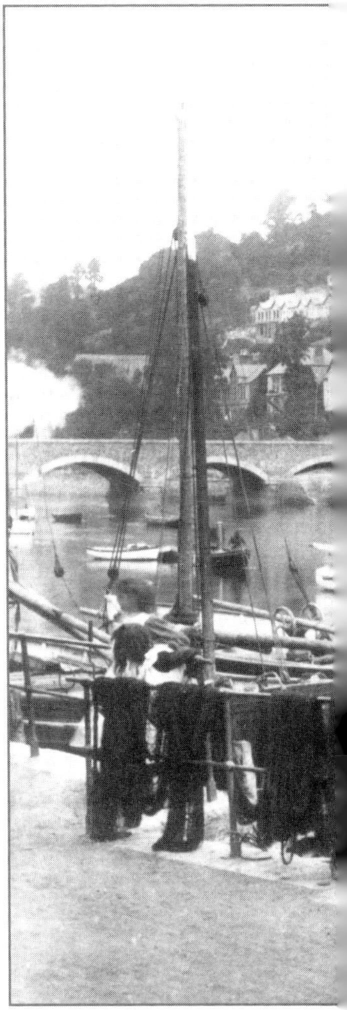

▲ **Looe, The Harbour 1906** 56404
Boys stand guard over fishing nets at West Looe. Across the harbour is Buller Quay at East Looe, where three railway trucks can be seen. Development is under way, and the higher terraces have been erected since photograph no 21296. Always a fishing harbour, Looe benefited from the well-built quays once the mineral traffic ceased.

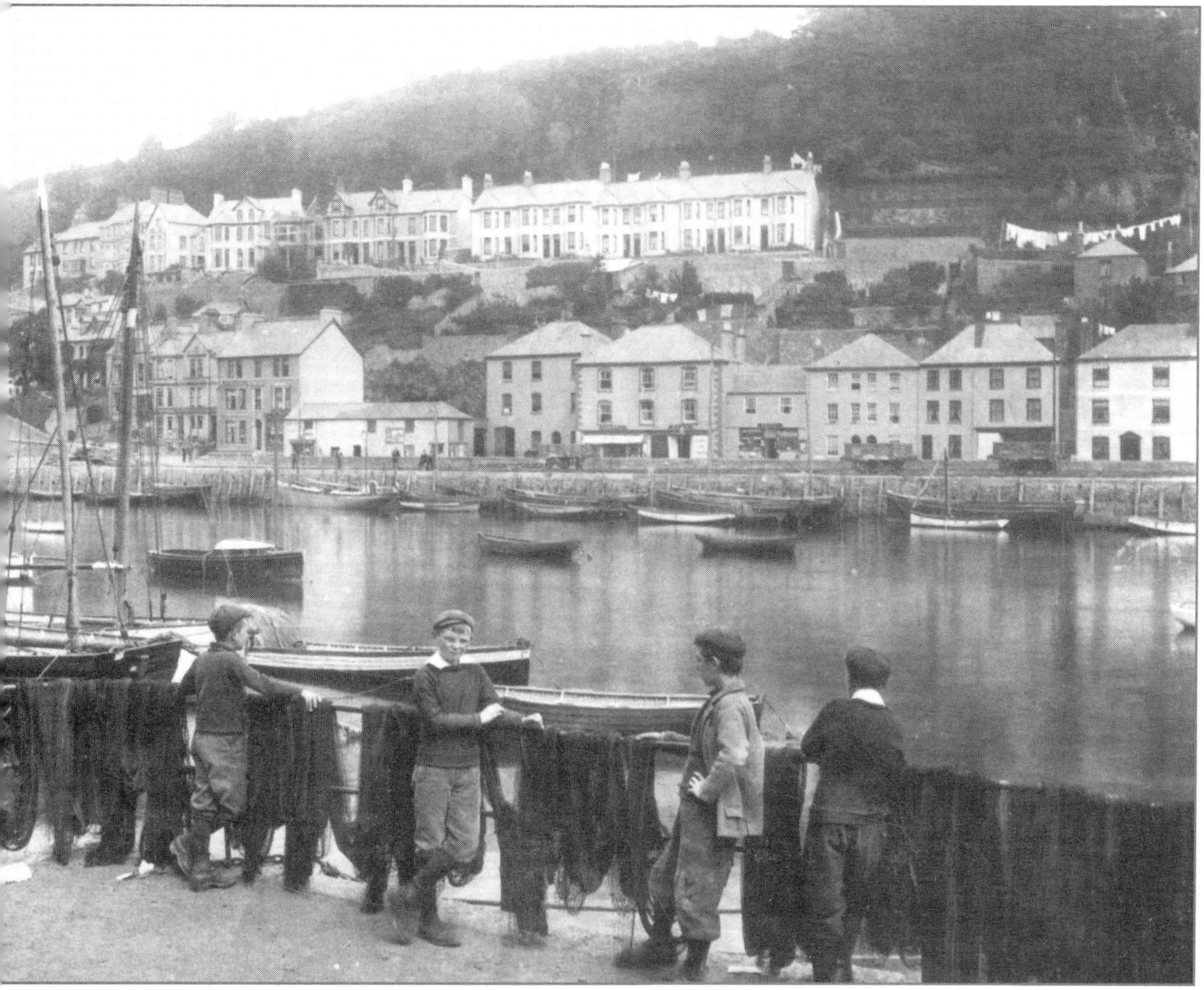

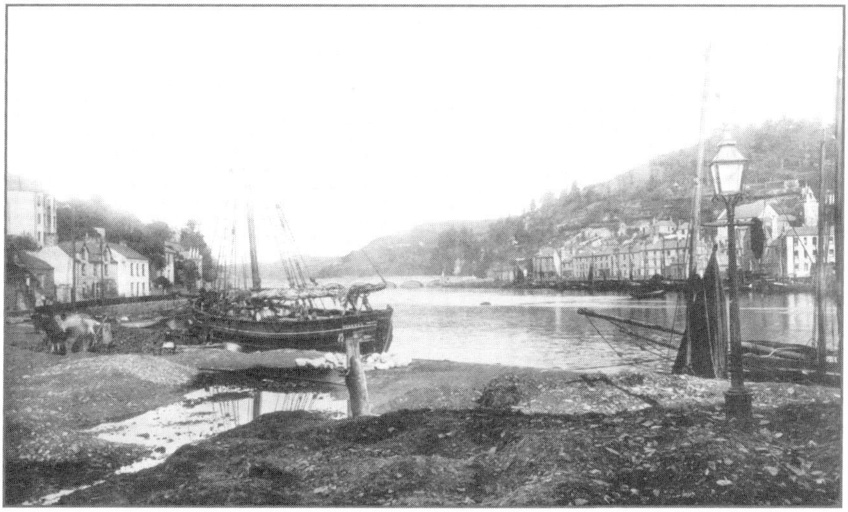

◄ **Looe, The View from the Church Steps 1888** 21302
The 'Pioneer' lies alongside the quay at West Looe; we are looking upstream towards the bridge. The church steps of St Nicholas's Church are behind the camara.

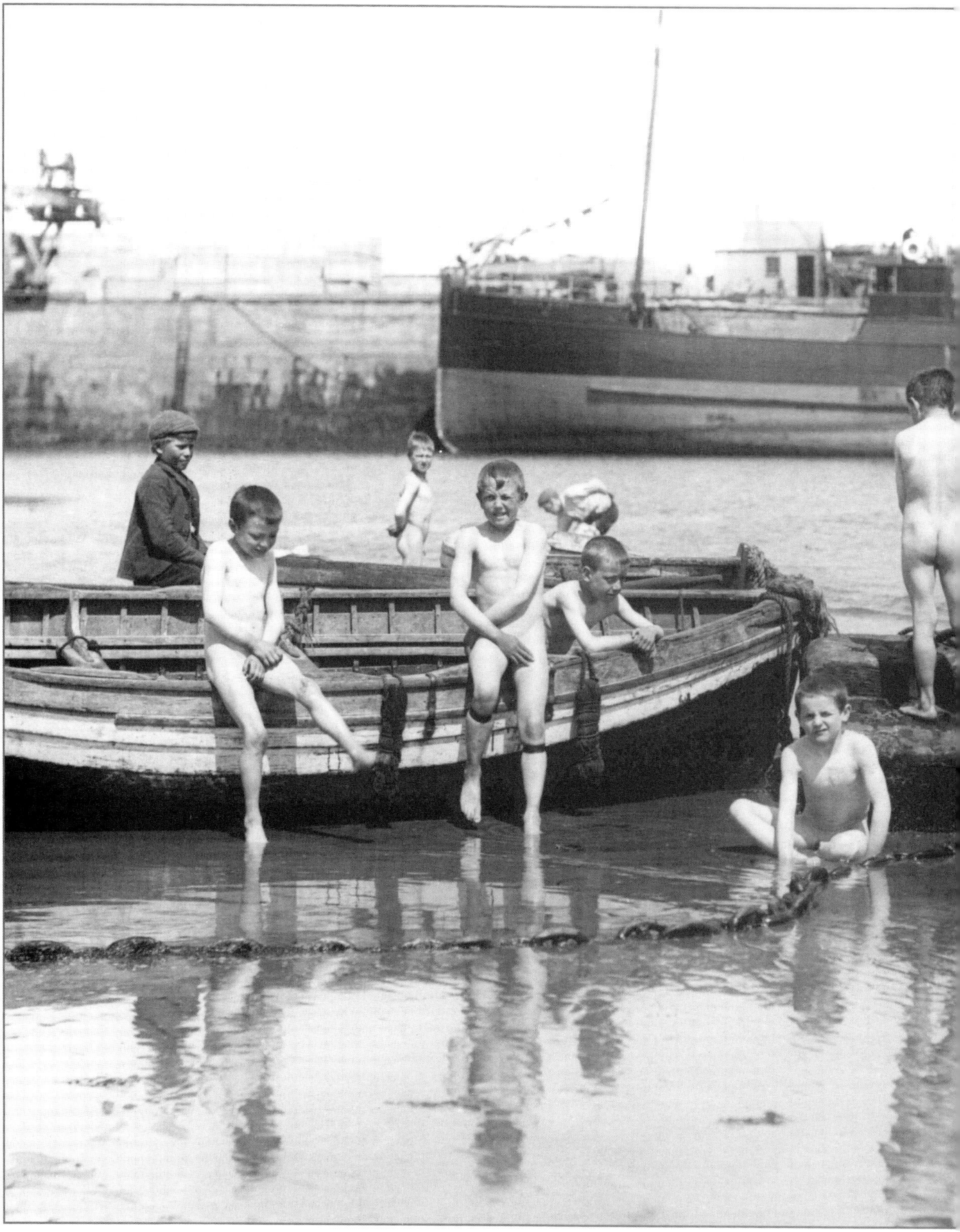

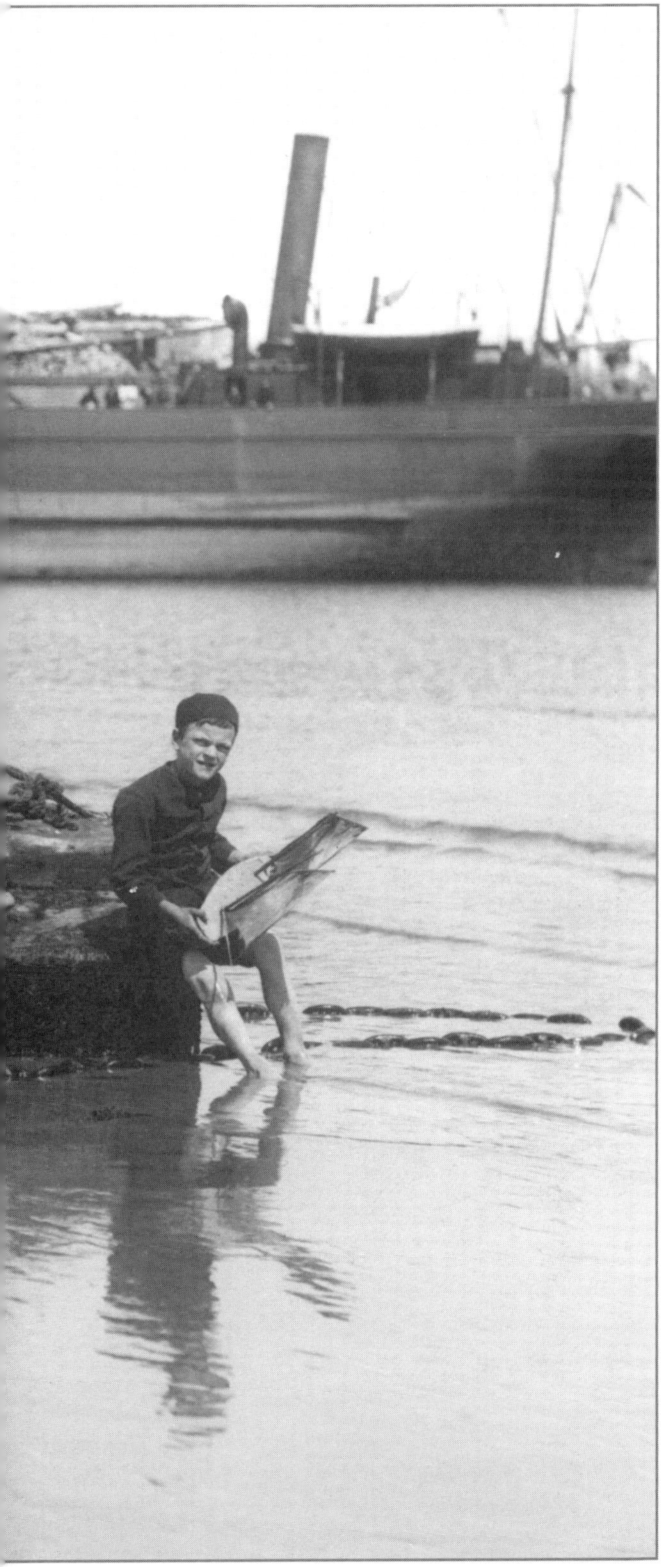

Fishing Coves and Harbours

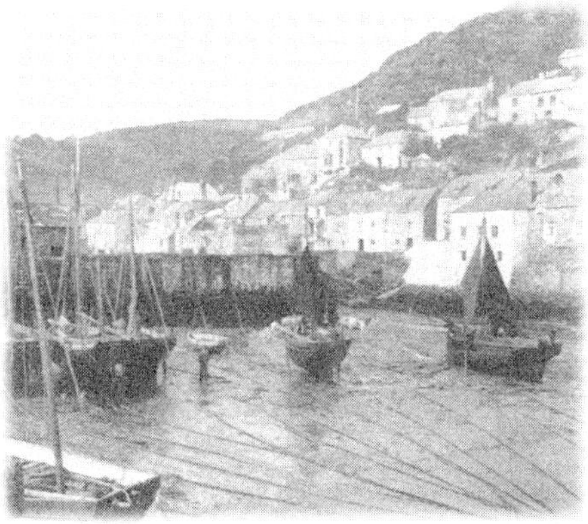

Newlyn, Water Babies 1893 31800
Although the bathing boys are the subject of this photograph, of particular interest is the steam coaster alongside the new pier in the background, where construction work still appears to be going on. The boy on the right holds a model fishing lugger.

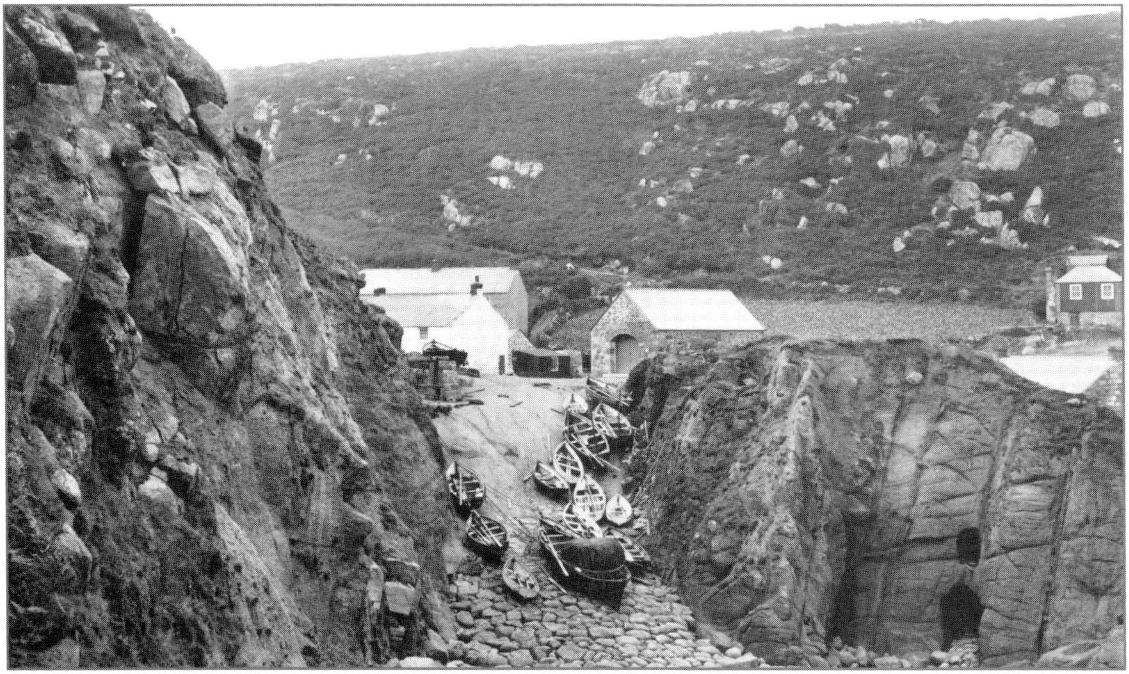

Porthgwarra, The Cove and the Caves 1908 61264
There is just room to draw up a few boats at this remote fishing cove down by the granite cliffs of Gwennap Head at the south-west corner of the Land's End peninsula.

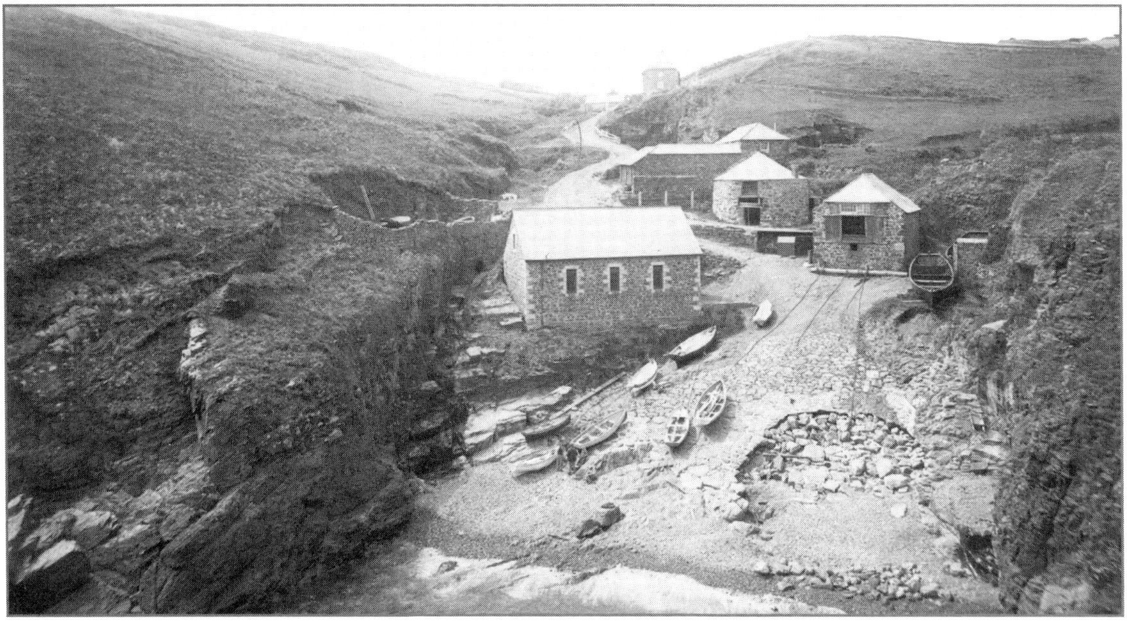

Landewednack, Church Cove 1895 36217
Church Cove is on the east side of the Lizard. The building on the left is the lifeboat station, erected in 1885; it is unusual that it is set at right angles to the beach. Difficulties in launching and retrieving the lifeboat led to its demise in 1899, in favour of Polpeor Cove on the Lizard itself. Note the capstan houses for hauling boats out of the water.

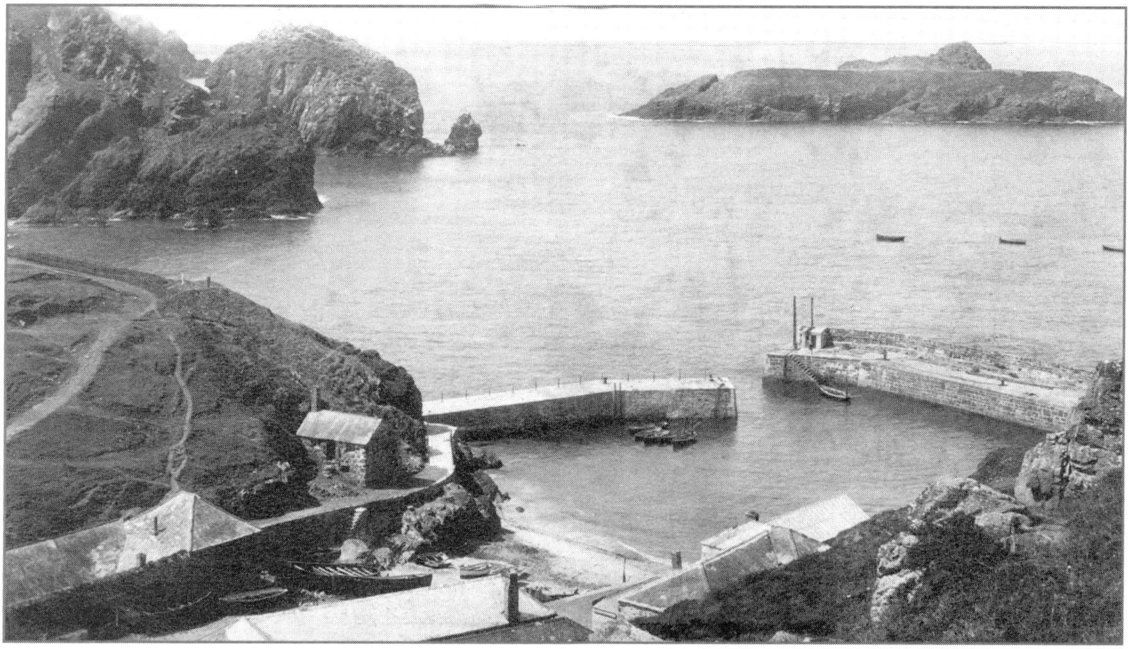

Mullion Cove 1899 43796

The two piers at Mullion had only just been built, in 1893-95, when this photograph was taken. Their purpose was to create a sheltered harbour on an otherwise rocky coast, in order to encourage crab and lobster fishing. Mullion Island lies offshore like a great whale.

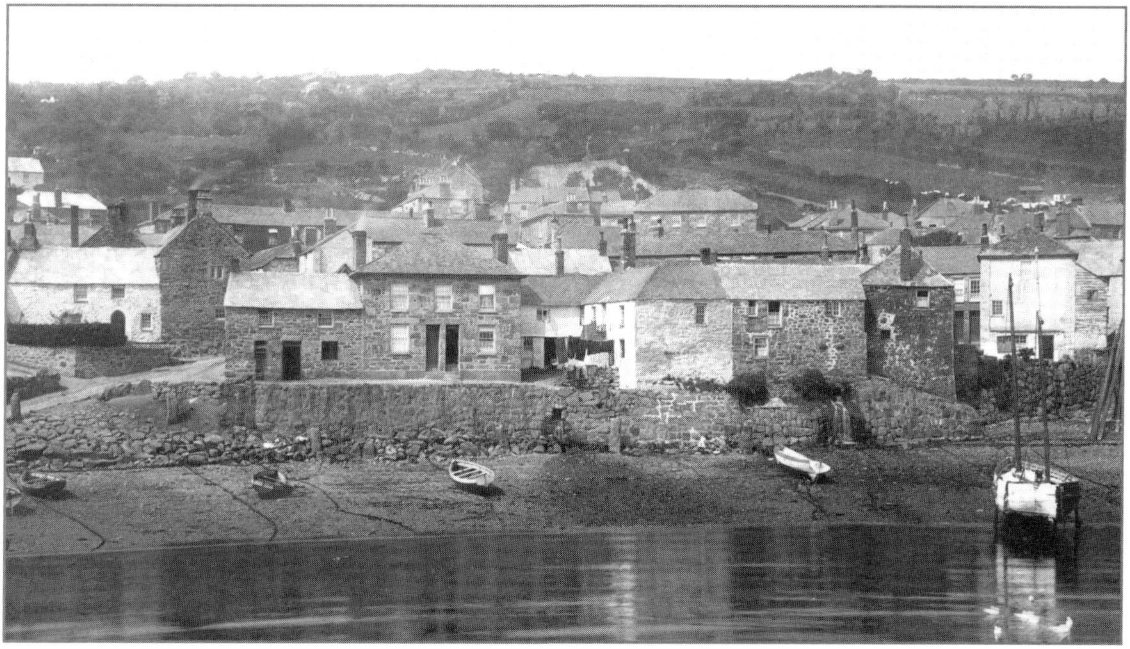

Mousehole, The Harbour 1893 31803

This photograph was taken from the harbour wall. From here we can see how the picturesque fishing village has been crammed into the flatter land between the sea and a steep hill. Although some houses have been altered, this view is recognisable today.

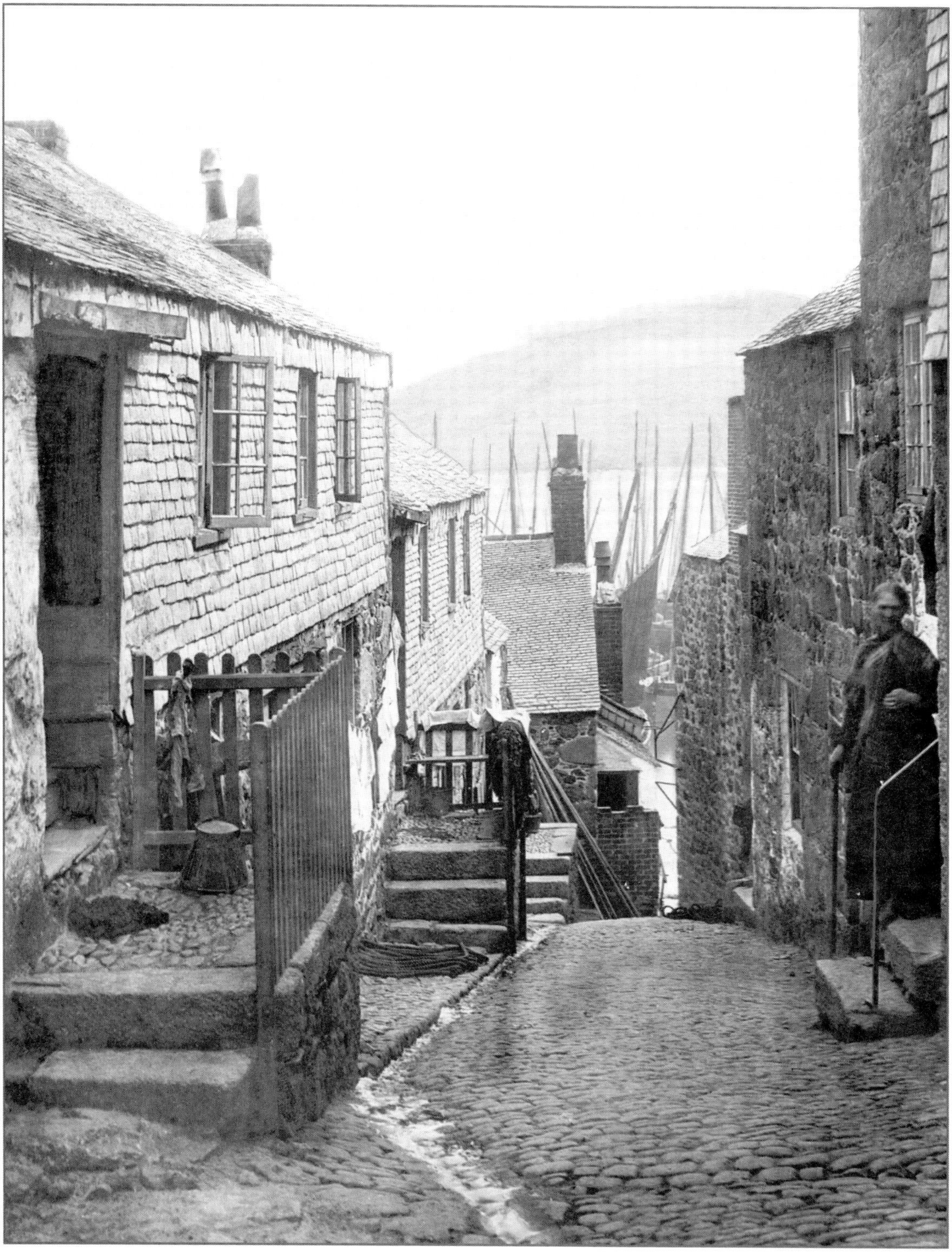

St Ives, Bethesda Hill 1890 24185
Here we see a narrow cobbled way with granite and slate-hung fishermen's cottages in the Downalong part of town. The masts of fishing boats moored in the harbour and the water beyond are glimpsed over the roof tops.

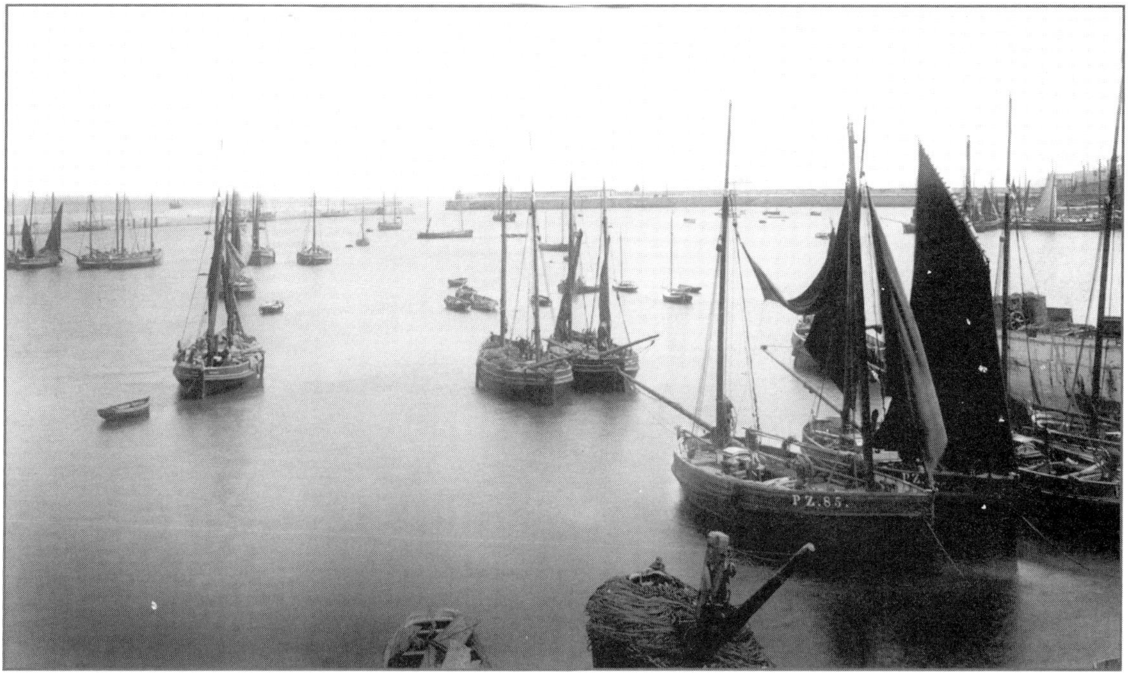

Newlyn, The Harbour 1895 36170
Cornwall's greatest fishing port is seen here at high tide with a number of fishing vessels. The newly-completed North or Victoria Pier is on the left, with the South Pier with its lighthouse at the back.

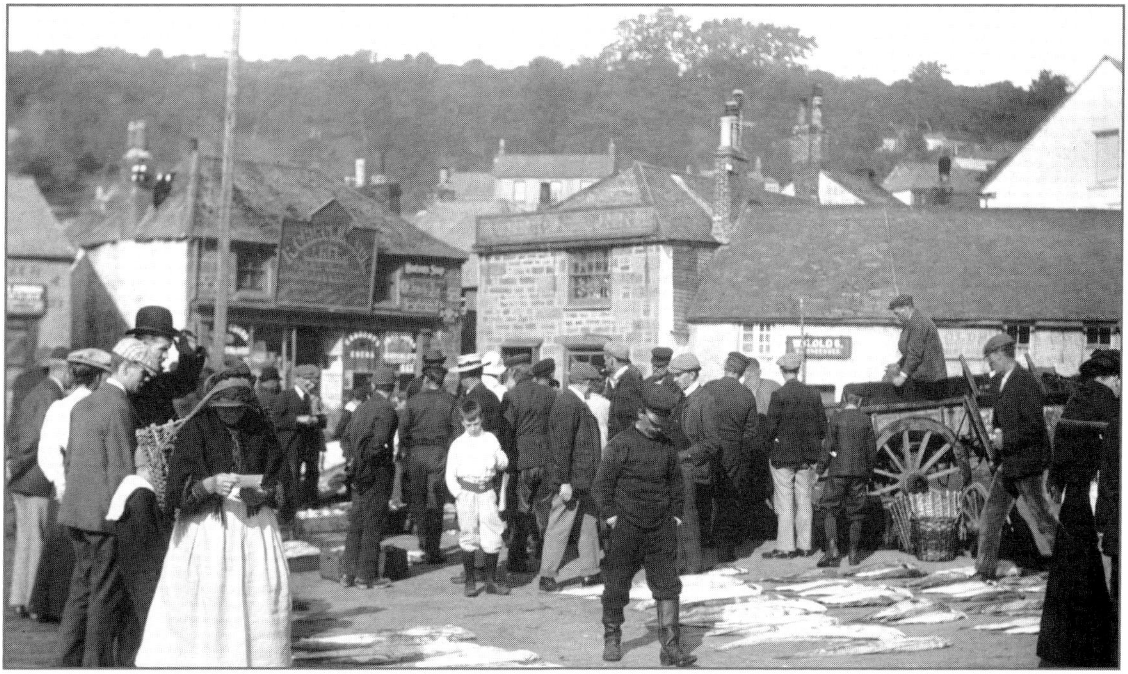

Newlyn, The Fish Market 1906 56525
Cod and ling laid out on the quayside create a great deal of interest. Behind the man on the cart is William Old's hairdressing establishment.

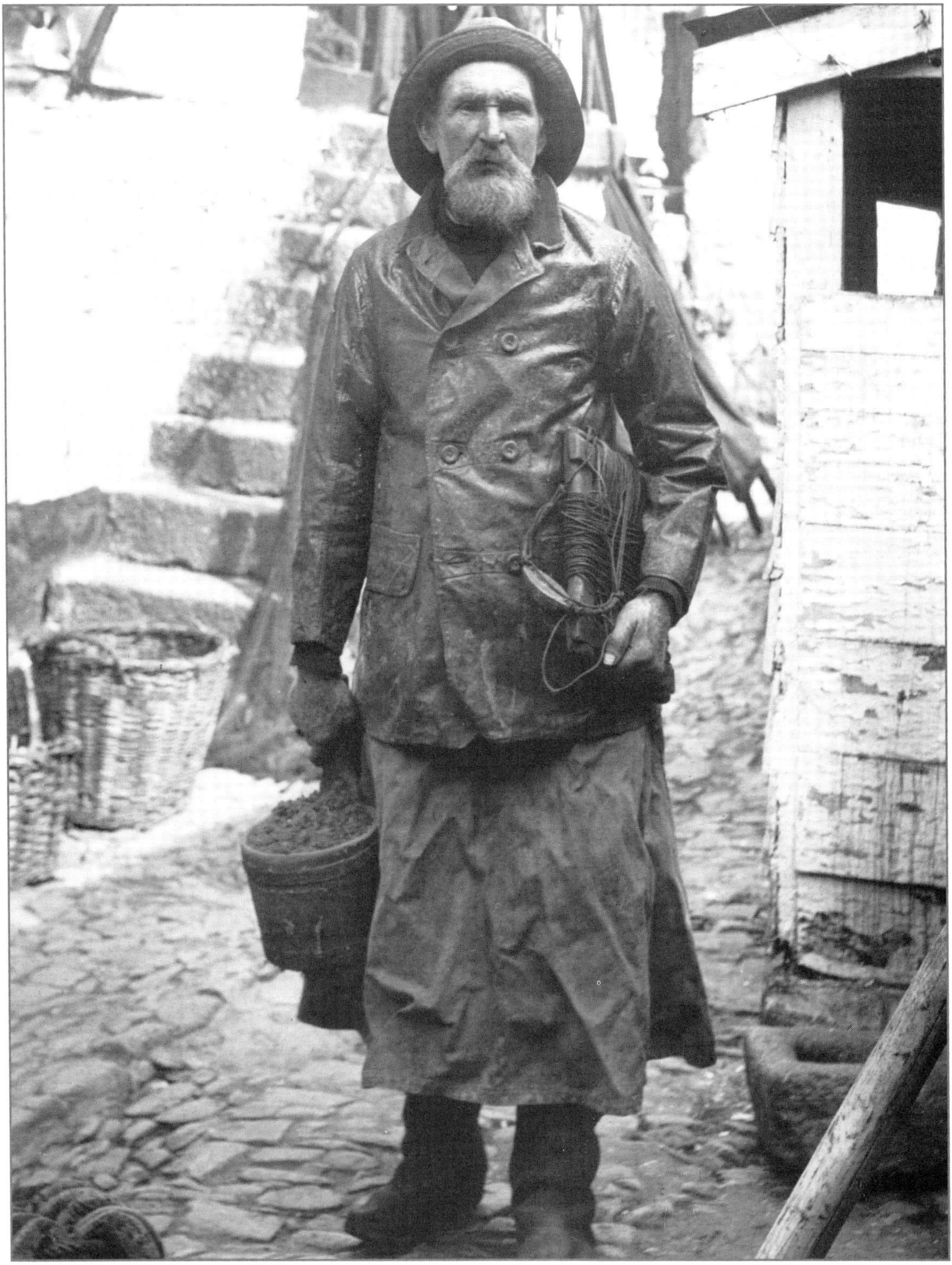

Newlyn, A Fisherman 1906 56528
A posed photograph of one of the local weather-beaten characters in his fisherman's oilskins.

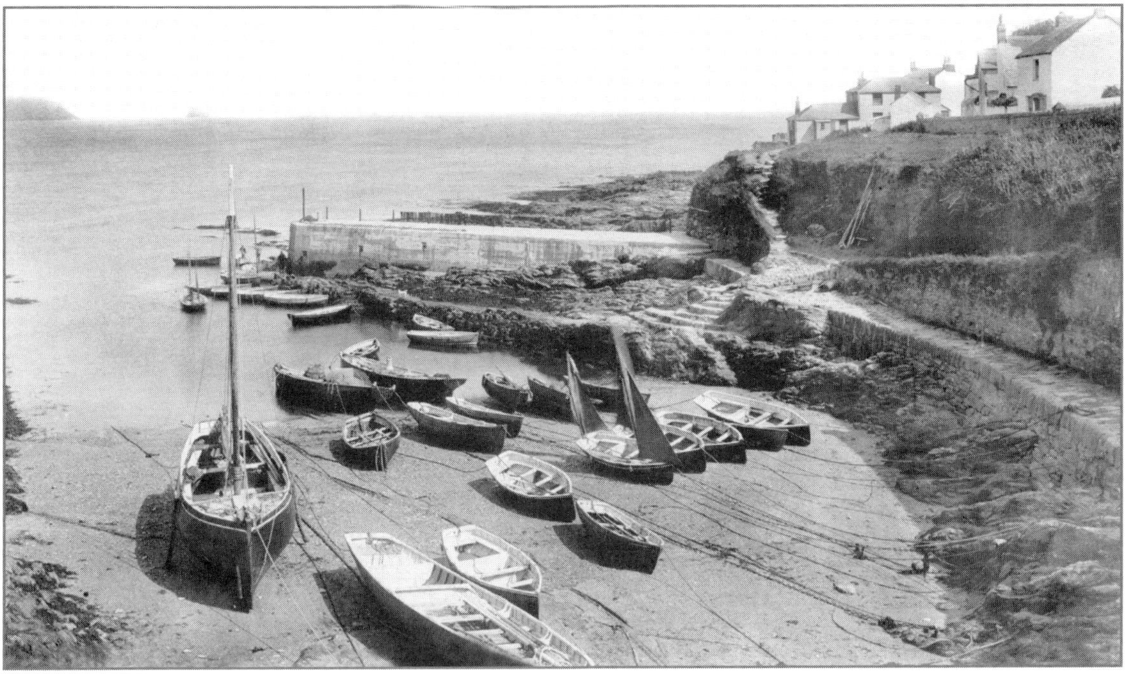

Portscatho, The Harbour 1895 37056
The little concrete pier affords some protection to the fishing boats at Portscatho, although it is barely a harbour. Nare Head and the Gull Rock can be seen across Gerrans Bay.

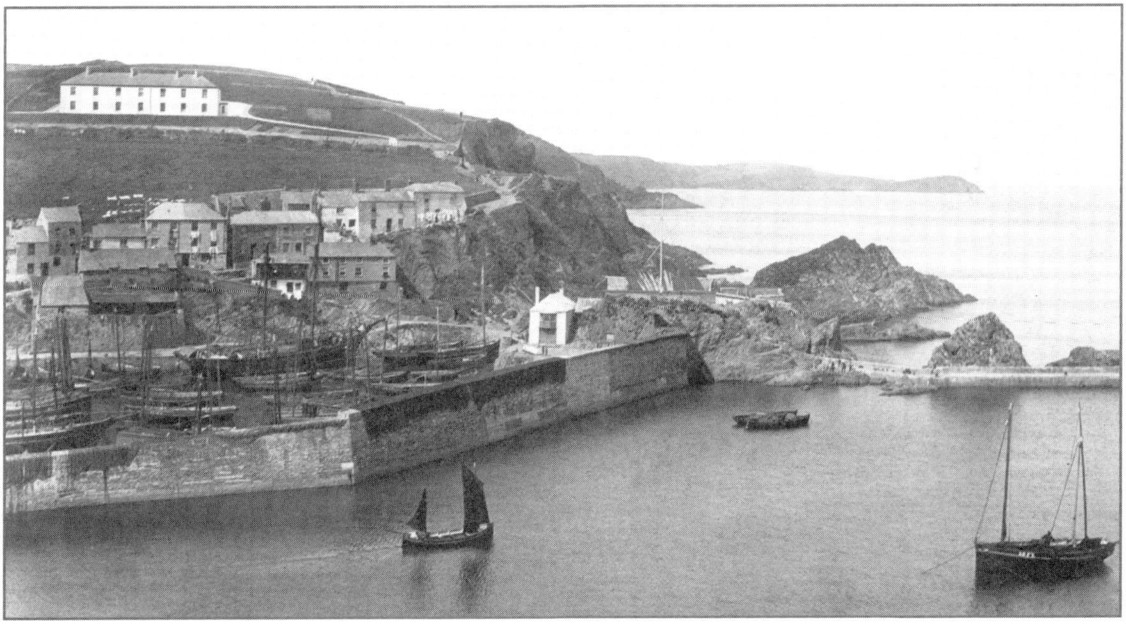

Mevagissey, East Cliff 1890 27552
A small fishing boat sails out into the calm waters of St Austell Bay, while larger boats remain packed into the inner harbour. A new harbour had just been constructed, only to be destroyed in March 1891 and then rebuilt in 1897. Black Head is in the distance. Apart from one white terrace, the hillside above the fishing village has since been fully developed for housing.

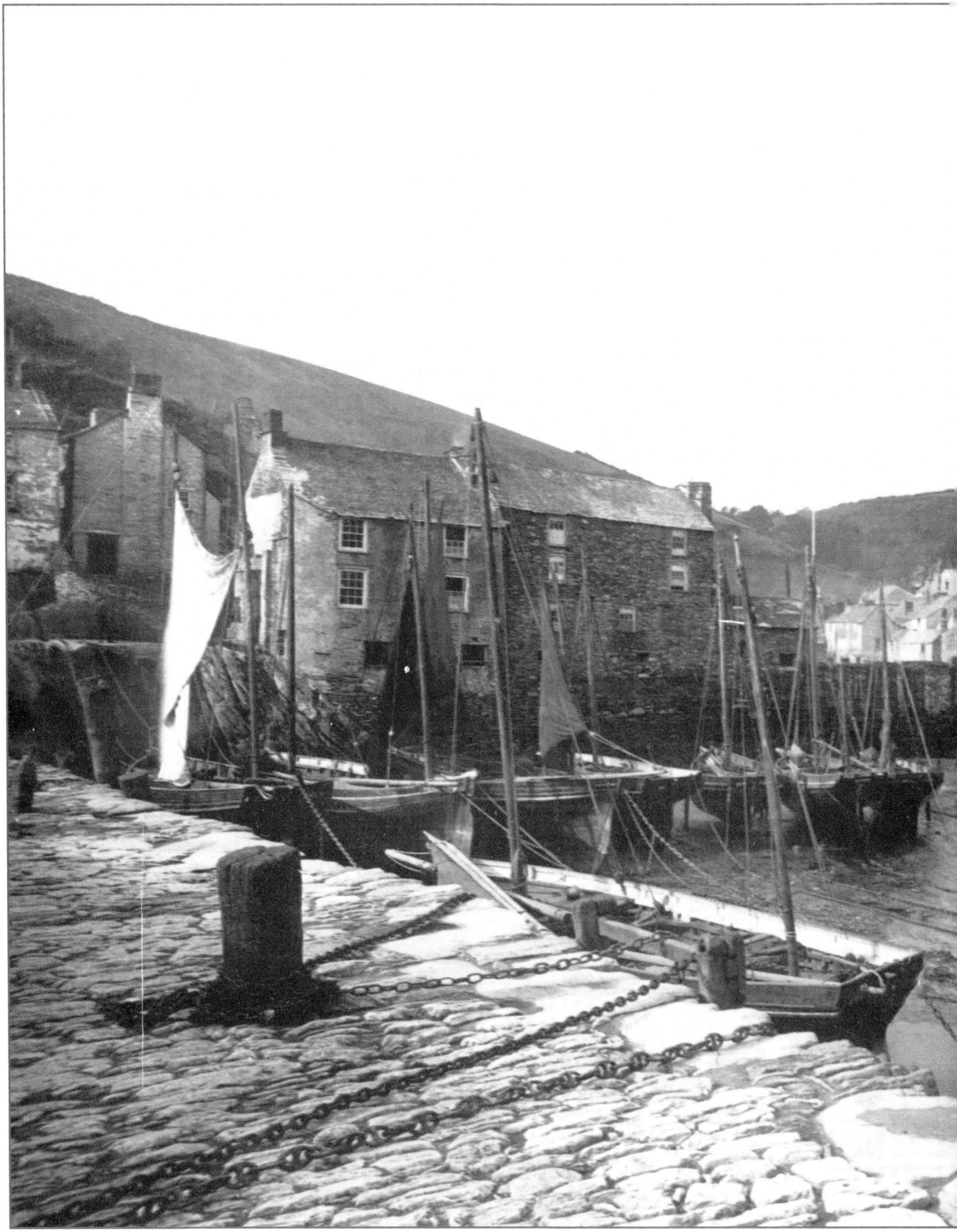

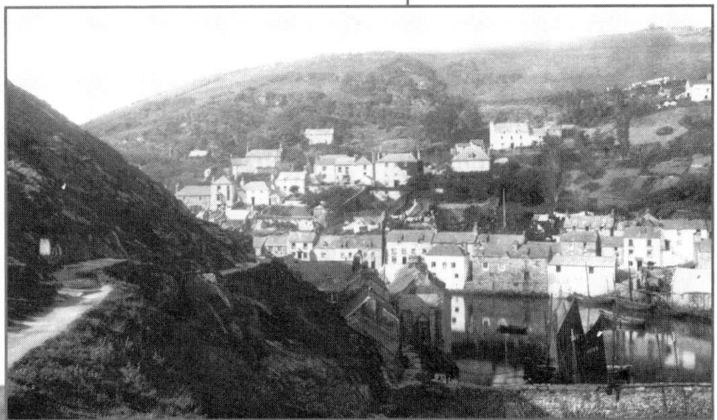

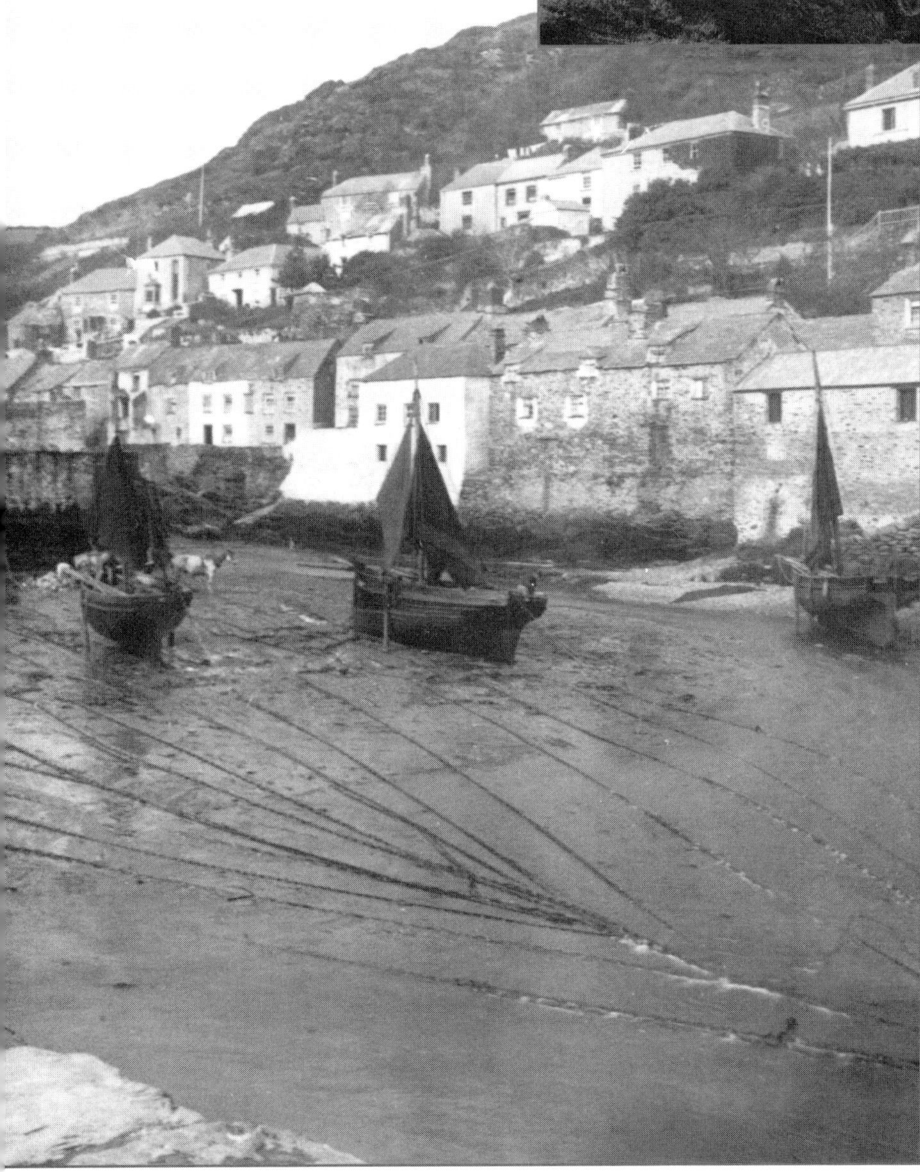

▲ **Polperro From Chapel Rock 1888** 21266

Apart from some more houses, this scene is still familiar today, viewed from the popular cliff walk out to the Chapel Rock near the harbour entrance. Dark sails of fishing boats are seen in the harbour.

◄ **Polperro The Harbour 1888** 21272

The tide is out, and Polperro's fishing fleet lies aground. Note the mooring chains on the harbour bed.

▼ **Polkerris, The Village and St Austell Bay c1876** 8449
The steep descent to the end of a lane gives a certain isolation to Polkerris, and this early view shows perfectly how the little village clings to the valley bottom behind a beach and stone pier. There was a pilchard fleet here, and the fish cellar claimed to be the largest in the county.

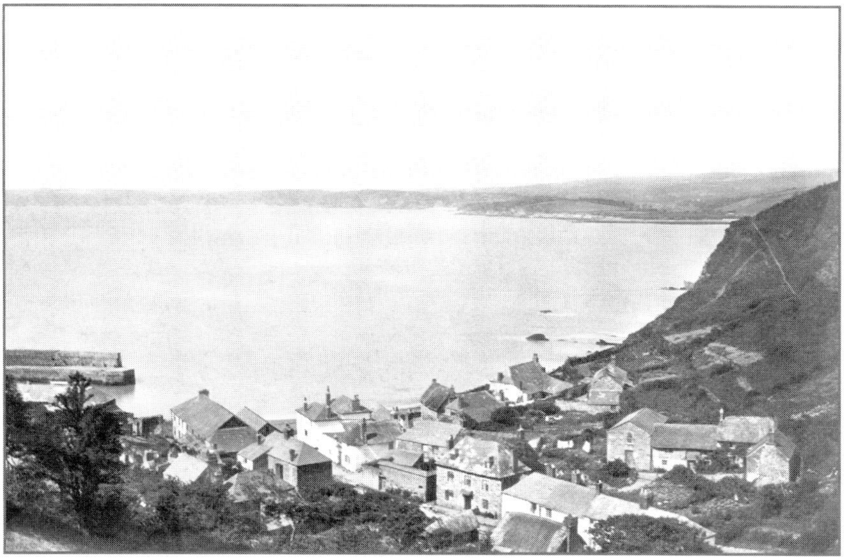

▼ **Port Isaac, The Harbour 1895** 37027
The Victorian school stands on the cliff top above the natural inlet where fishing boats and a trading boat are beached. A small pier to give some protection was not built until the early 20th century.

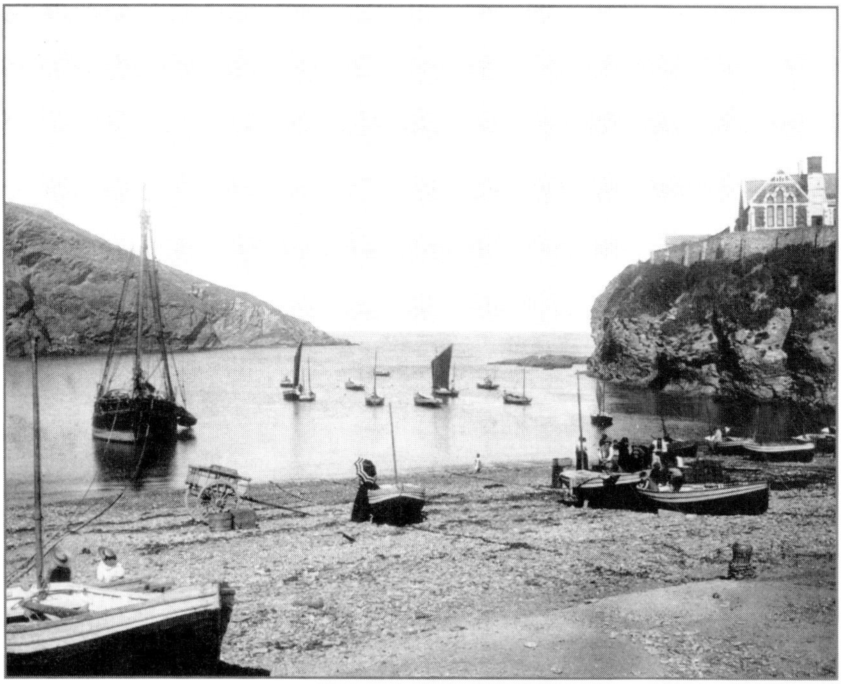

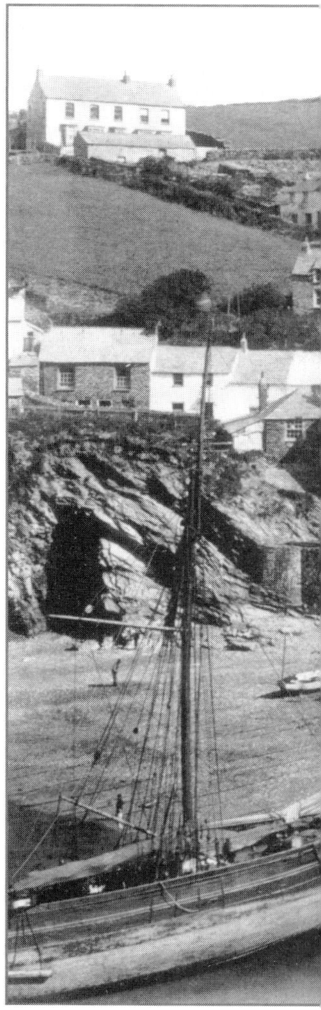

▲ **Port Isaac, The Village and the Harbour 1895**
37024
Port Isaac is one of Cornwall's least spoilt fishing villages; it grew up around the head of the sheltered harbour. There is a trading boat on the beach, either discharging coal or loading slate.

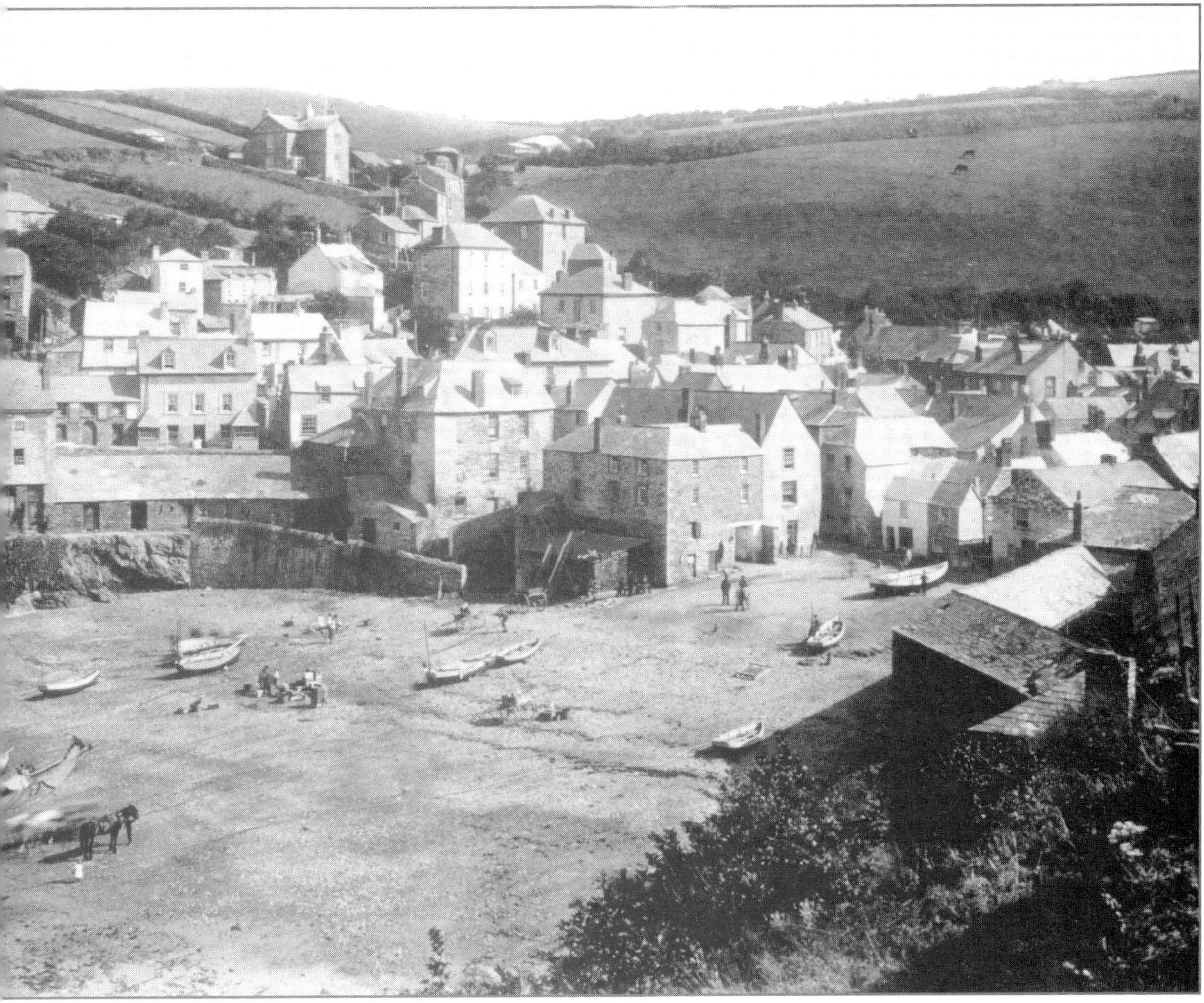

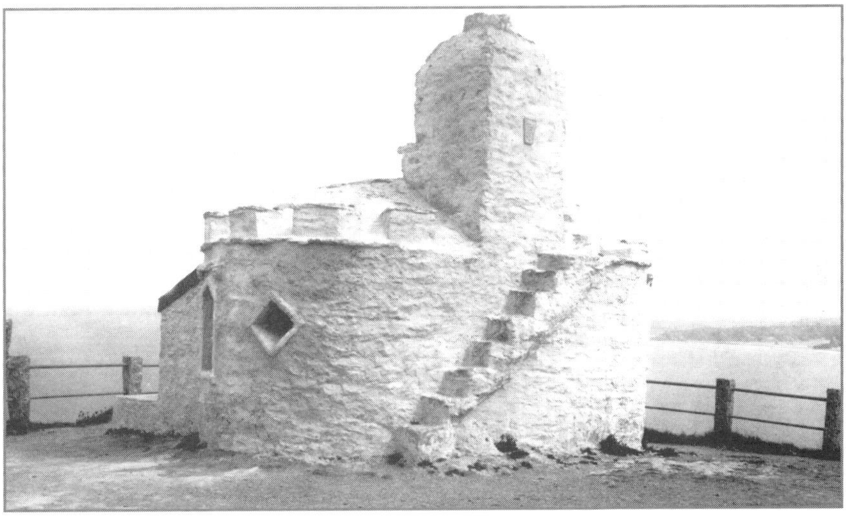

Newquay, The Huer's House 1907 59333
The Huer's House is identical today, even down to the granite railing posts. Sited up on the headland near the harbour, this is where the huer waited to spot incoming pilchard shoals. He would raise the alarm by crying 'heva! heva!', and would use signals to direct the fishing fleet to the shoal out in the bay.

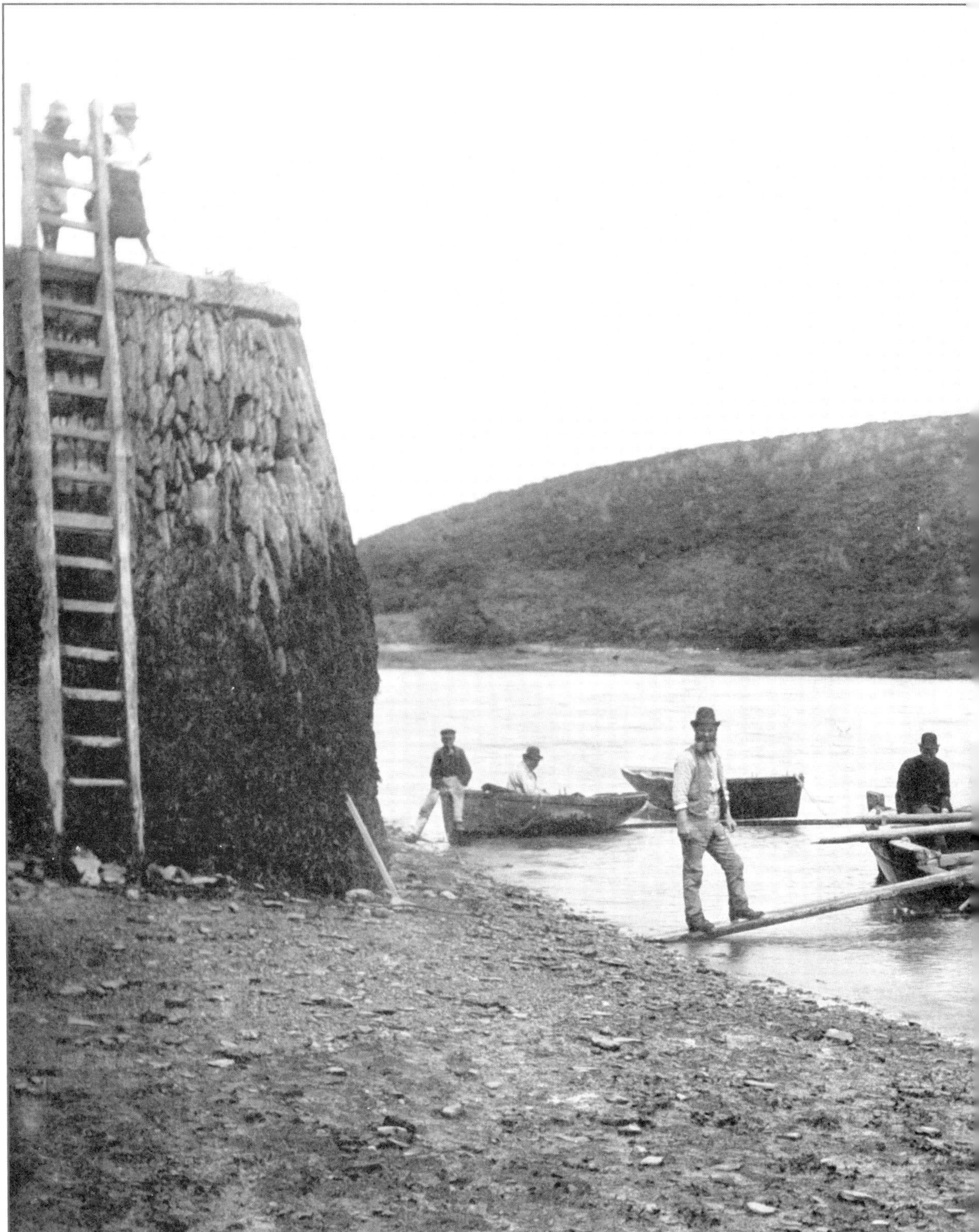

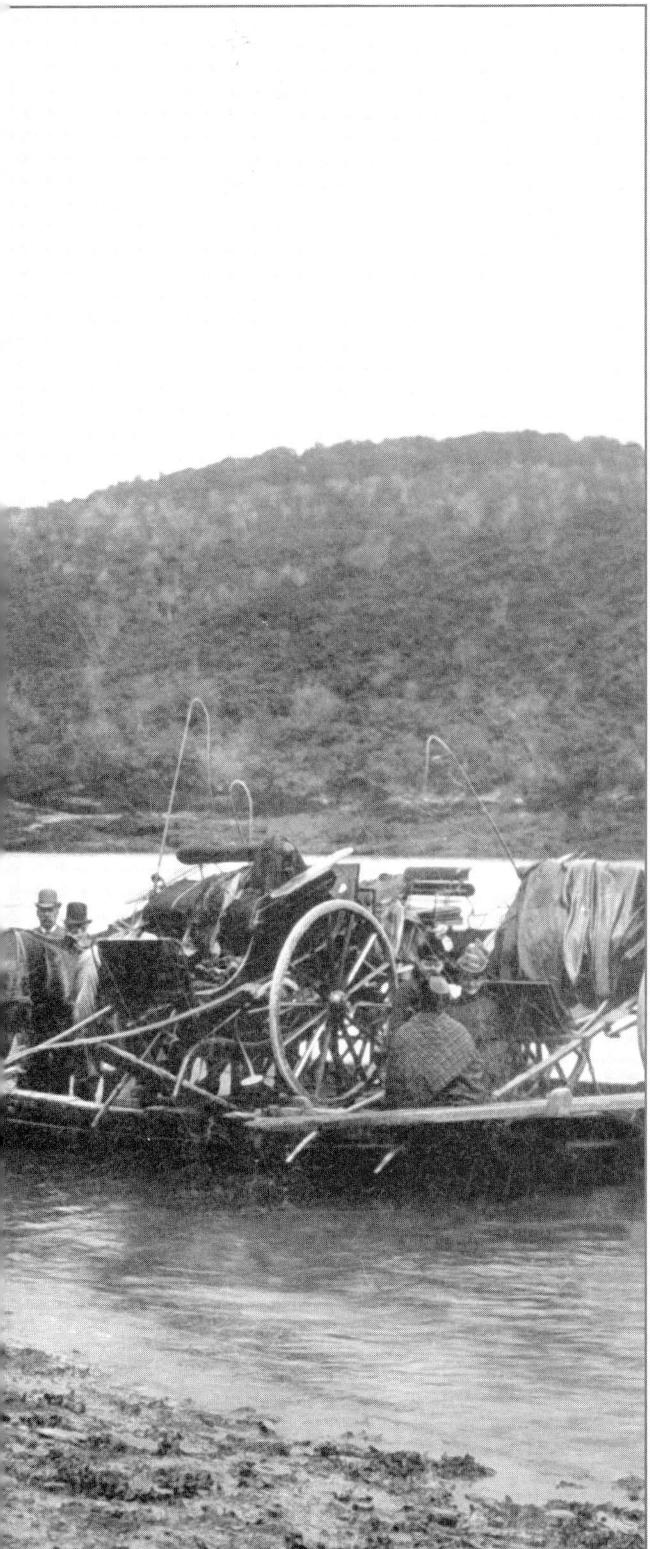

Travel in Cornwall

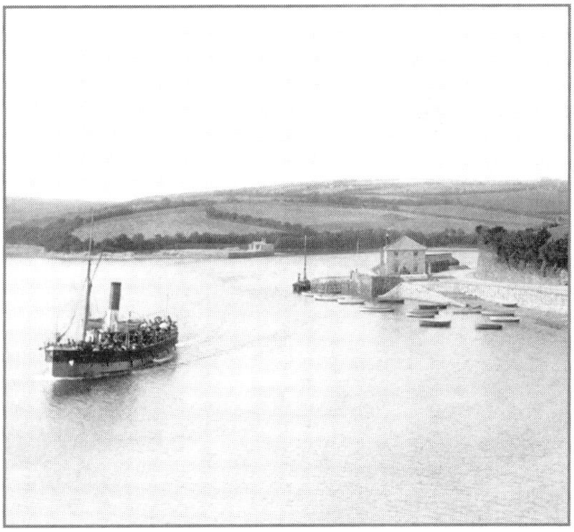

▲ **Truro, The 'Queen of the Fal' at Sunny Corner 1895** 37062
Ferry steamers plied regularly between Falmouth and Truro. Here this steamer is passing Sunny Corner on her return down the Truro River towards Malpas. Behind is Newham Quay, now much extended into a modern wharf.

◄ **Truro, King Harry Ferry Boats c1889** 24148
The King Harry Passage on the Fal at Trelissick was already an ancient crossing when this ferry was providing an important link to St Mawes and the Roseland peninsula. It was not easy to first get horses and vehicles on board and then row across the river. This photograph must date from the very last days of the old horse boat, because a new steam chain ferry was introduced in 1889; one of its successors still runs.

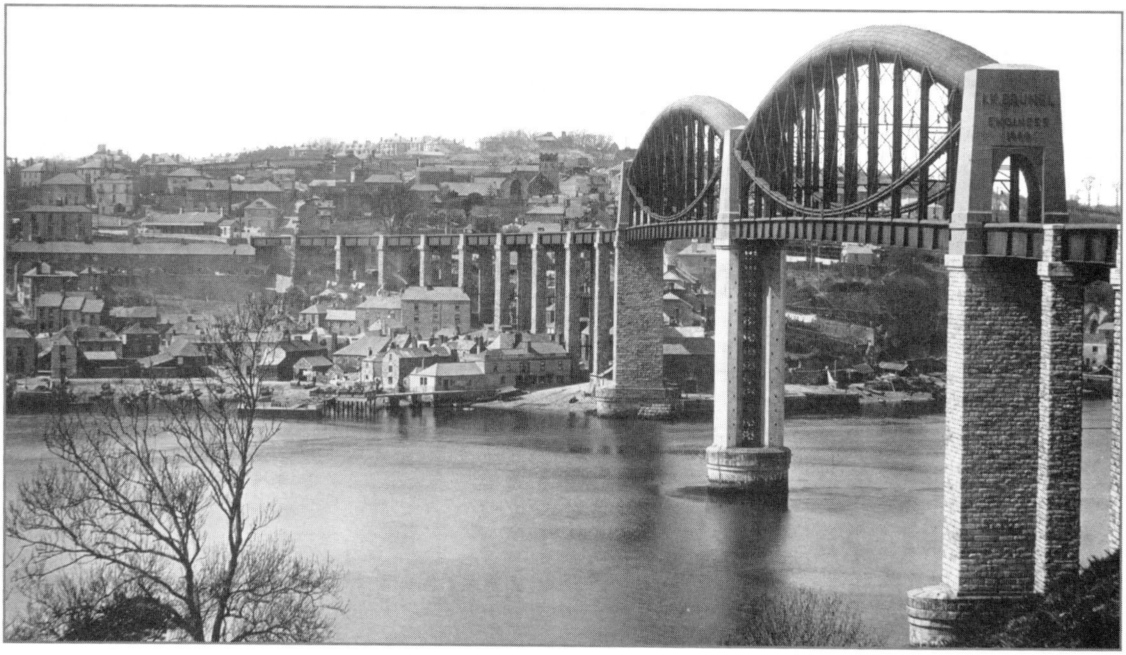

Saltash, The Royal Albert Bridge 1890 22476
Brunel's celebrated masterpiece across the Tamar estuary made the first direct rail link between Cornwall and the rest of England when it was opened by Prince Albert in May 1859. The bridge is only 31 years old in this view; it is taken from the Devon bank, looking over to Saltash with its railway station, left, and ferry slipway below the bridge.

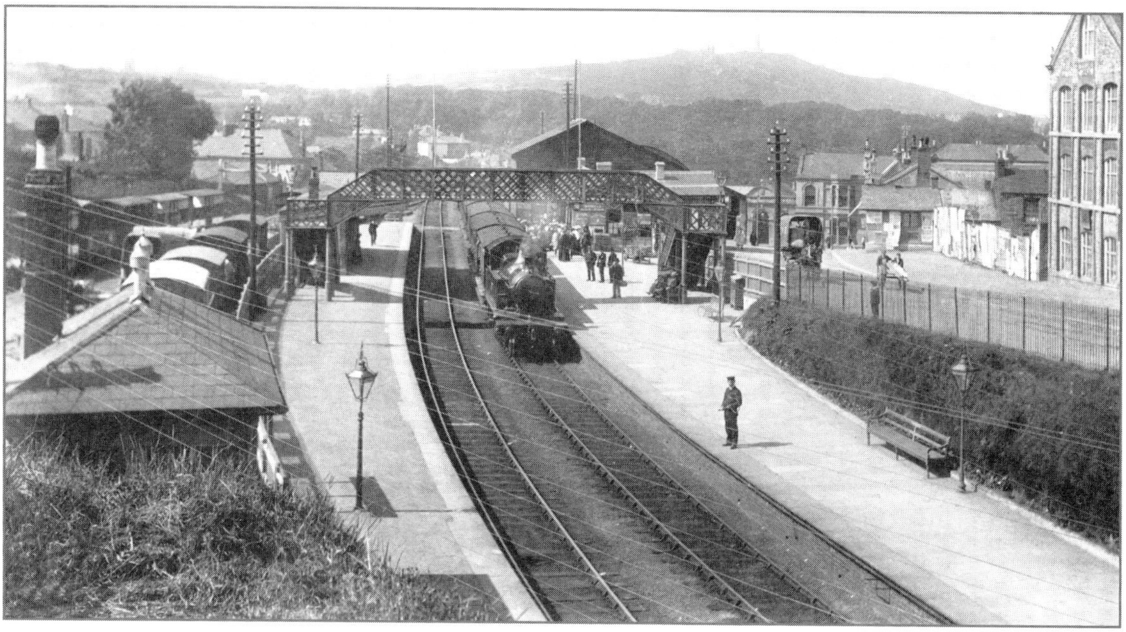

Redruth, The Railway Station 1906 56449
A train waits to leave for Truro, and perhaps Plymouth and Paddington. The goods sidings and the horse-drawn covered wagon complete this typical station scene. In the background rears Carn Brea, with its monument and castle. There are mine engine houses on the skyline, although the mining boom that made Redruth important in the 19th century is over.

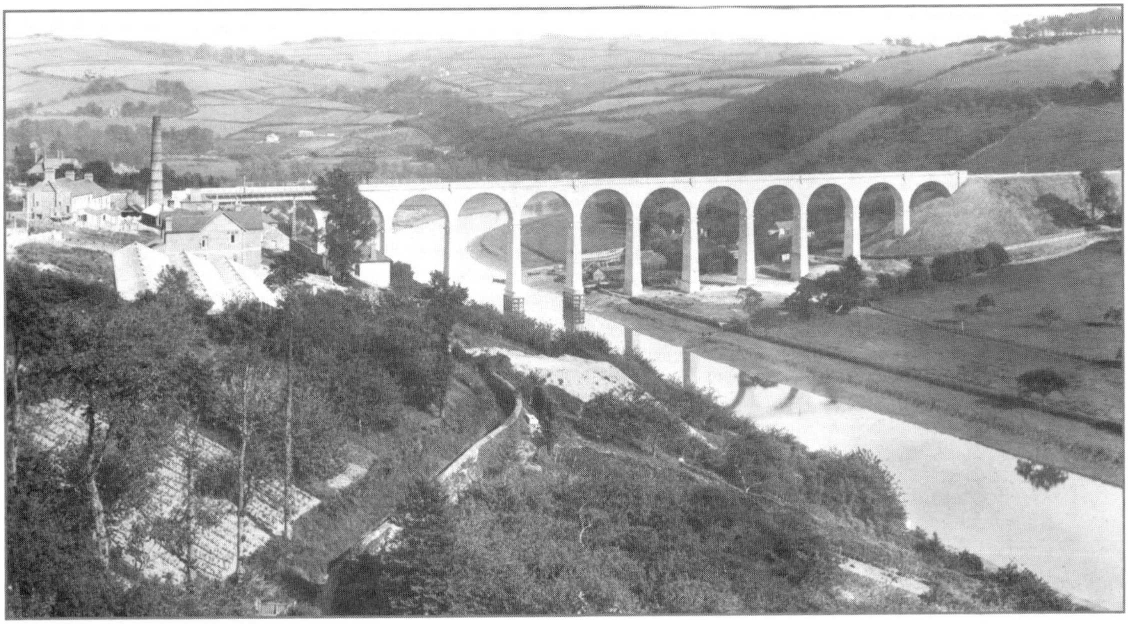

Calstock, The Viaduct 1908 59702
This new viaduct across the Tamar has just been opened, linking Plymouth to the district around Gunnislake and Callington. The construction workyard on the Devon bank has been cleared, but the wooden ketch 'Garlandstone' can be seen being built at James Goss's shipyard just behind the viaduct. The chimney of a fire brick works stands out in Calstock, and there is evidence of market gardening in the foreground.

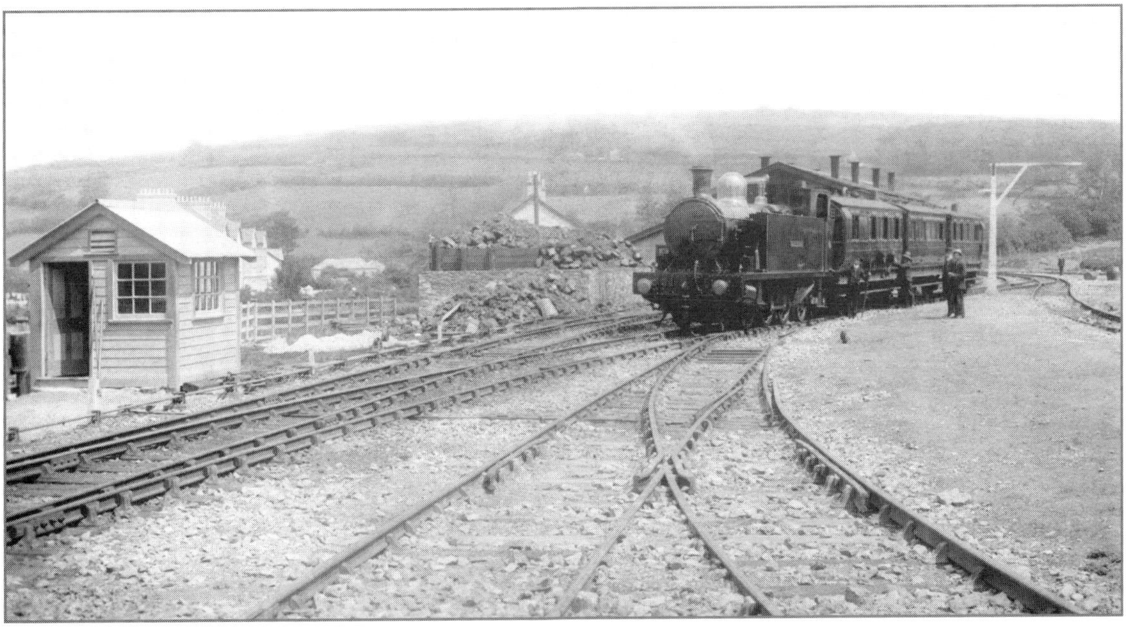

Callington, The Railway Station 1908 59722
The East Cornwall Mineral Railway, from Kelly Bray, near Callington, to Calstock Quay, opened in 1872, but in 1908 it was relaid to standard gauge and connected to Plymouth via the Calstock Viaduct. This picture was taken shortly after the opening on 2 March 1908; the locomotive could be the 'Lord St Levan'. This end of the line closed in 1966.

▼ **Sandplace, The Looe Valley 1901** 47779
This is the lower reach of the old Liskeard and Looe Canal; it was still used occasionally at this date to carry sea sand and limestone for burning in the kilns at Sandplace. On the left is the railway line, which was built in 1860 to replace most of the canal up the valley from Looe to Moorswater.

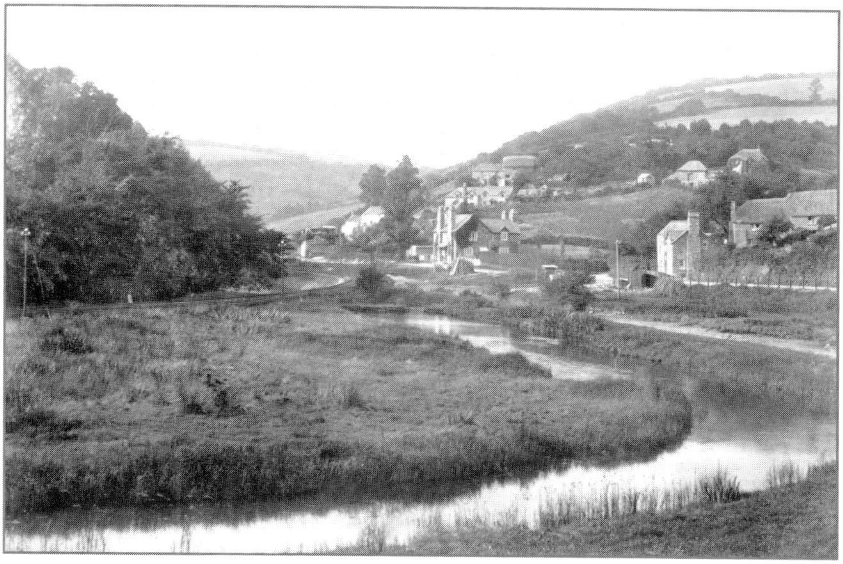

▼ **Bodmin, The Railway Station 1906** 56281
Approaching from the town centre, we are in front of the terminus of the Great Western Railway branch from Bodmin Road Station, opened in 1887. There is a spacious yard in front where neither traffic nor passengers wait, for presumably the next train is not due for a while.

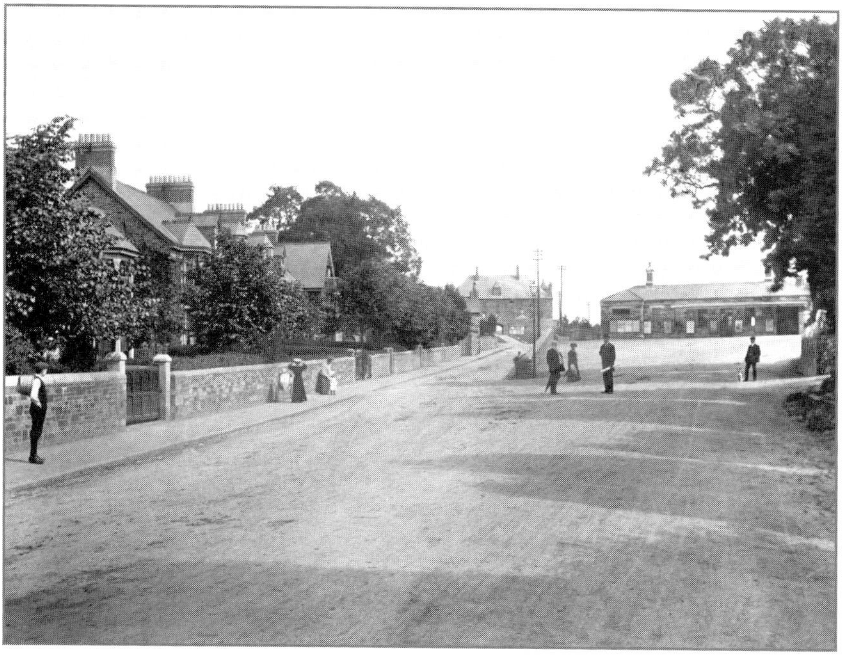

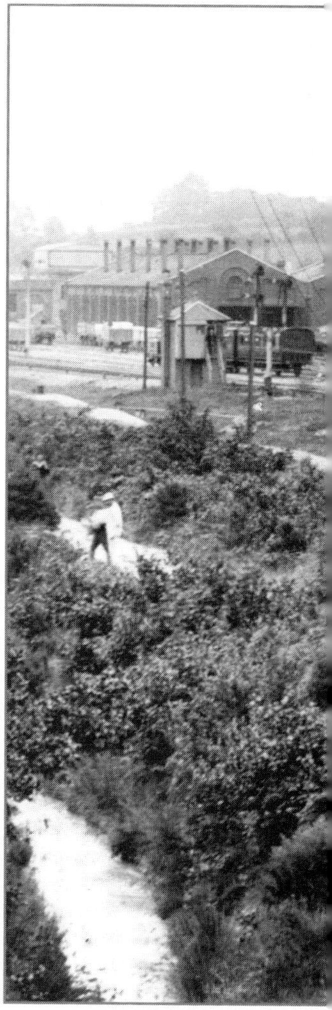

▲ **St Blazey, The Railway Station 1904** 52319A
This is a splendid railway photograph showing two passenger trains in St Blazey station. The train facing the camera is waiting to depart for the Luxulyan valley and Newquay. On the left are the extensive railway workshops erected by the Cornwall Mineral Railway, with the chimneys and waste tips of the old Par Consols Mine on the skyline.

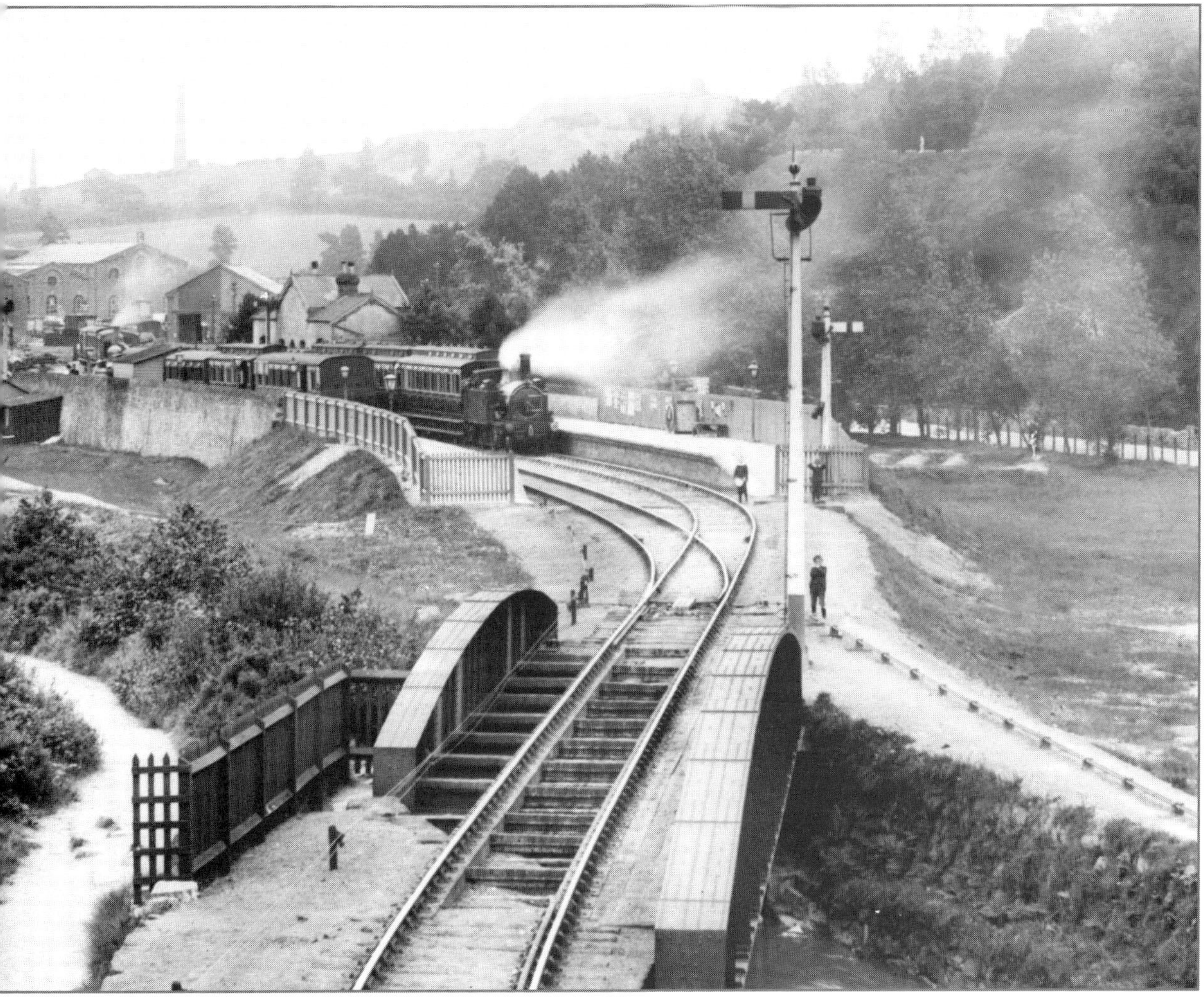

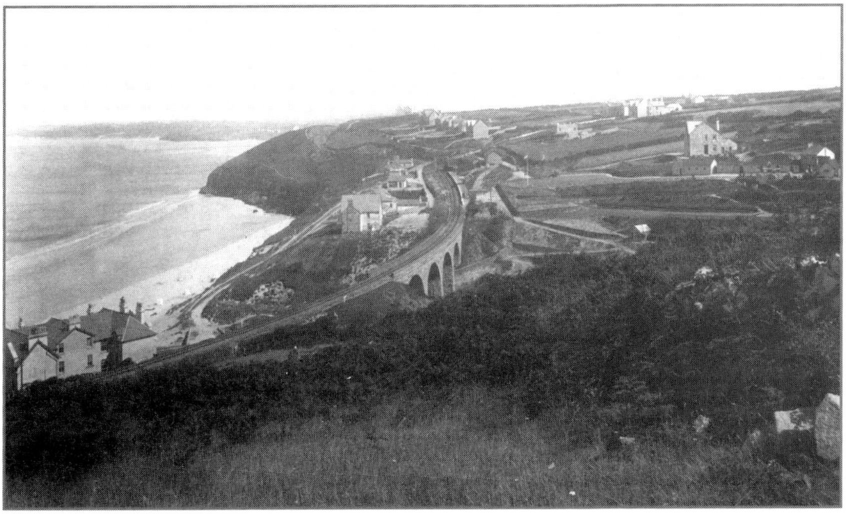

◀ **Carbis Bay, General View 1901** 47688
Cornwall's most westerly branch line, just 4 miles long, was opened from St Erth to St Ives in 1877. The railway viaduct crosses the little valley behind the beach, and the station platform is just beyond. Another major engineering feat on this scenic line is the rock cutting in the far headland. How things have changed at Carbis Bay - much of this scene has since been developed.

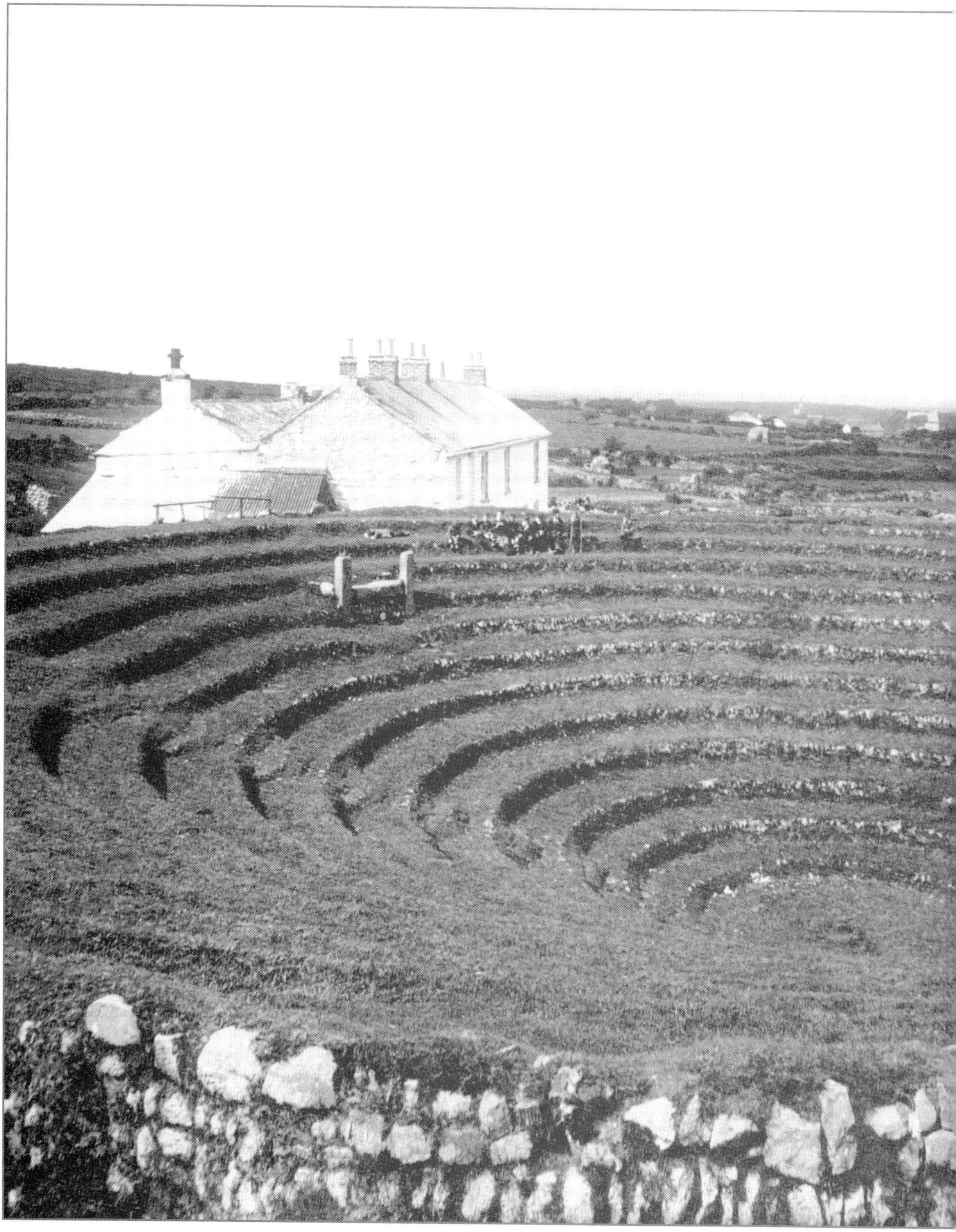

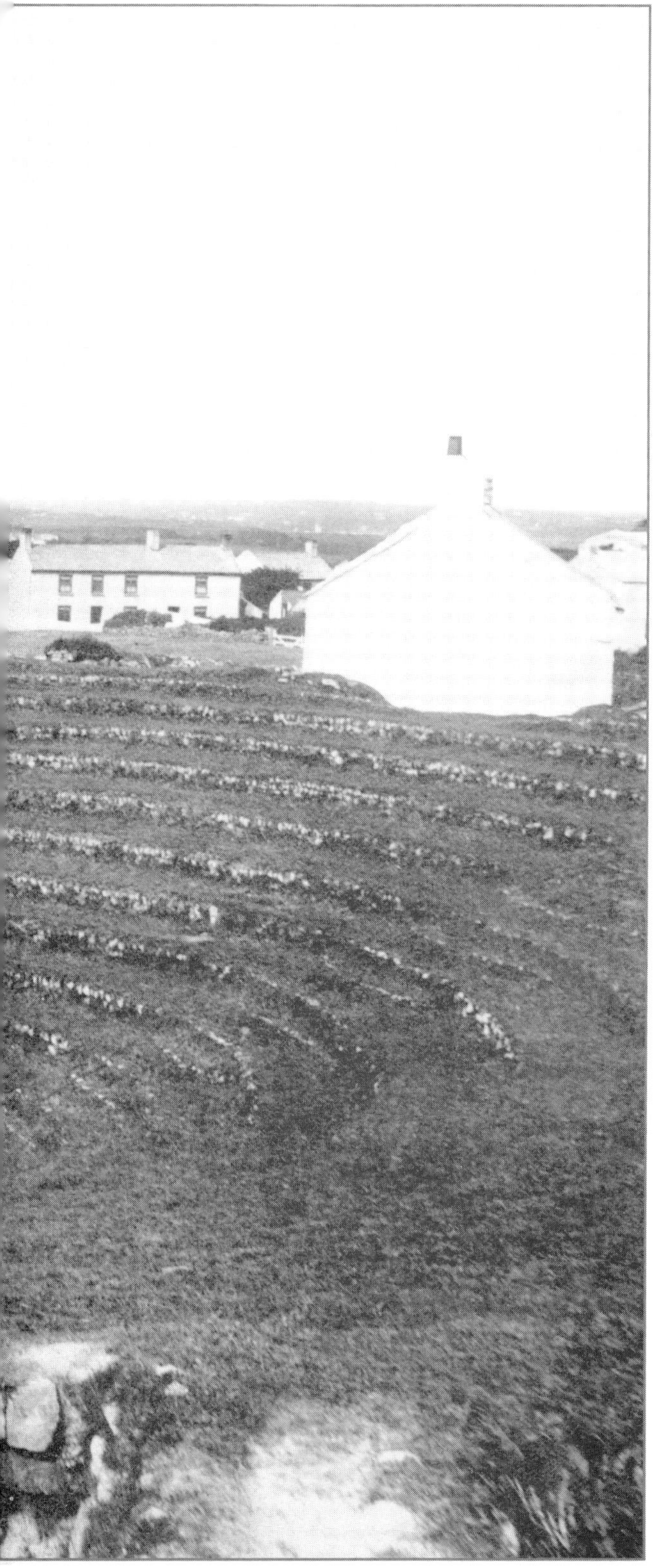

Industry and Commerce

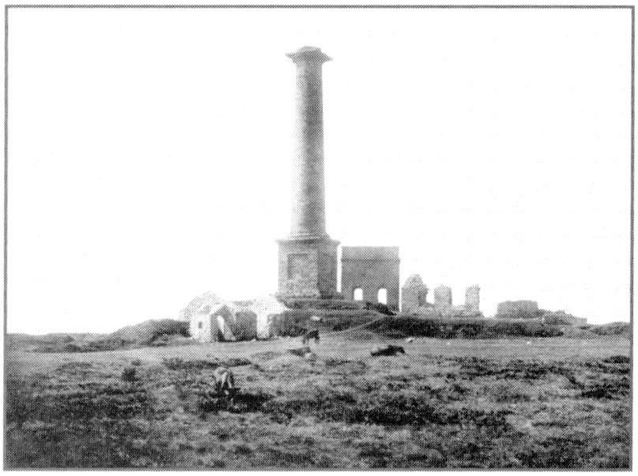

▲ **Callington, Kit Hill 1908** 59724
The 85-ft ornamental chimney stack for Kit Hill United Mine was built in 1858 as a summit landmark to be seen from many miles. After closure in the 1860s, the tin mine was re-opened as Kithill Great Consols in 1881-85. The stack dwarfs a beam engine house to the right, while less substantial buildings are already ruinous. Today the stack stands alone.

◀ **Redruth, Gwennap Pit 1898** 41623
Set in the mining landscape of West Cornwall, this famous amphitheatre was fashioned from collapsed mine workings on the slopes of Carn Marth. Ever since John Wesley preached here in the 18th century, it became important for open-air religious services for the non-conformist miners and their families.

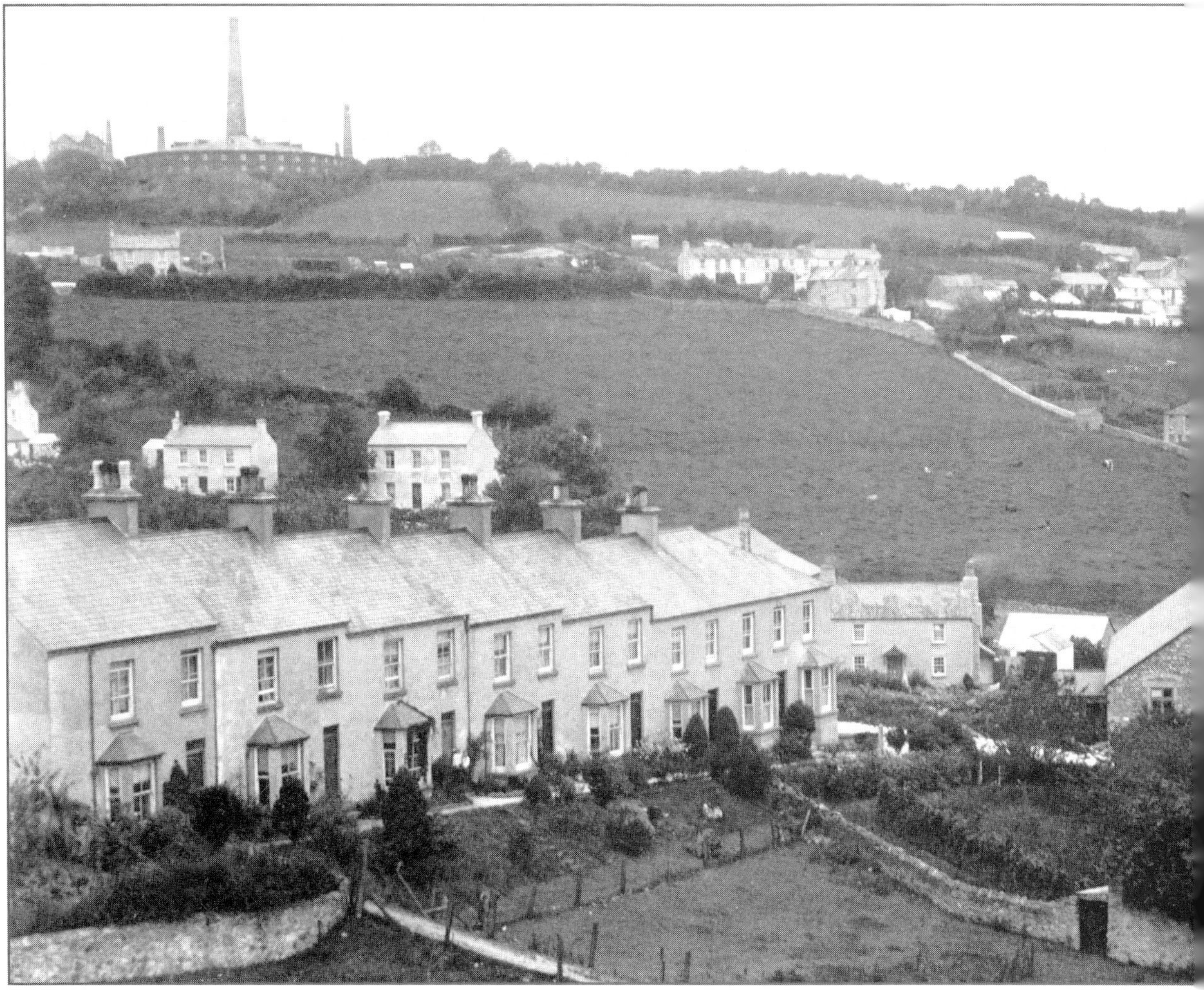

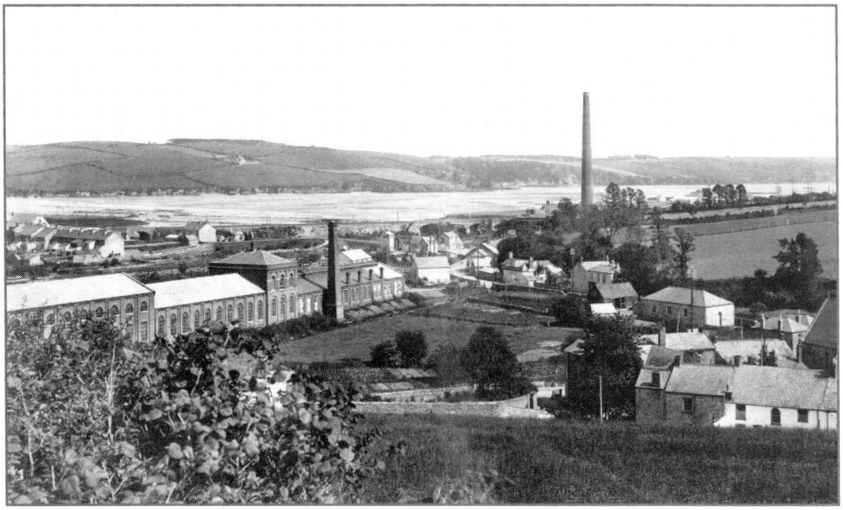

Par, The Bay 1898
41635
On the right are the masts of sailing vessels in Par harbour, while the very tall chimney was for a lead smelting works. Erected in 1866, this 'Par Stack' was demolished in 1907. The row of buildings on the left were the Cornwall Mineral Railway's depot, built in 1874 to the design of Sir Morton Peto.

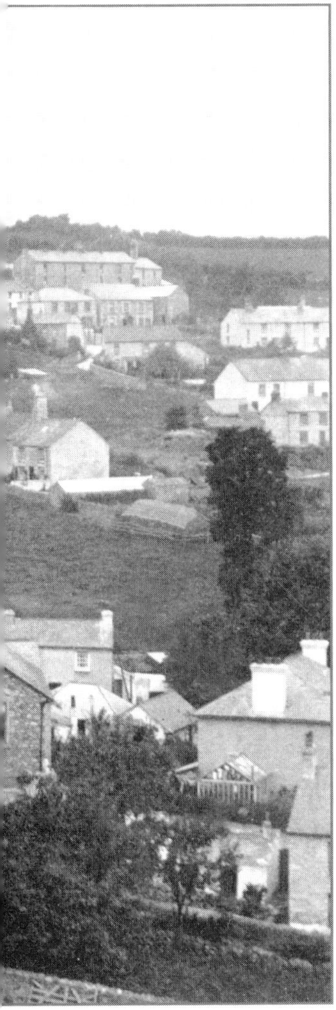

◀ **Gunnislake, Dimson 1906**
55184
Industrial housing is dominated by the tall chimney stack and circular kiln complex of the Plymouth Brickworks at North Dimson. Fire bricks were produced here in the second half of the 19th century.

▼ **Polperro, Crumplehorne, The Old Mill 1908** 59751A
Corn milling by water power is an ancient industry. The watermill at Crumplehorne, in the valley just above Polperro village, is a good example of an overshot waterwheel and its launder. Today it is a hostelry, and a replacement wheel has been installed.

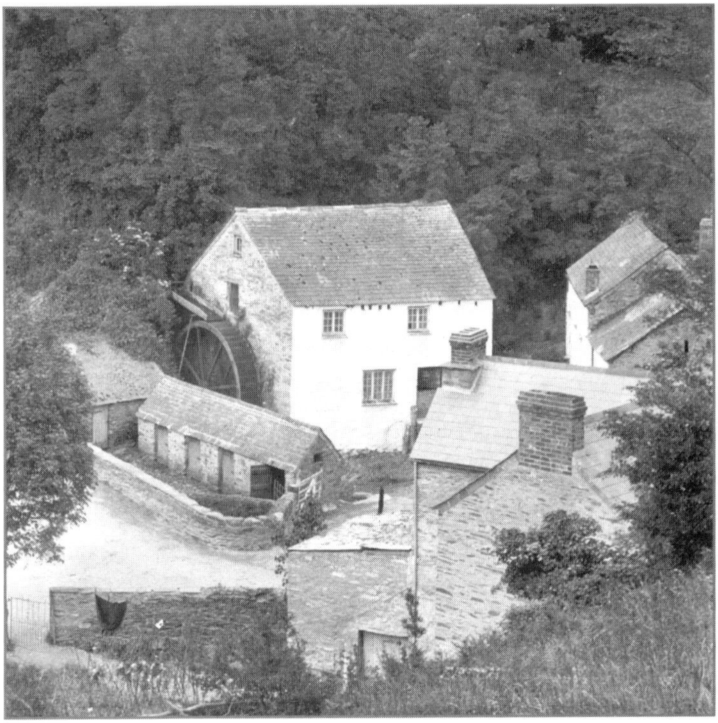

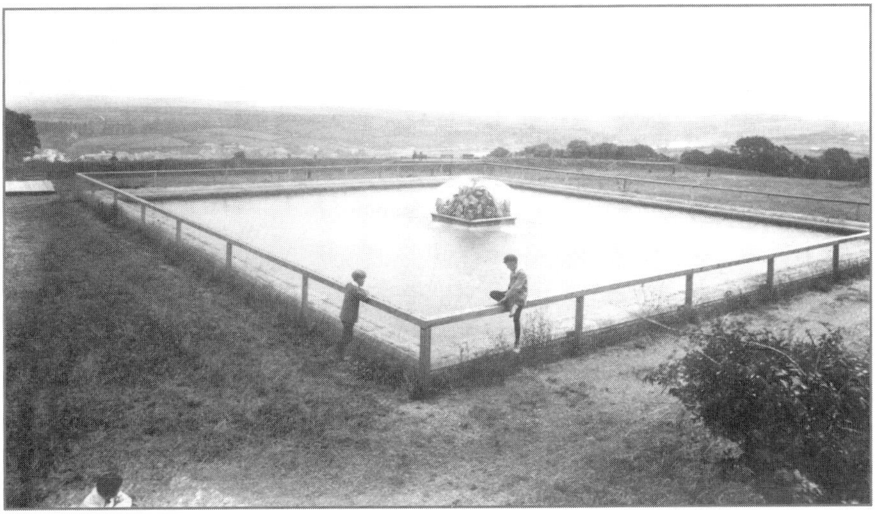

◀ **Wadebridge**
The Reservoir 1906
56258
The provision of public utilities became increasingly important from the Victorian period onwards. Wadebridge's clean water supply was fed by gravity from the reservoir with its central fountain, seen here high above the town in the valley below.

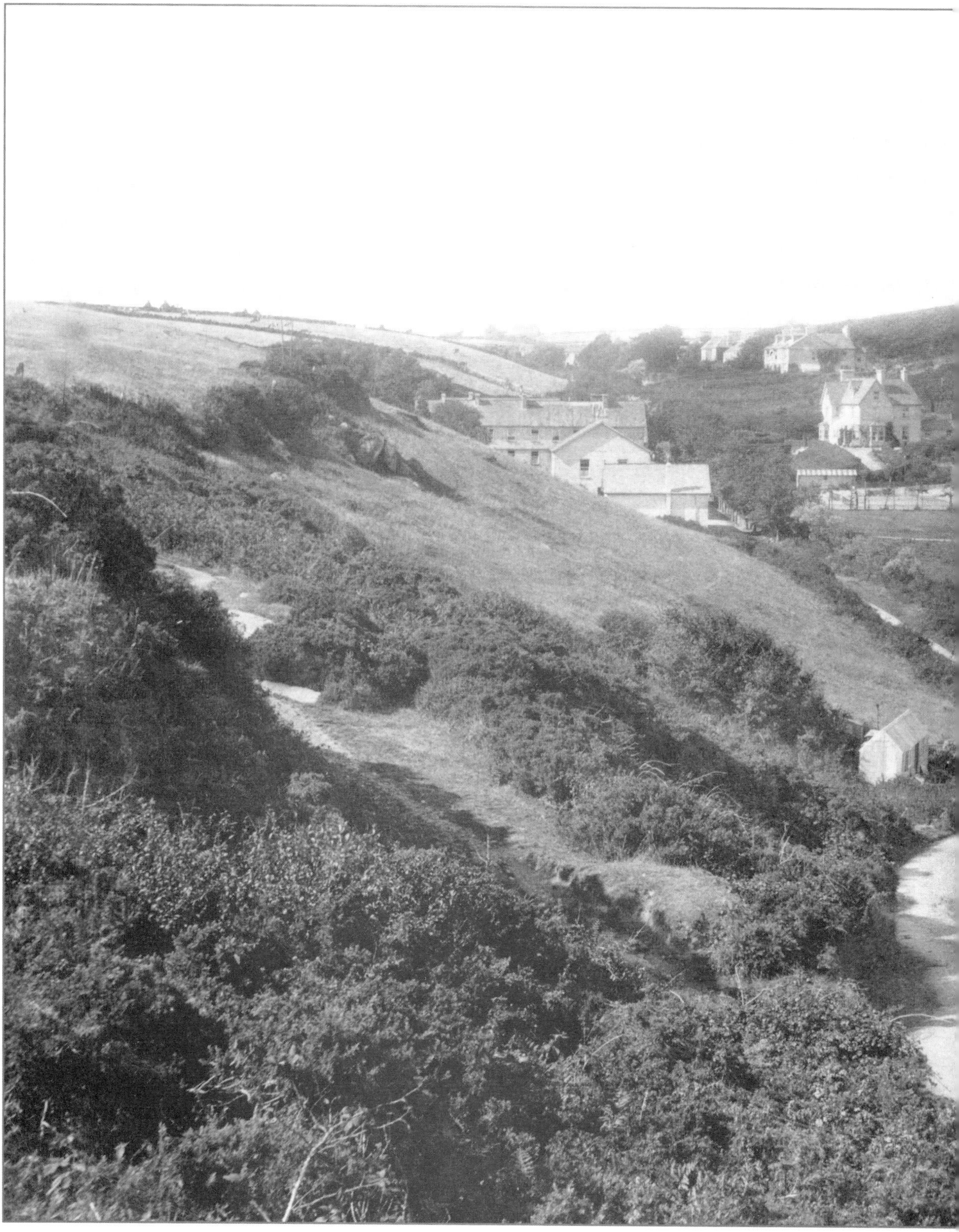

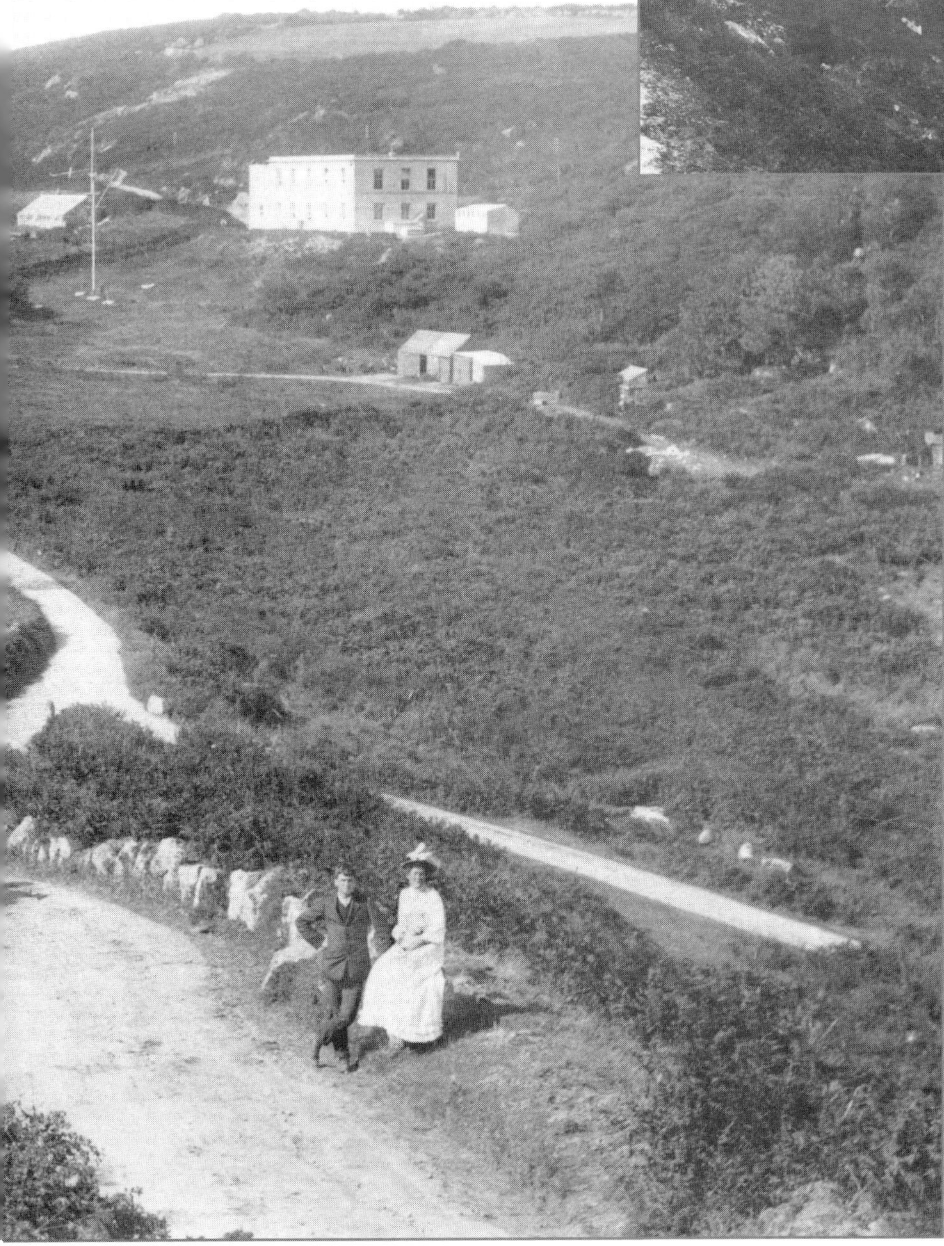

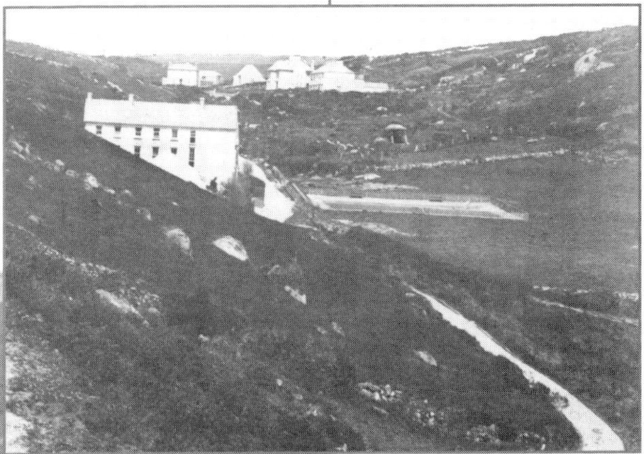

▲ **Porthcurno General View c1883**
16049
Ever since undersea cables came ashore on this far western coast, Porthcurno has played a major role in world communications and commerce. Here, in an otherwise lonely valley, we can see the Eastern Telegraph Co's large cable station in the centre, with employees' housing in the distance. A tennis court was provided for the workers who had been exiled here from London.

◄ **Porthcurno General View 1908**
61259
This view, similar to number 16049, is interesting, because it shows the square block of the new cable station on the right. In the centre is the cable stationmaster's house, with its own vinery just behind the flagpole. The Exiles Club has now been built just in front of the original cable station.

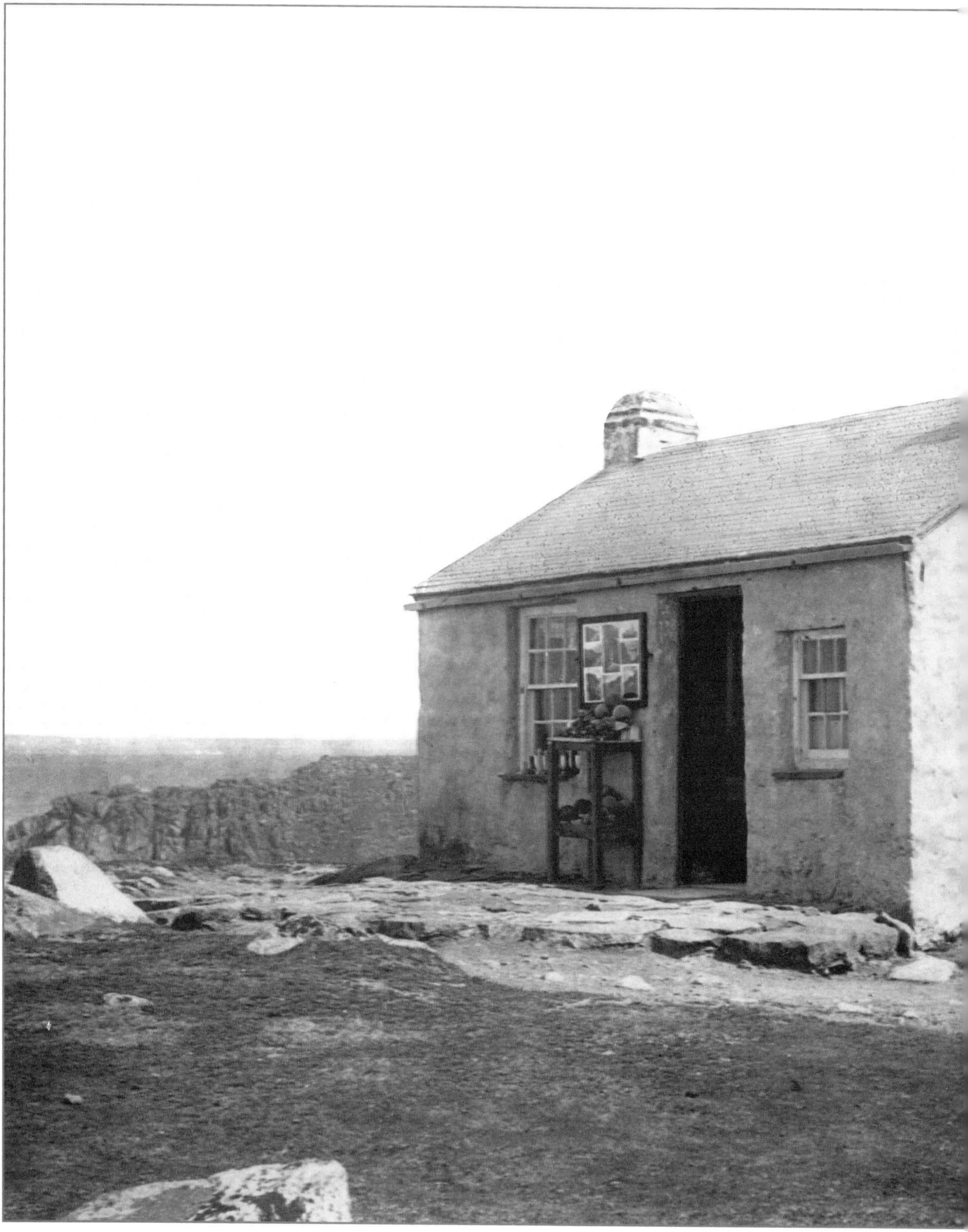

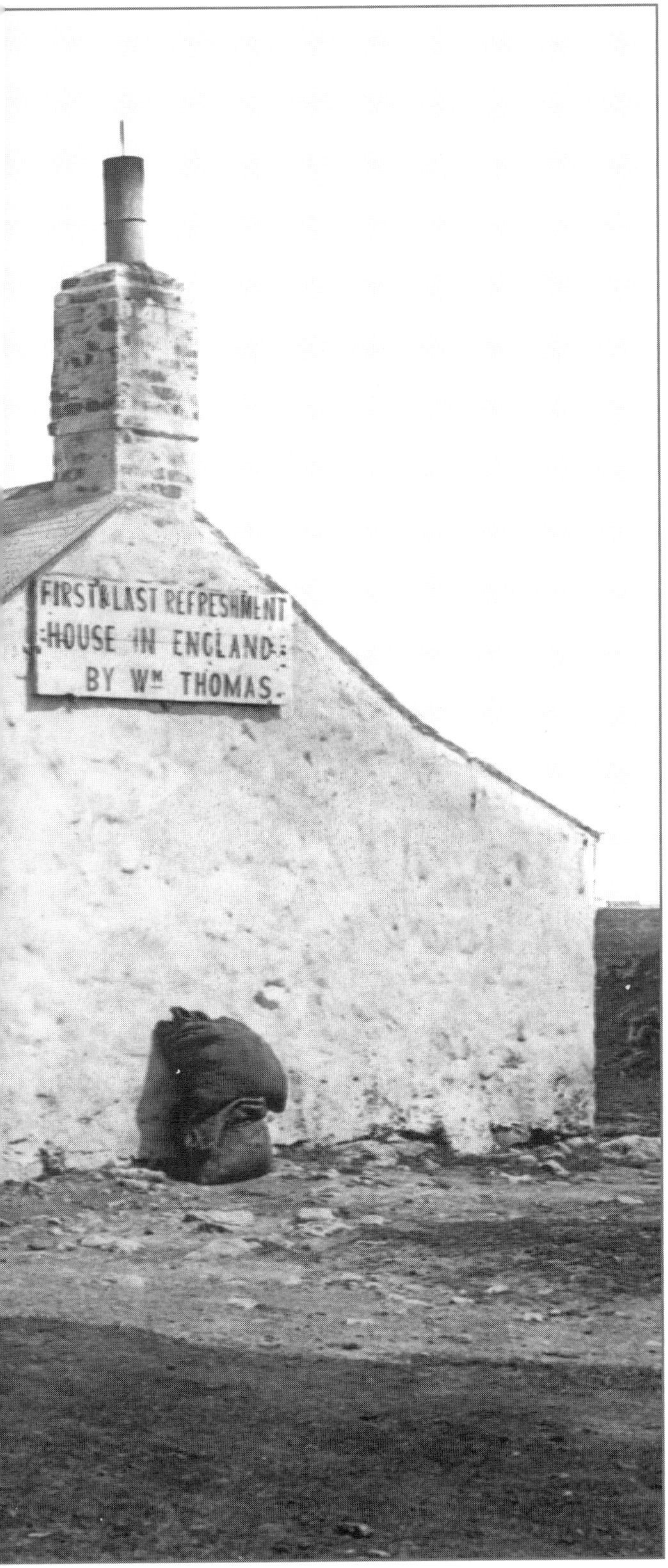

Tourism

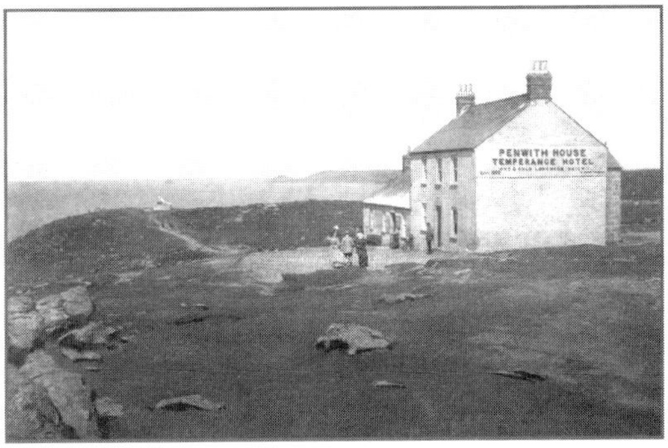

▲ **Land's End, Penwith House 1908** 61283
A few visitors are making the best of their visit to the bleak and windswept cliff top. The Penwith House Temperance Hotel, established in 1880, is providing hot or cold luncheons but there is no alcohol available to celebrate. We can see the First and Last House down by the Land's End, while in the far distance is the headland of Cape Cornwall.

◄ **Land's End, The First and Last House 1893** 31812
Souvenirs (including model lighthouses carved from serpentine stone) and postcards (perhaps Frith's) are displayed outside the most westerly house in England. William Thomas, named on the sign, was listed in a directory of the time as a carpenter and proprietor of the Land's End 'refreshment house'.

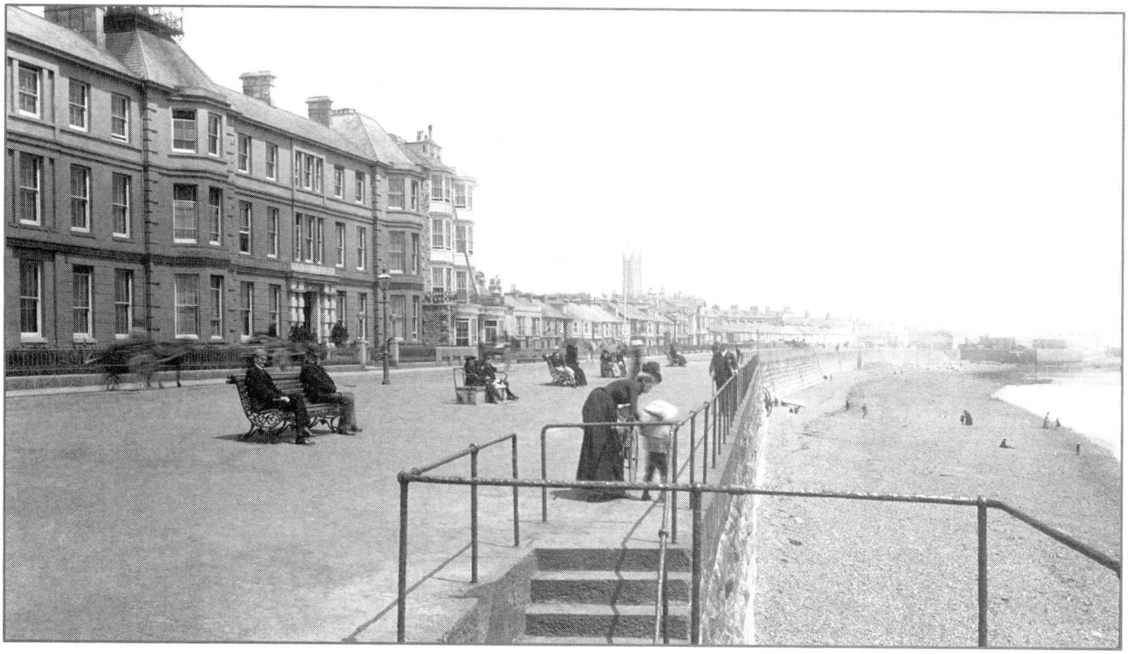

Penzance, The Esplanade 1890 27690A
The long esplanade is one of Penzance's great assets; here we look towards the harbour area, with the lofty church tower as a prominent landmark. A lady with a pram attends her child, while a few people are on the beach below. The major building is the Queens Hotel.

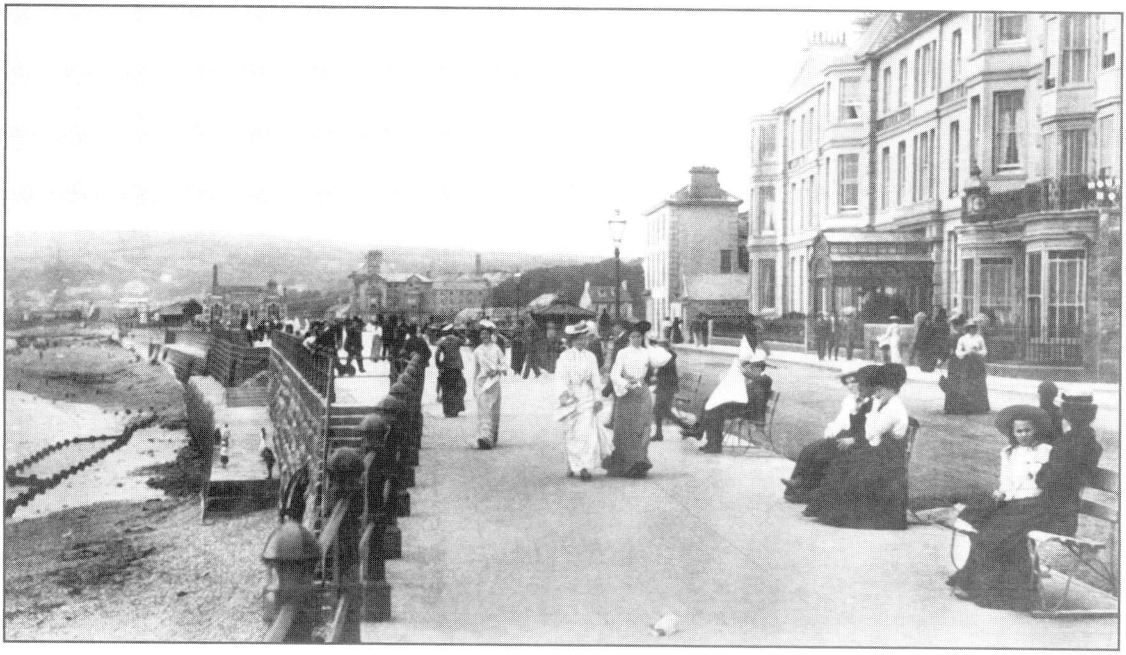

Penzance, The Esplanade 1904 52271
This photograph was taken from almost from the same viewpoint as No 27690A, but looking west. This is a busier scene, and the dresses are less sombre. Note that a covered porch has been added to the Queens Hotel, which in later years would take over the Mounts Bay Hotel on the right.

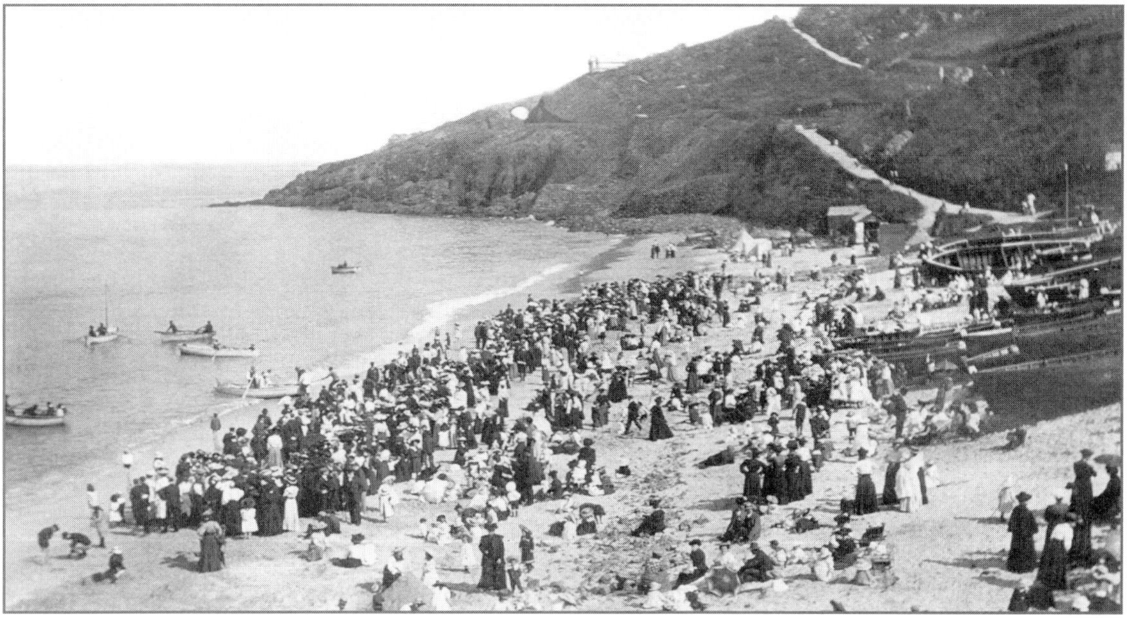

St Ives, The Beach 1901 47677A
Porthminster Beach, almost in the town and just below the railway station, was extremely popular even a century ago. The crowd appears to be there for an event - perhaps a Sunday-school outing. The late Victorian dresses are not the best garb for the beach. The pilchard fishing boats drawn up are a reminder that this was a working beach too.

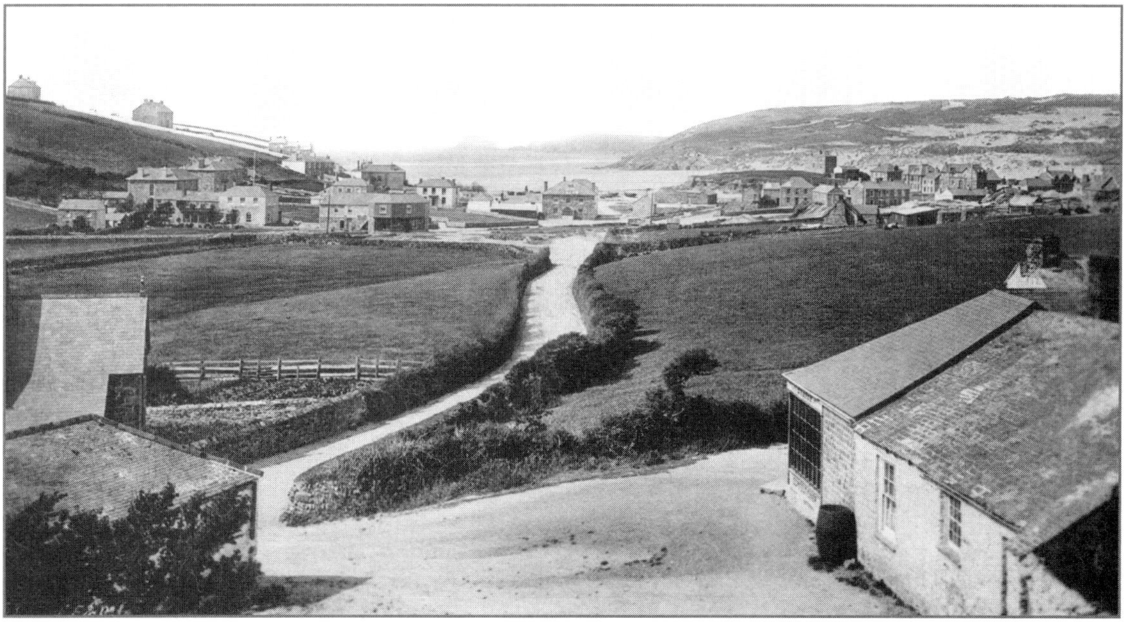

Perranporth, General View 1890 23963
By this date, Perranporth was becoming popular for bathing on account of its sandy beach. Pilchard fishing was also carried on, and a few boats are drawn up on the beach. Mining activities helped create the village, but the holiday trade really began to take off once the railway arrived in 1903. Penhale Point and Gull Rock are in the distance.

▼ **Perranporth, The Convalescent Home 1893** 31824
This is not exactly a holiday home, but the fresh environment and a view to the sea were deemed beneficial for the patients. This was financed by John Passmore Edwards, who also gave an endowment fund entrusted to the governors of the Royal Cornwall Infirmary in Truro. After becoming an old people's home, the building has been converted into flats. Perran Coombe is to the right.

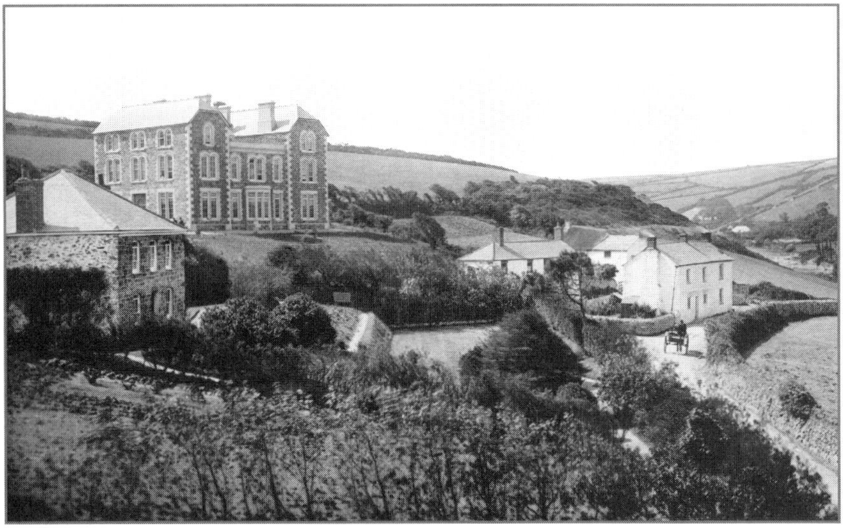

▼ **Newquay, From the Fish Cellars 1887** 20244
Here we have an early view of Towan Beach, with everyone overdressed for the seaside. A game of tennis is in progress on a court marked out in the sand. The masts of trading ships are seen in the harbour; its north pier was to be badly damaged in a north-east gale two years later. The Huer's House stands outlined on the slope above. The large Atlantic Hotel, which now dominates the headland, was not built until 1893.

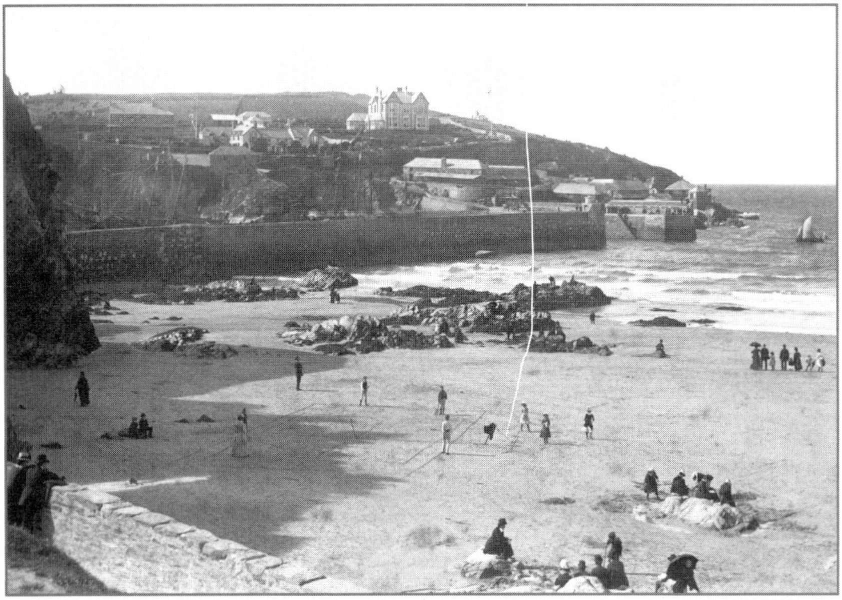

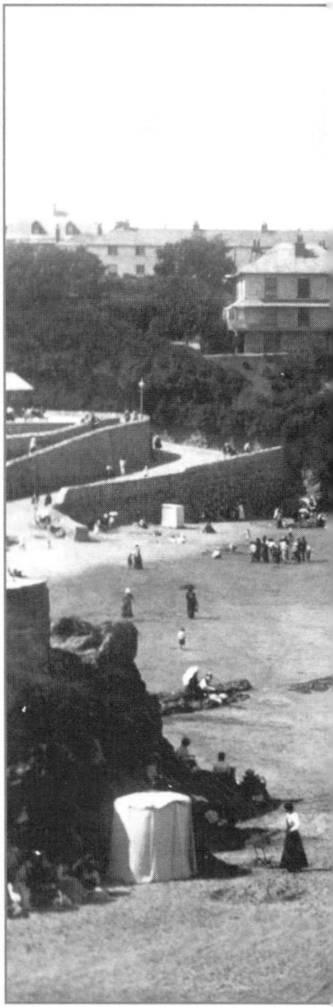

▲ **Newquay, Towan Beach 1901** 47734
This is a great place for a seaside holiday, with golden sand serviced by the growing resort of Newquay, with hotels and boarding houses built literally to the cliff edge. Note the wheeled bathing machines down by the sea, and the curious beach tents and a few deckchairs. Long skirts and parasols are the fashion for the ladies.

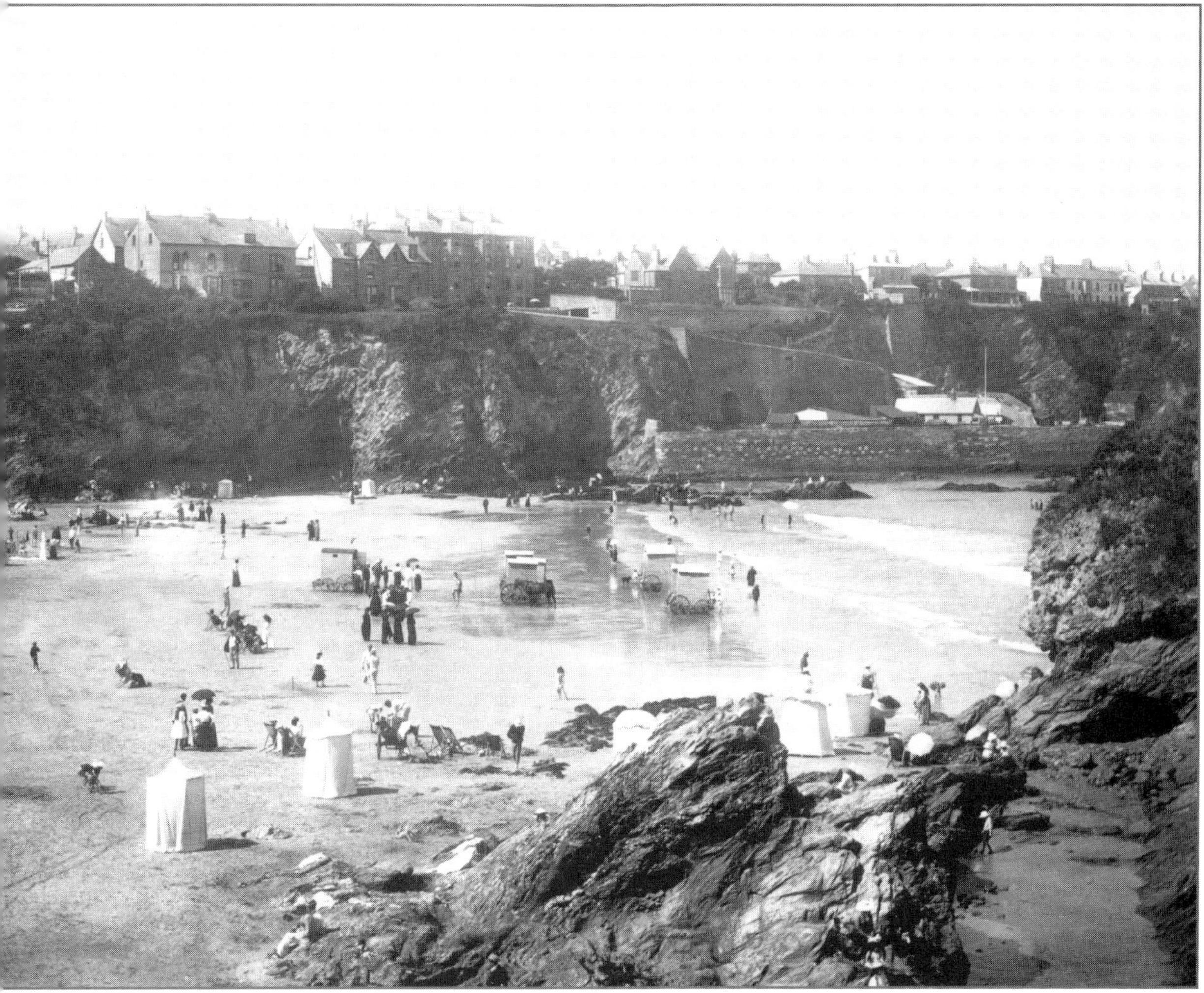

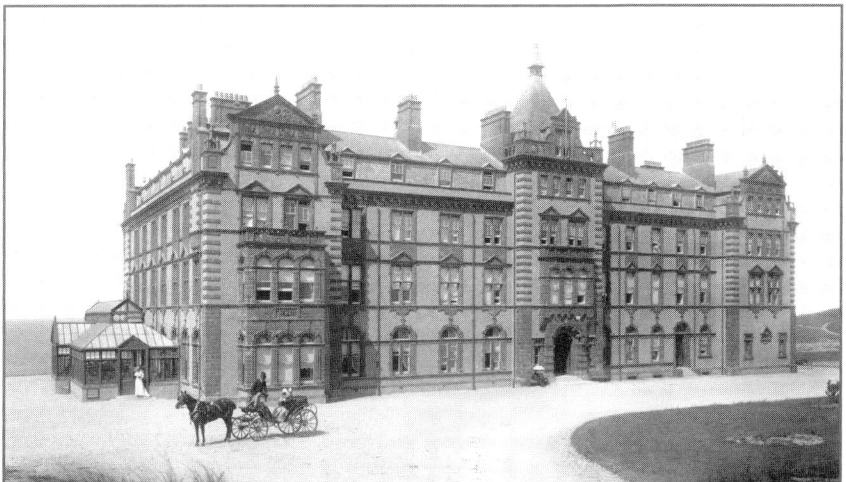

◀ **Newquay, The Headland Hotel and Fistral Bay 1901** 47744

Opened in June 1900, the immense hotel block dominates Fistral Beach on the edge of Newquay. A horse and open carriage are about to take guests on an excursion. This is a splendid example of a large hotel in the Cornish resort, built to rival the equally massive Atlantic Hotel of 1893.

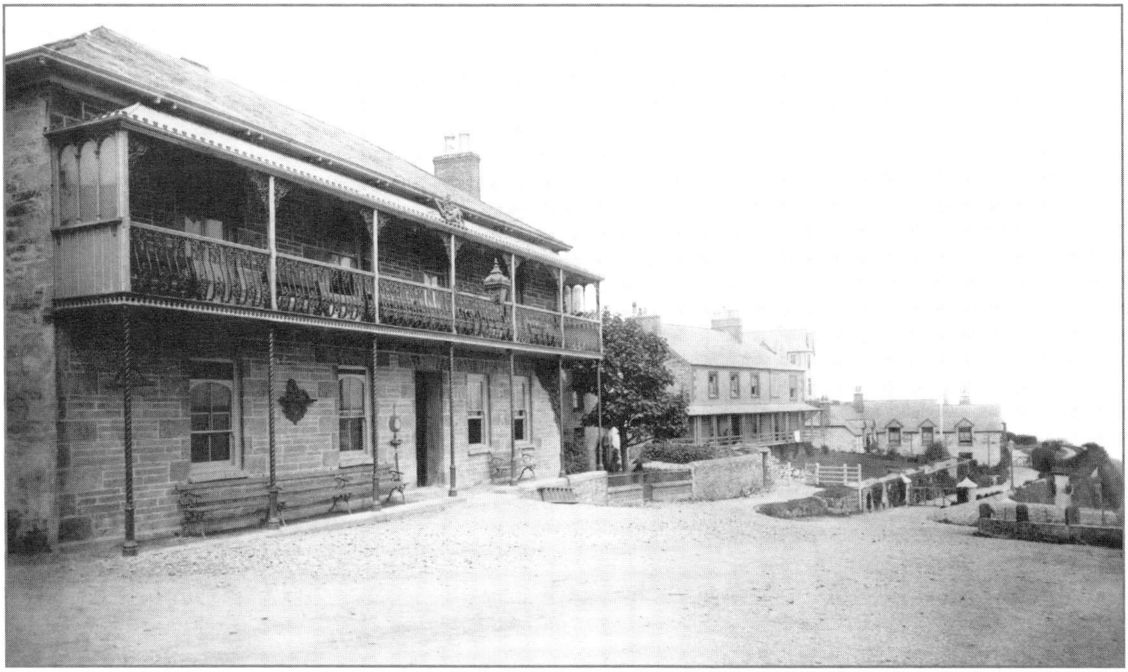

Newquay, The Red Lion Hotel 1888 21185
The modest hotel stands on North Quay Hill with a view over the harbour and bay. An almost colonial-style veranda with fancy railings is supported on cast-iron pillars with a twisted decoration.

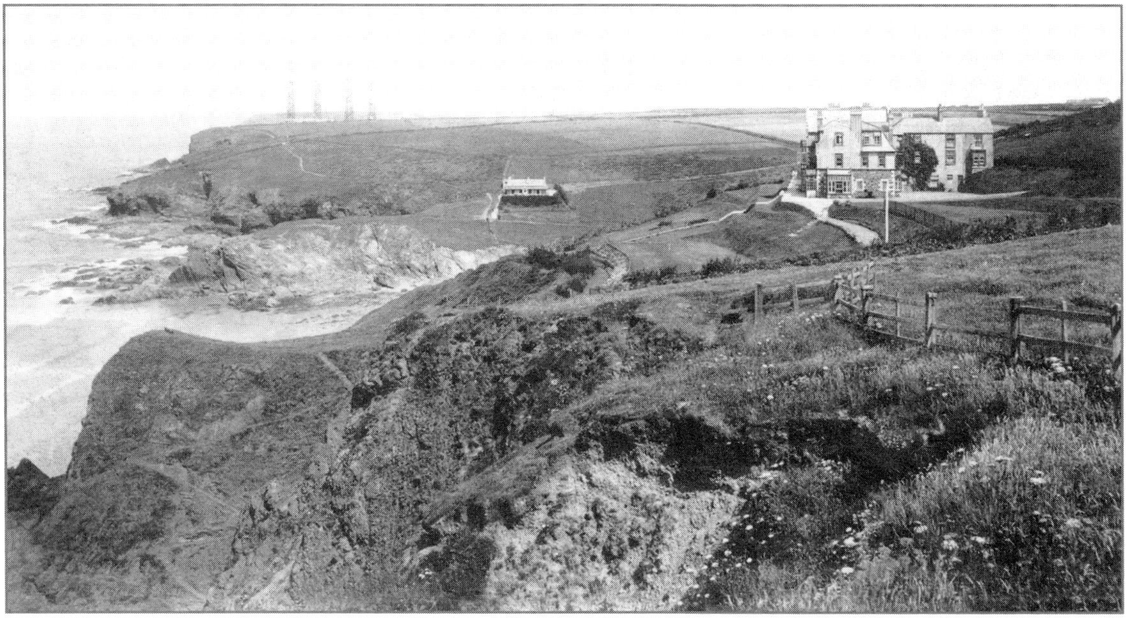

Polurrian Bay, The Polurrian Hotel 1903 49932
Although this photograph was taken for the view of the hotel above the bathing beach, of special interest here is the group of four new radio masts out on Poldhu cliffs. This was the wireless station where Guglielmo Marconi first transmitted signals to Newfoundland in December 1901. The hotel was built in 1890 as a large boarding house for tourists; it was close to the sea and the golf links.

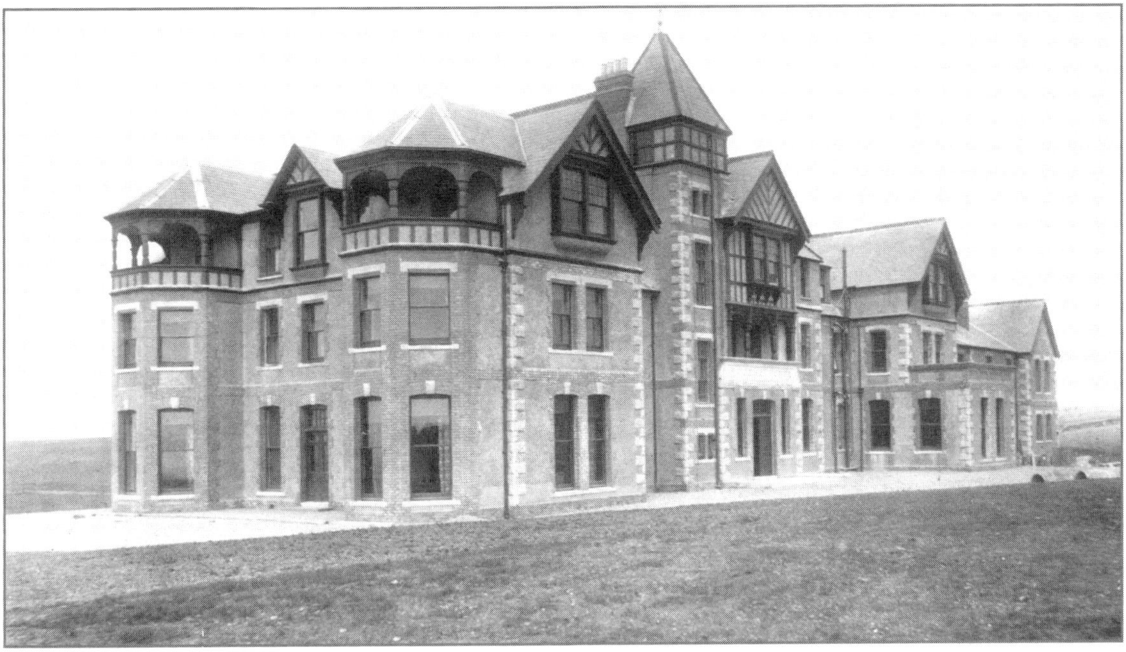

Mullion, The Poldhu Hotel 1899 43804

This very austere hotel is seen in the year it was opened, out on the cliff top just south of Poldhu Cove. It is on an extremely windswept location with not a tree or bush in sight, but no doubt the sea views and bracing air were deemed beneficial to guests.

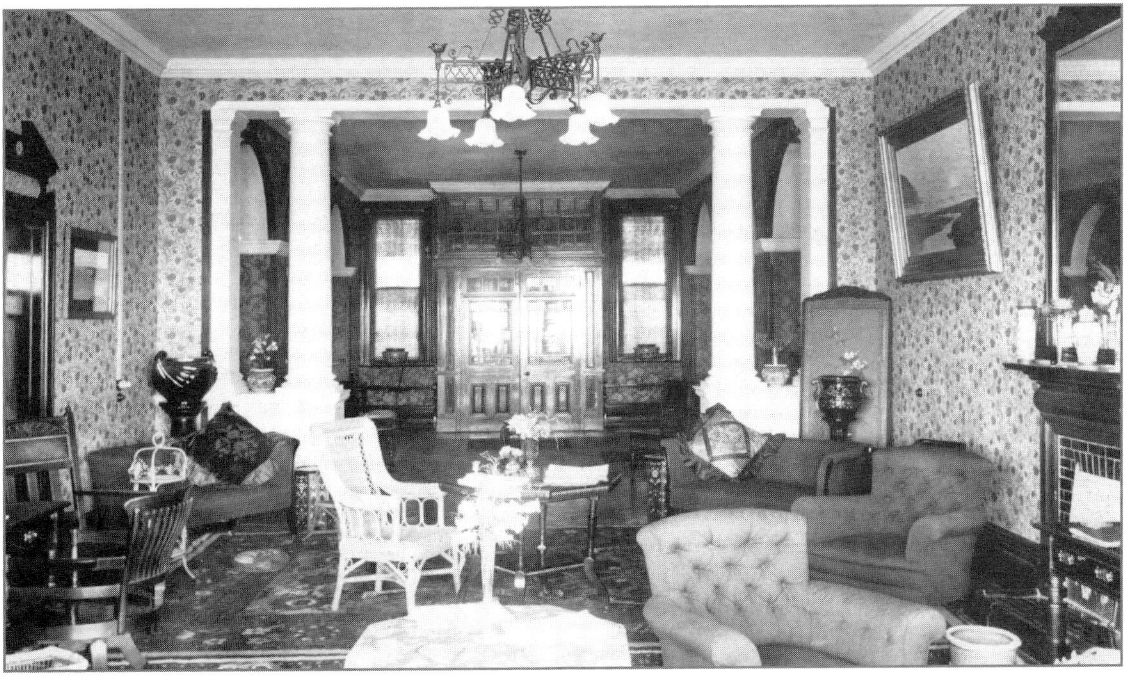

Mullion, The Poldhu Hotel, Interior 1899 43804A

A lavish late Victorian interior gives an idea of the comforts to be expected by guests at the hotel. A variety of furniture is provided, seemingly packed into the room.

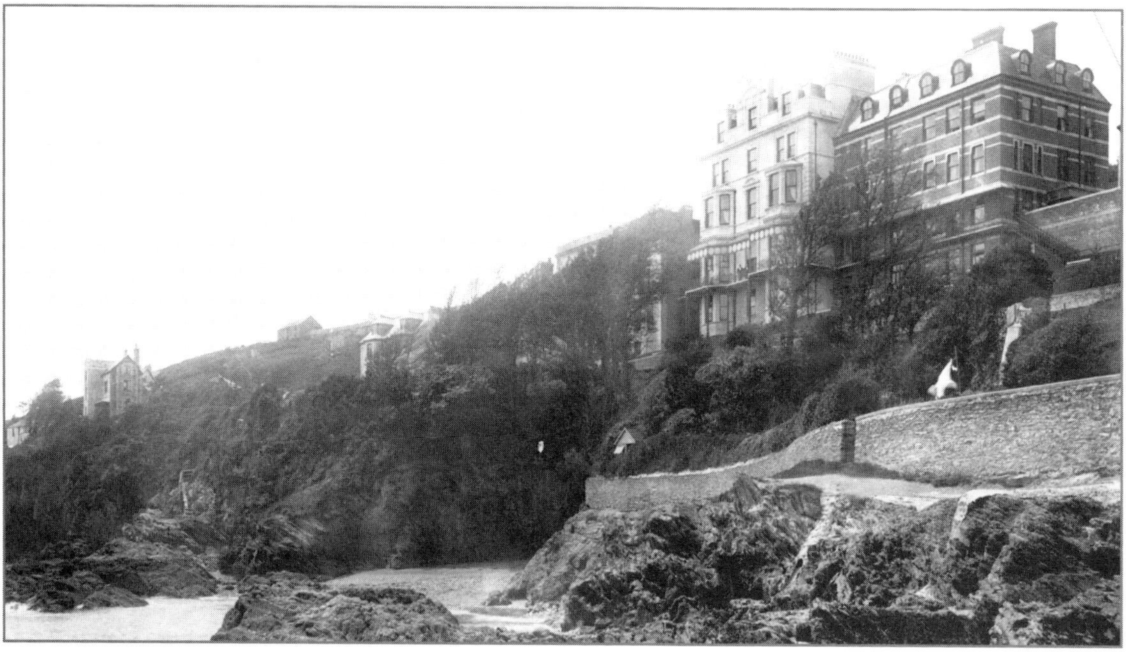

Fowey, The Fowey Hotel from the Rocks 1891 29829
This grand hotel is well-sited: it overlooks the interesting harbour of Fowey, where there is always some activity to watch, and there are more distant views out to the English Channel. Six years after this photograph, the hotel was advertised as having 'splendid suites of rooms ... now lighted by electricity'.

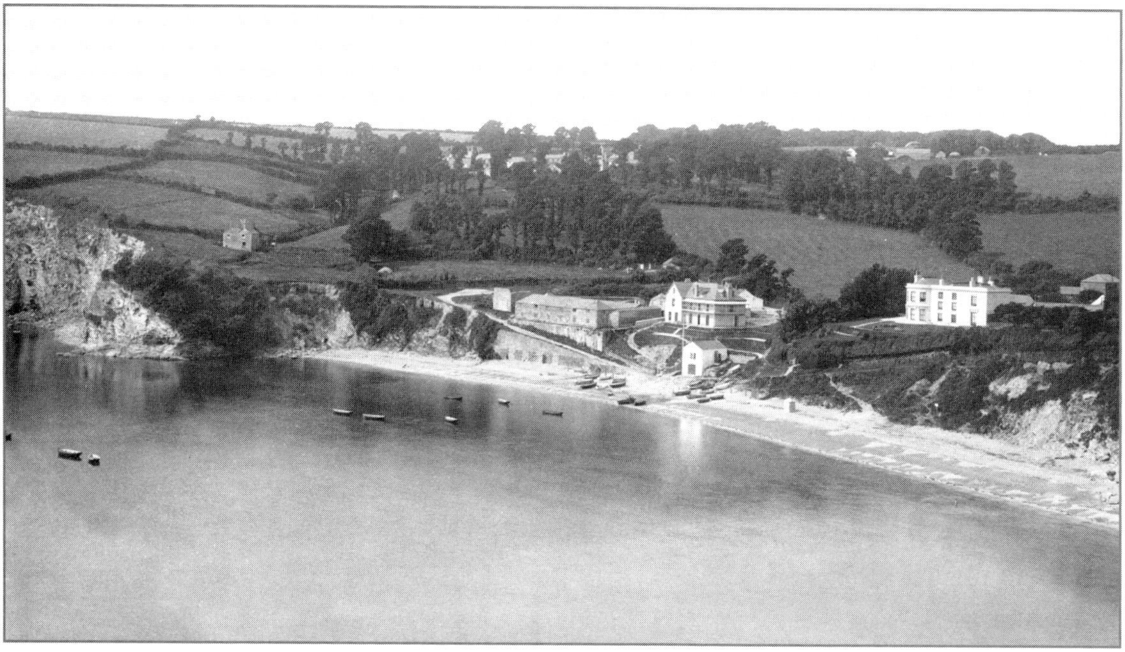

Porthpean, General View 1890 27635
Perhaps originally a retreat for the locals, being only a couple of miles from the town of St Austell, Porthpean had become a 'charming seaside resort, much frequented in the summer months as a boating and bathing place' by the late Victorian period. Its mild climate was considered almost equal to the south of France!

Index

Frith Book Co Titles

www.francisfrith.co.uk

The Frith Book Company publishes over 100 new titles each year. A selection of those currently available is listed below. For latest catalogue please contact Frith Book Co.

Town Books 96 pages, approximately 100 photos. ***County and Themed Books*** 128 pages, approximately 150 photos (unless specified). All titles hardback with laminated case and jacket, except those indicated pb (paperback)

Amersham, Chesham & Rickmansworth (pb)	1-85937-340-2	£9.99
Andover (pb)	1-85937-292-9	£9.99
Aylesbury (pb)	1-85937-227-9	£9.99
Barnstaple (pb)	1-85937-300-3	£9.99
Basildon Living Memories (pb)	1-85937-515-4	£9.99
Bath (pb)	1-85937-419-0	£9.99
Bedford (pb)	1-85937-205-8	£9.99
Bedfordshire Living Memories	1-85937-513-8	£14.99
Belfast (pb)	1-85937-303-8	£9.99
Berkshire (pb)	1-85937-191-4	£9.99
Berkshire Churches	1-85937-170-1	£17.99
Berkshire Living Memories	1-85937-332-1	£14.99
Black Country	1-85937-497-2	£12.99
Blackpool (pb)	1-85937-393-3	£9.99
Bognor Regis (pb)	1-85937-431-x	£9.99
Bournemouth (pb)	1-85937-545-6	£9.99
Bradford (pb)	1-85937-204-x	£9.99
Bridgend (pb)	1-85937-386-0	£7.99
Bridgwater (pb)	1-85937-305-4	£9.99
Bridport (pb)	1-85937-327-5	£9.99
Brighton (pb)	1-85937-192-2	£8.99
Bristol (pb)	1-85937-264-3	£9.99
British Life A Century Ago (pb)	1-85937-213-9	£9.99
Buckinghamshire (pb)	1-85937-200-7	£9.99
Camberley (pb)	1-85937-222-8	£9.99
Cambridge (pb)	1-85937-422-0	£9.99
Cambridgeshire (pb)	1-85937-420-4	£9.99
Cambridgeshire Villages	1-85937-523-5	£14.99
Canals And Waterways (pb)	1-85937-291-0	£9.99
Canterbury Cathedral (pb)	1-85937-179-5	£9.99
Cardiff (pb)	1-85937-093-4	£9.99
Carmarthenshire (pb)	1-85937-604-5	£9.99
Chelmsford (pb)	1-85937-310-0	£9.99
Cheltenham (pb)	1-85937-095-0	£9.99
Cheshire (pb)	1-85937-271-6	£9.99
Chester (pb)	1-85937-382 8	£9.99
Chesterfield (pb)	1-85937-378-x	£9.99
Chichester (pb)	1-85937-228-7	£9.99
Churches of East Cornwall (pb)	1-85937-249-x	£9.99
Churches of Hampshire (pb)	1-85937-207-4	£9.99
Cinque Ports & Two Ancient Towns	1-85937-492-1	£14.99
Colchester (pb)	1-85937-188-4	£8.99
Cornwall (pb)	1-85937-229-5	£9.99
Cornwall Living Memories	1-85937-248-1	£14.99
Cotswolds (pb)	1-85937-230-9	£9.99
Cotswolds Living Memories	1-85937-255-4	£14.99
County Durham (pb)	1-85937-398-4	£9.99
Croydon Living Memories (pb)	1-85937-162-0	£9.99
Cumbria (pb)	1-85937-621-5	£9.99
Derby (pb)	1-85937-367-4	£9.99
Derbyshire (pb)	1-85937-196-5	£9.99
Derbyshire Living Memories	1-85937-330-5	£14.99
Devon (pb)	1-85937-297-x	£9.99
Devon Churches (pb)	1-85937-250-3	£9.99
Dorchester (pb)	1-85937-307-0	£9.99
Dorset (pb)	1-85937-269-4	£9.99
Dorset Coast (pb)	1-85937-299-6	£9.99
Dorset Living Memories (pb)	1-85937-584-7	£9.99
Down the Severn (pb)	1-85937-560-x	£9.99
Down The Thames (pb)	1-85937-278-3	£9.99
Down the Trent	1-85937-311-9	£14.99
East Anglia (pb)	1-85937-265-1	£9.99
East Grinstead (pb)	1-85937-138-8	£9.99
East London	1-85937-080-2	£14.99
East Sussex (pb)	1-85937-606-1	£9.99
Eastbourne (pb)	1-85937-399-2	£9.99
Edinburgh (pb)	1-85937-193-0	£8.99
England In The 1880s	1-85937-331-3	£17.99
Essex - Second Selection	1-85937-456-5	£14.99
Essex (pb)	1-85937-270-8	£9.99
Essex Coast	1-85937-342-9	£14.99
Essex Living Memories	1-85937-490-5	£14.99
Exeter	1-85937-539-1	£9.99
Exmoor (pb)	1-85937-608-8	£9.99
Falmouth (pb)	1-85937-594-4	£9.99
Folkestone (pb)	1-85937-124-8	£9.99
Frome (pb)	1-85937-317-8	£9.99
Glamorgan	1-85937-488-3	£14.99
Glasgow (pb)	1-85937-190-6	£9.99
Glastonbury (pb)	1-85937-338-0	£7.99
Gloucester (pb)	1-85937-232-5	£9.99
Gloucestershire (pb)	1-85937-561-8	£9.99
Great Yarmouth (pb)	1-85937-426-3	£9.99
Greater Manchester (pb)	1-85937-266-x	£9.99
Guildford (pb)	1-85937-410-7	£9.99
Hampshire (pb)	1-85937-279-1	£9.99
Harrogate (pb)	1-85937-423-9	£9.99
Hastings and Bexhill (pb)	1-85937-131-0	£9.99
Heart of Lancashire (pb)	1-85937-197-3	£9.99
Helston (pb)	1-85937-214-7	£9.99
Hereford (pb)	1-85937-175-2	£9.99
Herefordshire (pb)	1-85937-567-7	£9.99
Herefordshire Living Memories	1-85937-514-6	£14.99
Hertfordshire (pb)	1-85937-247-3	£9.99
Horsham (pb)	1-85937-432-8	£9.99
Humberside (pb)	1-85937-605-3	£9.99
Hythe, Romney Marsh, Ashford (pb)	1-85937-256-2	£9.99
Ipswich (pb)	1-85937-424-7	£9.99
Isle of Man (pb)	1-85937-268-6	£9.99
Isle of Wight (pb)	1-85937-429-8	£9.99
Isle of Wight Living Memories	1-85937-304-6	£14.99
Kent (pb)	1-85937-189-2	£9.99
Kent Living Memories(pb)	1-85937-401-8	£9.99
Kings Lynn (pb)	1-85937-334-8	£9.99

Available from your local bookshop or from the publisher

Frith Book Co Titles (continued)

Lake District (pb)	1-85937-275-9	£9.99
Lancashire Living Memories	1-85937-335-6	£14.99
Lancaster, Morecambe, Heysham (pb)	1-85937-233-3	£9.99
Leeds (pb)	1-85937-202-3	£9.99
Leicester (pb)	1-85937-381-x	£9.99
Leicestershire & Rutland Living Memories	1-85937-500-6	£12.99
Leicestershire (pb)	1-85937-185-x	£9.99
Lighthouses	1-85937-257-0	£9.99
Lincoln (pb)	1-85937-380-1	£9.99
Lincolnshire (pb)	1-85937-433-6	£9.99
Liverpool and Merseyside (pb)	1-85937-234-1	£9.99
London (pb)	1-85937-183-3	£9.99
London Living Memories	1-85937-454-9	£14.99
Ludlow (pb)	1-85937-176-0	£9.99
Luton (pb)	1-85937-235-x	£9.99
Maidenhead (pb)	1-85937-339-9	£9.99
Maidstone (pb)	1-85937-391-7	£9.99
Manchester (pb)	1-85937-198-1	£9.99
Marlborough (pb)	1-85937-336-4	£9.99
Middlesex	1-85937-158-2	£14.99
Monmouthshire	1-85937-532-4	£14.99
New Forest (pb)	1-85937-390-9	£9.99
Newark (pb)	1-85937-366-6	£9.99
Newport, Wales (pb)	1-85937-258-9	£9.99
Newquay (pb)	1-85937-421-2	£9.99
Norfolk (pb)	1-85937-195-7	£9.99
Norfolk Broads	1-85937-486-7	£14.99
Norfolk Living Memories (pb)	1-85937-402-6	£9.99
North Buckinghamshire	1-85937-626-6	£14.99
North Devon Living Memories	1-85937-261-9	£14.99
North Hertfordshire	1-85937-547-2	£14.99
North London (pb)	1-85937-403-4	£9.99
North Somerset	1-85937-302-x	£14.99
North Wales (pb)	1-85937-298-8	£9.99
North Yorkshire (pb)	1-85937-236-8	£9.99
Northamptonshire Living Memories	1-85937-529-4	£14.99
Northamptonshire	1-85937-150-7	£14.99
Northumberland Tyne & Wear (pb)	1-85937-281-3	£9.99
Northumberland	1-85937-522-7	£14.99
Norwich (pb)	1-85937-194-9	£8.99
Nottingham (pb)	1-85937-324-0	£9.99
Nottinghamshire (pb)	1-85937-187-6	£9.99
Oxford (pb)	1-85937-411-5	£9.99
Oxfordshire (pb)	1-85937-430-1	£9.99
Oxfordshire Living Memories	1-85937-525-1	£14.99
Paignton (pb)	1-85937-374-7	£7.99
Peak District (pb)	1-85937-280-5	£9.99
Pembrokeshire	1-85937-262-7	£14.99
Penzance (pb)	1-85937-595-2	£9.99
Peterborough (pb)	1-85937-219-8	£9.99
Picturesque Harbours	1-85937-208-2	£14.99
Piers	1-85937-237-6	£17.99
Plymouth (pb)	1-85937-389-5	£9.99
Poole & Sandbanks (pb)	1-85937-251-1	£9.99
Preston (pb)	1-85937-212-0	£9.99
Reading (pb)	1-85937-238-4	£9.99
Redhill to Reigate (pb)	1-85937-596-0	£9.99
Ringwood (pb)	1-85937-384-4	£7.99
Romford (pb)	1-85937-319-4	£9.99
Royal Tunbridge Wells (pb)	1-85937-504-9	£9.99
Salisbury (pb)	1-85937-239-2	£9.99
Scarborough (pb)	1-85937-379-8	£9.99
Sevenoaks and Tonbridge (pb)	1-85937-392-5	£9.99
Sheffield & South Yorks (pb)	1-85937-267-8	£9.99
Sherborne (pb)	1-85937-301-1	£9.99
Shrewsbury (pb)	1-85937-325-9	£9.99
Shropshire (pb)	1-85937-326-7	£9.99
Shropshire Living Memories	1-85937-643-6	£14.99
Somerset	1-85937-153-1	£14.99
South Devon Coast	1-85937-107-8	£14.99
South Devon Living Memories (pb)	1-85937-609-6	£9.99
South East London (pb)	1-85937-263-5	£9.99
South Somerset	1-85937-318-6	£14.99
South Wales	1-85937-519-7	£14.99
Southampton (pb)	1-85937-427-1	£9.99
Southend (pb)	1-85937-313-5	£9.99
Southport (pb)	1-85937-425-5	£9.99
St Albans (pb)	1-85937-341-0	£9.99
St Ives (pb)	1-85937-415-8	£9.99
Stafford Living Memories (pb)	1-85937-503-0	£9.99
Staffordshire (pb)	1-85937-308-9	£9.99
Stourbridge (pb)	1-85937-530-8	£9.99
Stratford upon Avon (pb)	1-85937-388-7	£9.99
Suffolk (pb)	1-85937-221-x	£9.99
Suffolk Coast (pb)	1-85937-610-x	£9.99
Surrey (pb)	1-85937-240-6	£9.99
Surrey Living Memories	1-85937-328-3	£14.99
Sussex (pb)	1-85937-184-1	£9.99
Sutton (pb)	1-85937-337-2	£9.99
Swansea (pb)	1-85937-167-1	£9.99
Taunton (pb)	1-85937-314-3	£9.99
Tees Valley & Cleveland (pb)	1-85937-623-1	£9.99
Teignmouth (pb)	1-85937-370-4	£7.99
Thanet (pb)	1-85937-116-7	£9.99
Tiverton (pb)	1-85937-178-7	£9.99
Torbay (pb)	1-85937-597-9	£9.99
Truro (pb)	1-85937-598-7	£9.99
Victorian & Edwardian Dorset	1-85937-254-6	£14.99
Victorian & Edwardian Kent (pb)	1-85937-624-X	£9.99
Victorian & Edwardian Maritime Album (pb)	1-85937-622-3	£9.99
Victorian and Edwardian Sussex (pb)	1-85937-625-8	£9.99
Villages of Devon (pb)	1-85937-293-7	£9.99
Villages of Kent (pb)	1-85937-294-5	£9.99
Villages of Sussex (pb)	1-85937-295-3	£9.99
Warrington (pb)	1-85937-507-3	£9.99
Warwick (pb)	1-85937-518-9	£9.99
Warwickshire (pb)	1-85937-203-1	£9.99
Welsh Castles (pb)	1-85937-322-4	£9.99
West Midlands (pb)	1-85937-289-9	£9.99
West Sussex (pb)	1-85937-607-x	£9.99
West Yorkshire (pb)	1-85937-201-5	£9.99
Weston Super Mare (pb)	1-85937-306-2	£9.99
Weymouth (pb)	1-85937-209-0	£9.99
Wiltshire (pb)	1-85937-277-5	£9.99
Wiltshire Churches (pb)	1-85937-171-x	£9.99
Wiltshire Living Memories (pb)	1-85937-396-8	£9.99
Winchester (pb)	1-85937-428-x	£9.99
Windsor (pb)	1-85937-333-x	£9.99
Wokingham & Bracknell (pb)	1-85937-329-1	£9.99
Woodbridge (pb)	1-85937-498-0	£9.99
Worcester (pb)	1-85937-165-5	£9.99
Worcestershire Living Memories	1-85937-489-1	£14.99
Worcestershire	1-85937-152-3	£14.99
York (pb)	1-85937-199-x	£9.99
Yorkshire (pb)	1-85937-186-8	£9.99
Yorkshire Coastal Memories	1-85937-506-5	£14.99
Yorkshire Dales	1-85937-502-2	£14.99
Yorkshire Living Memories (pb)	1-85937-397-6	£9.99

See Frith books on the internet at www.francisfrith.co.uk

FRITH PRODUCTS & SERVICES

Francis Frith would doubtless be pleased to know that the pioneering publishing venture he started in 1860 still continues today. Over a hundred and forty years later, The Francis Frith Collection continues in the same innovative tradition and is now one of the foremost publishers of vintage photographs in the world. Some of the current activities include:

Interior Decoration

Today Frith's photographs can be seen framed and as giant wall murals in thousands of pubs, restaurants, hotels, banks, retail stores and other public buildings throughout the country. In every case they enhance the unique local atmosphere of the places they depict and provide reminders of gentler days in an increasingly busy and frenetic world.

Product Promotions

Frith products are used by many major companies to promote the sales of their own products or to reinforce their own history and heritage. Frith promotions have been used by Hovis bread, Courage beers, Scots Porage Oats, Colman's mustard, Cadbury's foods, Mellow Birds coffee, Dunhill pipe tobacco, Guinness, and Bulmer's Cider.

Genealogy and Family History

As the interest in family history and roots grows world-wide, more and more people are turning to Frith's photographs of Great Britain for images of the towns, villages and streets where their ancestors lived; and, of course, photographs of the churches and chapels where their ancestors were christened, married and buried are an essential part of every genealogy tree and family album.

Frith Products

All Frith photographs are available Framed or just as Mounted Prints and Posters (size 23 x 16 inches). These may be ordered from the address below. From time to time other products - Address Books, Calendars, Table Mats, etc - are available.

The Internet

Already fifty thousand Frith photographs can be viewed and purchased on the internet through the Frith websites and a myriad of partner sites.

For more detailed information on Frith companies and products, look at these sites:

www.francisfrith.co.uk
www.francisfrith.com
(for North American visitors)

See the complete list of Frith Books at:
www.francisfrith.co.uk
This web site is regularly updated with the latest list of publications from the Frith Book Company. If you wish to buy books relating to another part of the country that your local bookshop does not stock, you may purchase on-line.

For further information, trade, or author enquiries please contact us at the address below:
The Francis Frith Collection, Frith's Barn, Teffont, Salisbury, Wiltshire, England SP3 5QP.
Tel: +44 (0)1722 716 376 Fax: +44 (0)1722 716 881 Email: sales@francisfrith.co.uk

See Frith books on the internet at www.francisfrith.co.uk

FREE MOUNTED PRINT

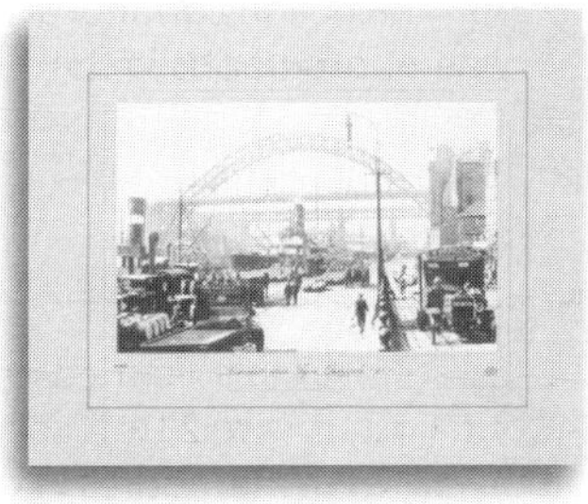

Mounted Print
Overall size 14 x 11 inches

Fill in and cut out this voucher and return *it with your remittance for £2.25 (to cover postage and handling). Offer valid for delivery to UK addresses only.*

Choose any photograph included in this book. *Your SEPIA print will be A4 in size. It will be mounted in a cream mount with a burgundy rule line (overall size 14 x 11 inches).*

Order additional Mounted Prints at HALF PRICE (only £7.49 each*)
If you would like to order more Frith prints from this book, possibly as gifts for friends and family, you can buy them at half price (with no additional postage and handling costs).

Have your Mounted Prints framed
For an extra £14.95 per print* you can have your mounted print(s) framed in an elegant polished wood and gilt moulding, overall size 16 x 13 inches (no additional postage and handling required).

> *** IMPORTANT!**
>
> **These special prices are only available if you order at the same time as you order your free mounted print. You must use the ORIGINAL VOUCHER on this page (no copies permitted). We can only despatch to one address.**

Send completed Voucher form to:
The Francis Frith Collection, Frith's Barn, Teffont, Salisbury, Wiltshire SP3 5QP

CHOOSE ANY IMAGE FROM THIS BOOK

Voucher
*for **FREE** and Reduced Price Frith Prints*

Please do not photocopy this voucher. Only the original is valid, so please fill it in, cut it out and return it to us with your order.

Picture ref no	Page no	Qty	Mounted @ £7.49	Framed + £14.95	Total Cost
		1	Free of charge*	£	£
			£7.49	£	£
			£7.49	£	£
			£7.49	£	£
			£7.49	£	£
			£7.49	£	£
Please allow 28 days for delivery			* Post & handling (UK)		£2.25
			Total Order Cost		£

Title of this book ....
I enclose a cheque/postal order for £ ....
made payable to 'The Francis Frith Collection'

OR please debit my Mastercard / Visa / Switch / Amex card
(credit cards please on all overseas orders), details below

Card Number

Issue No (Switch only) Valid from (Amex/Switch)

Expires Signature

Name Mr/Mrs/Ms ....
Address ....
....
....
.... Postcode ....
Daytime Tel No ....
Email ....

Valid to 31/12/05

Free Print - see overleaf

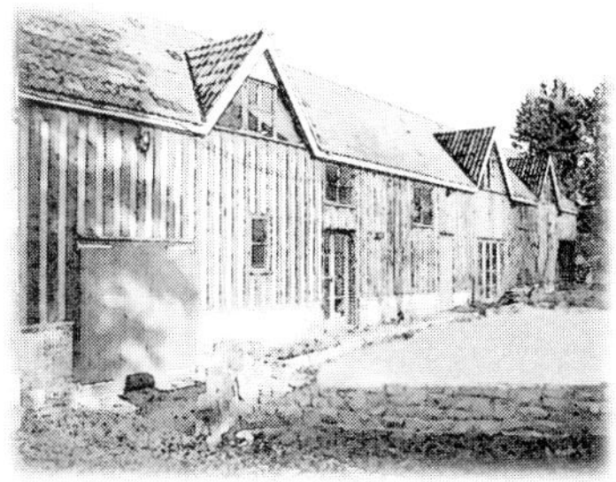

Would you like to find out more about Francis Frith?

We have recently recruited some entertaining speakers who are happy to visit local groups, clubs and societies to give an illustrated talk documenting Frith's travels and photographs. If you are a member of such a group and are interested in hosting a presentation, we would love to hear from you.

Our speakers bring with them a small selection of our local town and county books, together with sample prints. They are happy to take orders. A small proportion of the order value is donated to the group who have hosted the presentation. The talks are therefore an excellent way of fundraising for small groups and societies.

Can you help us with information about any of the Frith photographs in this book?

We are gradually compiling an historical record for each of the photographs in the Frith archive. It is always fascinating to find out the names of the people shown in the pictures, as well as insights into the shops, buildings and other features depicted.

If you recognize anyone in the photographs in this book, or if you have information not already included in the author's caption, do let us know. We would love to hear from you, and will try to publish it in future books or articles.

Our production team

Frith books are produced by a small dedicated team at offices in the converted Grade II listed 18th-century barn at Teffont near Salisbury, illustrated above. Most have worked with the Frith Collection for many years. All have in common one quality: they have a passion for the Frith Collection. The team is constantly expanding, but currently includes:

Jason Buck, John Buck, Ruth Butler, Heather Crisp, David Davies, Isobel Hall, Julian Hight, Peter Horne, James Kinnear, Karen Kinnear, Tina Leary, Stuart Login, Amanda Lowe, David Marsh, Sue Molloy, Kate Rotondetto, Dean Scource, Eliza Sackett, Terence Sackett, Sandra Sampson, Adrian Sanders, Sandra Sanger, Julia Skinner, Claire Tarrier, Lewis Taylor, Shelley Tolcher and Lorraine Tuck.